BEAUTY TIPS *from* MOOSE JAW

EXCURSIONS IN THE GREAT WEIRD NORTH

WILL FERGUSON

CANONGATE

Edinburgh · New York · Melbourne

First published in Great Britain in 2005 by
Canongate Books Ltd, 14 High Street,
Edinburgh EH1 1TE

This edition published in 2006

Origin   ada,
a

ISBN-10 1 84195 690 2
ISBN-13 978 184195 690 9

The author gratefully acknowledges permission to reproduce the material in
this book. Every reasonable effort has been made to contact the copyright holders;
in the event of an inadvertent omission or error, please notify the publisher

From "All Star", *Smash Mouth*, words and music by Greg Camp,
© Warner-Tamerlane Publishing Corp and Squish Moth Music, 1999

From *The Irish in Newfoundland, 1600–1900*, © Michael McCarthy, 1999.
Reprinted by permission of Creative Book Publishing

From *Old Newfoundland: A History to 1843*, © Patrick O'Flaherty, 1999.
Reprinted by permission of Long Beach Press

From "Canadians", *Collected Poems*, © Miriam Waddington, 1986.
Reprinted by permission of Oxford University Press Canada

Printed and bound in Great Britain by Clays Ltd, St Ives plc
Jacket and text design by Kelly Hill
Typeset in Fairfield Light
Map on pp viii–ix by Jim Lewis
Other maps by Susan Thomas/Digital Zone

www.canongate.net

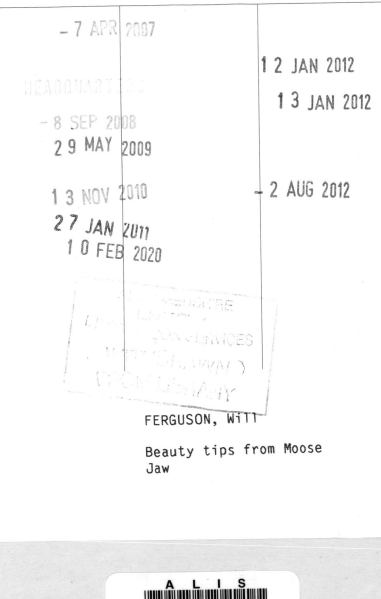

Also By Will Ferguson

Hokkaido Highway Blues
Happiness™

for Alex

CONTENTS

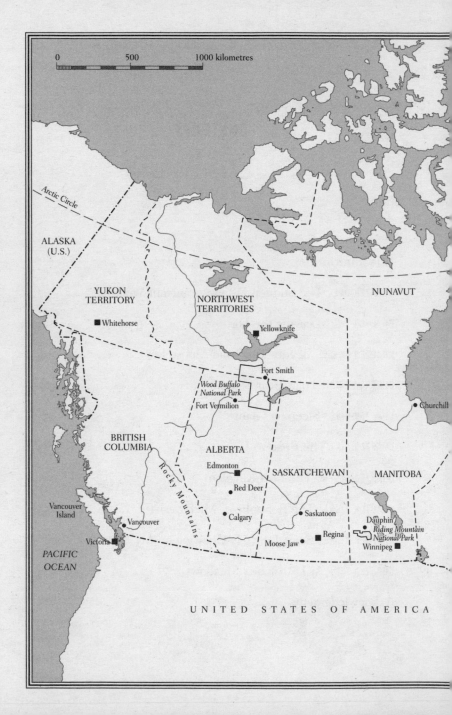

Arctic Circle

ALASKA
(U.S.)

YUKON
TERRITORY

NUNAVUT

NORTHWEST
TERRITORIES

■ Whitehorse

■ Yellowknife

Fort Smith

Wood Buffalo
National Park

Fort Vermilion

• Churchill

BRITISH
COLUMBIA

ALBERTA

SASKATCHEWAN

MANITOBA

Edmonton ■

Rocky Mountains

• Red Deer

• Calgary

• Saskatoon

Dauphin
Riding Mountain
National Park

Vancouver
Island

• Vancouver

Victoria ■

Moose Jaw

■ Regina

Winnipeg ■

PACIFIC
OCEAN

UNITED   STATES   OF   AMERICA

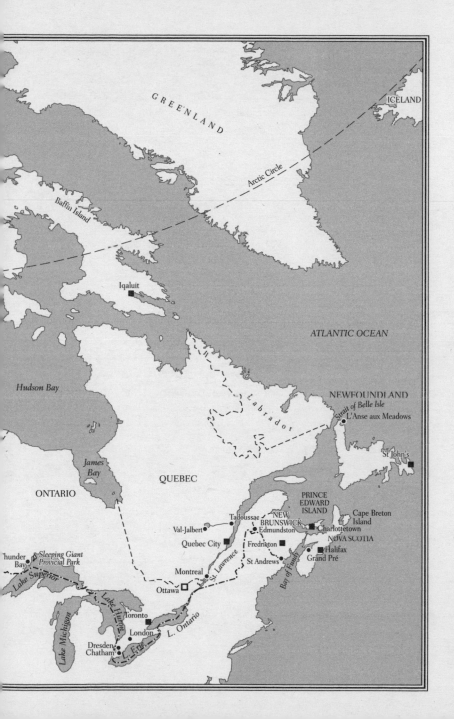

INTRODUCTION

This is a book about arrivals, not departures—and therein lies
the great divide between the Old World and the New.

I once spent two months in Northern Ireland, following
the Ulster Way through every valley and county, through
small villages and tattered industrial cities, and I was struck
by how often the stories there ended with ships departing,
and with vessels disappearing into the mist. Like so many
countries in Europe, Ireland is an *emigrant* nation.

But I am from Canada and we see things differently; we
see them from the other side of the ocean. Our stories begin
when these vessels re-appear, *out* of the mist. Our stories
begin with landfall. We are an immigrant nation, and ours is
the story of worlds colliding, of foreigners wading ashore, of
beachheads established, of colonies embedded in a landscape, of outposts taking root.

Canada is, in fact, not so much a country as it is a collection of outposts. In *Beauty Tips from Moose Jaw* alone, you will
come upon outposts of Denmark, England, Ireland, France,
Finland, Norway, Italy, Germany, Scotland, China, Africa and
the Ukraine—all re-invented and re-imagined in a new land.
These outposts, in turn, are set against the larger context of
Canada's aboriginal First Nations. This was not an empty

continent that the Europeans discovered, and that is something worth remembering.(*Note to readers outside of Canada*:
The term "tribes" is rarely used anymore and has been
replaced by the more accurate "First Nations"—these were,
after all, complex cultures with their own trade networks, military alliances, languages and religions. The term "Metis"—
the "s" is silent—refers to someone of mixed Native and white
heritage, usually French; and "Inuit" has now replaced the
out-dated term "Eskimos.")

Essayist and scholar Northrop Frye noted that what set
Canada apart from other countries in the western hemisphere
is that it lacked a distinguishable frontier—a line that
advanced purposefully across the map like an isobar separat-
ing one world from the next, with "settlement" on one side and
"vanishing wilderness" on the other. In this, the Canadian
experience diverged drastically from that of the United States.
The American *frontier thesis*—a heavily symbolic narrative of
progress and order steamrolling over an untamed land, imposing order onto chaos—may be historically suspect, but the
psychological impact it has had on American society cannot be
underestimated. By contrast, historians in Canada wrote of a
metropolitan thesis, in which the flow of ideas and goods
fanned outward from various urban centres to small scattered
pockets of civilization—to outposts, in effect: clusters of light
separated by a vast, brooding darkness.

The effect of this upon the Canadian psyche, Frye argued,
was something he called *the garrison mentality*: a sense of dread
and loneliness that comes from cowering behind palisaded
walls, far from "home" in a land as savage as it is indifferent.
The existential heebie-jeebies, as it were. But "garrison" is too

dark a word; garrison suggests gnawing despair and the threat of impending attack. I prefer the term "outpost," because it includes a wider range of possibilities. Outposts are not only geographic; they can be linguistic, political, cultural. They are small triumphs of survival. Mini-epics of continuity. The French fact in Canada is an enduring example of this.

I have spent the last three-and-a-half years travelling among the outposts and enclaves of Canada. I began at the Pacific and worked my way east, across the continent, from the southern end of Vancouver Island to the northern tip of Newfoundland. This book is meant to be accessible to anyone, without presuming any in-depth knowledge of Canadian society on the part of the reader. A few references did stump my UK publisher, however, and I have been asked to explain the following "Canadianisms."

I. "How about them Leafs?" This refers to sports. Which is, to say, ice hockey. In Canada, all references to sport and/or leisure are automatically assumed to be about hockey unless otherwise noted. In this case, it is the Toronto Maple Leafs hockey team I am referring to—and no, that is not a typo. It really is spelled "Leafs," not *Leaves*. Why? I have no idea.

II. "Toque"(pronounced "two" with a quick "k" at the end): what would be referred to as a "wooly hat" in the UK; official Canadian headgear; iconic attire (see: front cover).

III. "Tim Hortons" (aka. "Dead Tim's"): object of veneration; candidate for Canadian sainthood. Tim Horton was a hockey player who started a chain of doughnut shops, thereby combining Canada's two great passions: toothless men on skates, and fried dough glazed in sugar. Tim Horton died in a car crash, but his name—and his legacy—lives on. "Tim Bits," meanwhile, refers not to some sort of macabre, quasi-religious communion with the Body of the Departed Tim. No. Tim Bits are simply the holes from the doughnuts, sold separately in Canada.

IV. "Turning right on a red light" (that is, with the flow of oncoming traffic). In the UK, this is considered running a red, but in North America—Montreal and New York aside—it is perfectly permissible. Dangerous, but permissible.

V. "Loonie": a one-dollar coin. This refers not to mental instability, but to the depiction of a waterfowl "loon" on one side. (When a two-dollar coin was introduced it was named, with perfect Canadian logic, "the twoonie.")

I was also asked to give a quick explanation of the Quebec separatist movement, so here goes: Canada is divided into ten provinces and three northern territories, and although 25% of Canadians are francophone, 80% of this population is concentrated in a single province: Quebec. A movement among the Quebecois to separate from the rest of Canada and form their own country has led to two provincial referendums on independence, one in 1980 and a second in 1995. In both cases, the pro-unity federalist side won, though in the second referendum it was only by the narrowest of margins. Separatism in Quebec continues to flare up and die down, leading the country from one constitutional crisis to the next.

Unlike the Basques in Spain or the IRA in Northern Ireland, the separatists in Quebec have long since abandoned violence as a political tool. (The "October Crisis" alluded to in Chapter Eight refers to the 1970 kidnapping and murder of a Canadian government minister by terrorists in Quebec, the last such act of political violence to occur there.)

The central problem is this: the territorial borders of the province of Quebec do not line up with the linguistic and cultural boundaries of the larger francophone population. In fact, the entire northern half of Quebec is not francophone at all, but is inhabited by the Inuit and Cree First Nations. The southern and western areas, meanwhile, have sizeable English-speaking populations, and—outside of Quebec's provincial boundaries—there are other large French-speaking populations, such as the Acadians and Brayons in the province of New Brunswick. It's a very messy situation.

Now, if Quebec can separate from the rest of Canada, you would think that the Native and Anglo regions in that province could in turn separate from Quebec. Separatist "intellectuals," however, go into a sputtering fury at such a suggestion, declaring that Quebec's borders are sacrosanct. By their logic, explicitly stated, "Canada is divisible, but Quebec is not."

Its sounds ridiculous, because it is. Fortunately, Canada—this glorious collection of outposts, where doughnut-eating dead hockey players are elevated to the level of deity—has a way of blithely carrying on, in spite of its many internal contradictions. This is, after all, a country where one of the major political parties was known, until just recently, as "The Progressive Conservatives." It's an apt description of Canadians as a whole.

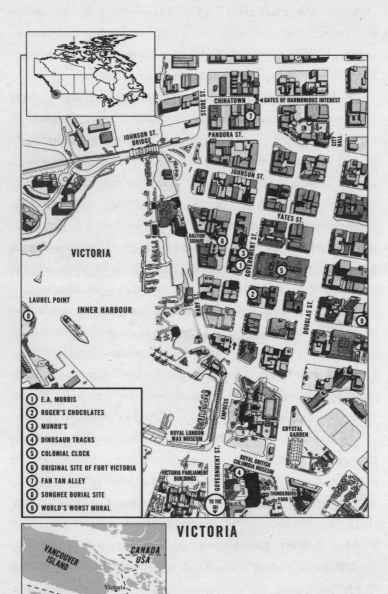

CHINATOWN ◄GATES OF HARMONIOUS INTEREST

STORE ST.

PANDORA ST.

CITY HALL

JOHNSON ST. BRIDGE

JOHNSON ST.

YATES ST.

BASTION SQUARE

GOVERNMENT ST.

VICTORIA

LAUREL POINT

INNER HARBOUR

WARF ST.

DOUGLAS ST.

① E.A. MORRIS
② ROGER'S CHOCOLATES
③ MUNRO'S
④ DINOSAUR TRACKS
⑤ COLONIAL CLOCK
⑥ ORIGINAL SITE OF FORT VICTORIA
⑦ FAN TAN ALLEY
⑧ SONGHEE BURIAL SITE
⑨ WORLD'S WORST MURAL

ROYAL LONDON WAX MUSEUM

EMPRESS

CRYSTAL GARDEN

ROYAL BRITISH COLUMBIA MUSEUM

VICTORIA PARLIAMENT BUILDINGS

GOVERNMENT ST.

IMAX

THUNDERBIRD PARK

TO THE 181

VICTORIA

VANCOUVER ISLAND

CANADA
USA

Victoria

chapter one

THE SUDDEN DISAPPEARANCE OF VICTORIA

SUNDAY NIGHT AT THE JAMES BAY INN, amid the click and clack of billiard balls. I am in sunny British Columbia, in the city of Victoria, and this is what I see: yellowing walls and low ceilings, chalky pool cues and pitchers of beer, boozy dartboards riddled with punctures. (The sideboards around the dartboards are also needle-pocked, a testament to the wisdom of having drunk people throw sharp objects in dark, crowded rooms.)

I am here against my better judgment. Tonight, you see, is the big poetry event, and as I am about to learn, both darts and poems are flung with a certain irresponsible élan here in the James Bay Inn.

Roy McFarlane, the organizer of tonight's event, is surprised to see me. "Wow," he says as he pulls up a chair. "You actually showed up."

With his greying goatee and a wardrobe that is disproportionately denim, Roy is the embodiment of West Coast calm. A bookseller by trade, an arts promoter and activist by inclination, Roy has helped coordinate Earth Day events, Green Party fundraisers, Greenpeace protests—if the words "green" or "earth" are in the title, Roy is there. Now, normally I avoid Green

Party, Earth Day vegan types in the same way I avoid Christian proselytizers: both groups take their personal preoccupations far too seriously. But Roy never tries to convert me, and I never make inappropriate comments about his quixotic political crusades. Or at the very least, I keep them to a minimum.

In the James Bay Inn on this Sunday night, Emily Carr is hovering in the shadows. Offspring of an anglophile merchant, painter of Native villages, lover of overgrown totem poles, Emily Carr—"the laughing one"—died at the inn more than fifty years ago. They say she still drops by from time to time. Mind you, it was neither a pub nor a hotel when Carr was here, but a home for the elderly. She lived in a room where the pub washroom is currently located, and painted her canvases in what is now the upstairs lobby. She has apparently proved very sociable since her demise. But much as I admire her work, I am not here to stake out Emily Carr.

I am here for the poetry slam. Tomorrow, I will take a train up Vancouver Island and then drive across to Nootka Sound, where I will catch a ride on a working freighter along the island's west coast. Tonight, on the eve of my departure, I have come for the poetry. Finally. I might as well get it over with. And who knows? There may be a newspaper article in this, which would thereby qualify any beer or onion rings I consume as tax-deductible. (My journalistic integrity is second to none.)

Every time I've come to Victoria, Roy McFarlane has tried to steer me away from the tourist-friendly, sunlight-saturated inner harbour. Roy speaks of a different Victoria, a parallel city, largely nocturnal and stubbornly uncolonized by images of Olde Englande. "There's a strong alternative arts scene here. I run a regular event at the James Bay Inn," he told me on our first meeting. "You should come."

"And what sort of event would that be?" I inquired. "Poetry," he replied. *Public* poetry.

"A poetry reading?" Just one small problem: I hate poetry. Or rather, I hate poets. (If you are a poet reading this, I don't mean you, of course. I mean other poets.) Like many a cynic, I have long suspected that the number of people reading poetry is *exactly the same* as the number of people writing poetry—and I say that as a reformed poet myself.

"It's not a poetry reading," Roy said. "It's a poetry slam. But it's not so much poetry as it is *spoken word*."

Oh. Well then.

"And technically, it's more of a sweat than a slam." Roy went on to explain the difference between a *slam* and a *sweat* in great detail, none of which I have retained. You'll just have to take my word for it that there is indeed a difference, and that neither constitutes "a reading," which is something else entirely.

Since then, whenever I come through Victoria, I promise Roy I will show up at the James Bay Inn, and I never do. Why on earth would I want to attend a poetry slam in Victoria? It's like going to High Tea at the Empress Hotel and ordering coffee. When I am in Victoria, I want to be in Victoria. I want the rainy days and the mists, the sunlight and the seaplanes; I want the inner harbour, I want the stately vine-draped edifices. I don't want a bunch of black-clad artistes and finger-snapping poets mumbling mumbo-jumbo into a microphone.

But at last I have relented, and here I am. "Are you going to get up on stage?" he asks. "No? Well, if you change your mind, let me know. Beer?"

"Please."

I'll need it. The James Bay Inn is already filling up with a mix of patrons and poets, pool players and performers. "The bar atmosphere, with the billiards in the background and the beer, creates its own effect," says Roy. "It can get a little strange."

Vancouver Island lies moored off the coast of British Columbia like a giant waterlogged tree, thick with moss and ferns. Here, land and water meet in a dramatic fashion, coming together in a cymbal crash of salt spray. Mountains fall into the sea. Waves roll in with all of the Pacific Ocean behind them.

Rising up from a partially submerged chain of mountains, dripping with condensation, this is the largest island on the Pacific coast of North America, and one of the most rugged. On the southern tip of this rainforest isle, as far away from Great Britain as you can possibly go and still be in Canada, the oddest of outposts has taken root.

Here in the charmed city of Victoria, the sun of Empire has yet to set. Victoria—provincial capital, colonial stronghold—has been hailed as "more English than the English," and the description is apt. For this is England in the mind of God, England as a Platonic ideal. England as it never really existed. While the rest of the country grapples with the problems of a postmodern identity, Victoria, snug in its flannel comforter, has yet to move into post-colonialism.

If this sounds disparaging, it isn't meant to be, for I am in love with Victoria. I come whenever I can, twisting flight paths and travel schedules in order to bring myself to the end of the island. I love the illusion of Victoria. I experience the city as though through layers of gauze, veils that soften and dull its edges. As I fight my way through one layer, another entangles, like lace curtains that filter the sun, rendering the world in slightly surreal pastels.

Light fills Victoria's inner harbour the way brandy fills a glass. Seaplanes lift off, leaving spreading V's in their wake. Early-morning whale-watching boats are returning from wider waters, ruddy-faced passengers grinning into the wind. Mini-armadas of sea kayakers windmill away. Seagulls scatter. A fleet of pedestrian ferries, little bigger than bathtub toys, bobs along on the water. Tourists graze, buskers busk. A flurry of jugglers flirts with fire, drawing applause and spare change from the audience.

Hanging baskets, overspills of lilac. In Victoria, the scent of flowers is stronger than the sea. In Victoria, even the hustle and bustle is languid. A soulful cowboy crooner, his open guitar case dotted with coins, wails, "Good-time Charley's got the blues." But in Victoria, the blues—the very *idea* of the blues—is more an abstraction than an emotion. Surely the danger here is narcolepsy, not depression.

Three statues stand on guard in the harbourfront heart of Old Victoria, and between them they tell a story. In front of the Parliament Buildings is Queen Victoria herself, crown on head, frown on face, clublike sceptre in hand. Farther down, a scowling colonial soldier wields a bayonet and rifle. And facing the Empress Hotel stands Captain Cook, clutching a scroll of nautical charts. There you have it. The crown, the map and the gun: the three pillars of Empire. Exploration, military might and royal assent.

Where is Victoria? It is here. In the harbour, within sight of the Empress Hotel and the Parliament Buildings. Weighty arrangements of copper and stone, they represent the two key elements without which today's Victoria would not exist: tourism and government. Together with the stark white CPR Steamship Terminal, they form a trio of buildings—like the statues, a triumvirate, if you will—that dominates the inner harbour.

Entering the lobby of the Empress Hotel, with its cold warmth of marble and its pith-helmet potted palms, is like stepping into a BBC costume drama. "Anyone for scones and clotted cream?" And yet the building itself is quintessentially Canadian, rendered in the Château style of CPR hotels everywhere. (Actually, the Empress resembles nothing so much as an oversized English manor with steep French chalet rooftops plonked on top, but that too is a distinctly Canadian blend.)

In the Empress Hotel there was once a room without an exit. If you stand outside the main lobby and look up, towards the left turret, you'll see a line of thin windows. Legend has it that two of these used to mark a room with no door. Whether this was an architectural oversight or an intentional dead end is unknown, but the hotel room lay undisturbed for more than seventy years. Before the wing was dismantled and renovated, a workman peered in through the window and saw pillows and blankets, carefully arranged and grey with dust. It seemed like a metaphor—a metaphor for something unstated.

The Parliament Buildings sit at a sharp angle to the Empress Hotel. High green domes and sweeping stairways. The tiny gilded statue of Captain Vancouver perched up top. (Technically it is a provincial legislature, but "parliament" sounds so much more officious.) The side windows are embedded with dour stained-glass slogans: "Great effects come from industry and perseverance." "The virtue of prosperity is temperance." "*Splendor Sine Occasu* (splendour without dimin-ishment):" This last message, British Columbia's motto, might well have been penned as the civic mission statement of Victoria itself.

Across the street from the Parliament Buildings, at the third point in the triangle, are the clean lines and towering pillars of the CPR Steamship Terminal, complete with Neptune, God of the Sea, entwined in the building's façade. Victoria was once a keystone of Pacific transportation, but no more. The building is now a wax museum, complete with paraffin queens and counterfeit crowns.

The Empress Hotel, erected to accommodate the steamship passengers, is built upon a swamp. It is constructed on reclaimed land in an area the Songhee people called Whosaykum, "the muddy place," a fetid pool that was dammed and drained by CPR engineers. The Empress stands on invisi-ble stilts of Douglas fir, the trunks stripped down and driven through the sludge to the hardpan below. A drained swamp, a drowned forest, an imperial foothold. The Empress sits atop this rainforest of timber but, more important, it sits upon a bedrock of imperial certainties: part hotel, part palanquin.

The Songhee who lived here before the British arrived numbered at least 1200, probably more. The site of their main village is now home to the Royal Victoria Yacht Club. During my stay at the inn on Laurel Point, I learn that the building was erected on an ancient Indian burial ground. Life-sized wooden effigies representing great Songhee warriors and orators once stood guard over the dead at Laurel Point. The burial sheds and the carved statues are gone now, replaced by an inn with a wide view of the harbour and a lavish breakfast buffet.

The history of Victoria is the transformation of Songhee village into yacht club, of burial shed into hotel lobby.

The totem poles of Thunderbird Park, quite literally in the shadow of the Empress, are reminders of this. The past here is a recent past, and the Victoria we know is an invention.

On Government Street, just up from Victoria's inner harbour, lies another architectural triptych, one that perhaps better explains the city's enduring appeal.

The best tobacconist in Canada. The best chocolate shop. The finest bookstore. All three are located in Victoria, all within a single block.

I start at the Old Morris Tobacconist Company, which, more than a mere purveyor of cigars, is in fact a complete gentlemen's shop. It was established in 1892, with the last major renovations done in 1910. When you enter the Old Morris, you enter a world rich in aromas. The smell of cigars fills the air like the warmth from a fireplace. It is the scent of tobacco leaves soaked in rum and maple, steeped in wine, flavoured with cherry and nutmeg.

The shop is laden with the necessary superfluities of a refined male life: ornamental shaving kits, walking sticks, handcrafted chess sets, cigar cutters and pipe-cleaning instruments that unroll in leather cases, like a Victorian surgical set. This is leisure as an expression of status: arcane and elitist and deeply personal, all at the same time.

"Exactly," says the clerk, a soft-spoken wisp of a man who moves like a trail of smoke along the counter. "Gentlemen's requisites," he whispers. "*Accoutrements.*"

I don't smoke, but I could linger in the Old Morris all day, inhaling deeply, sampling the air.

"When I polish the counter," the clerk says with a strangely serene smile, "I almost get lost in its grain."

A sepia-toned display in the window demonstrates how one's character is revealed by how one holds one's cigarette. If you hold your cigarette with your thumb and forefinger you are "modest and good-natured." If you hold it inward, towards your palm, "you are likely to have hobbies." If you hold it between the knuckles of your fist you are, not surprisingly I suppose, "hard to deal with." If you hold it loosely you are "apt to be lazy." Being a nonsmoker, I consider instead how I hold my pen. I discover that I am "aloof and meticulous," which describes me to a T, except for the "aloof" and "meticulous" part.

In the beautiful glass display cases of the Old Morris, the cigars are kept at a humidity of exactly 70 percent, in a small pocket of tropical mist. "The best cigar?" says the clerk.

"No, the most expensive," I say, repeating my query.

"With cigars," he purrs, "it amounts to the same thing." Like a curator in a museum, he carefully unwraps a hand-rolled Monte Cristo A Habana. "A three-hour smoke," he says with a sigh.

It makes one lament for the days when men regularly had three hours to kill, not to mention sixty-four dollars to spare for a single cigar.

In the centre of the small shop sits an alabaster pillar with a glowing lamp on top and a flicker of live flame below. It is a cigar lighter, the wonderfully named *electrolier*, and it has been in the Old Morris since 1910. There is only one other like it in the world, located in a hotel lobby in Singapore. And on the front of this elegant pillar sits a cartoon drawing of a cigarette with an ugly orange bar drawn across it. *NO SMOKING.*

I live in a country where you can't smoke in a tobacco shop, where you can't light a cigar from the flame of an almost century-old work of art created specifically for that purpose. I live in a country where a beautifully handcrafted wooden cigar box from Havana is slapped with stickers displaying photos of diseased lungs and dissected human brains. These graphic, paternalistic warnings, distinctly Canadian: what purpose do they serve in a shop like Old Morris? None.

Oddly enough, the boxes at Rogers' Chocolatier, across the street and down a bit from the Old Morris, are not plastered with stickers showing close-ups of cellulite and clogged arteries. Still, the tobacconist and chocolate shops feel remarkably similar. Rogers' too is filled with a richly layered aroma, in this case of cocoa and almonds.

Rogers' Chocolates began in 1885, and it moved into its present building in 1918. The amber glass and bronze panels, the gold-leaf script on the windows, the art nouveau interior—it is a very chocolatey sort of place. And if the curved glass counters inside suggest a jewellers', there is a reason: the display cases were originally built to hold diamonds. "Chocolate. A girl's *second*-best friend," the clerk behind the counter quips. He is as robust and friendly as the Old Morris clerk was thin and whispery.

"The most expensive item?" He points to a tray on the top shelf. "The chocolate orange peels. Definitely."

I study a display of these. "But they're just orange peels dunked in chocolate," I say, stating the obvious.

"Well, they cost twenty-eight dollars a pound, and the price is low considering they're handmade and take about four hours to boil down."

I try a sample. They taste exactly like orange peels dunked in chocolate.

"Orangey," I say.

The clerk beams. "Aren't they, though?"

I work my way around the room—in the interests of journalistic authenticity, you understand—sampling chocolate almond clusters and creamy rum-filled squares, savouring the tastes and textures like a kid in a, well, you know.

I come to the second-most expensive item in the store, a five-pound box of Rogers' legendary Victoria creams, which sells for $100. "Can I try some?" I say recklessly, drunk on chocolate.

The clerk, however, is catching on, and he raises an eyebrow at my request. "I suppose. . . . How many did you want to try?"

"Oh, about five pounds' worth."

"Ha ha," he says. But he isn't laughing.

There's a crack in one of the display cases, and above this fault line a sign informs us:

> Some fifty years ago, a rather diminutive patron, feeling she had not been afforded prompt service, rapped her walking stick smartly against the display case, causing the glass to crack. Every few years we consider having it repaired, but someone always suggests we leave it as a silent reminder to "listen to our customers."

In Victoria, even cracks in the surface are lovingly maintained. In my quest for five pounds of "sample," I consider rapping my own walking stick smartly against the glass—except that I don't have one. There's that, and also the fact that I am completely sated by this point.

Back across Government Street and just thirty-three paces past the Old Morris lies Munro's, "the bookstore in a bank." And any city that turns a bank into a bookstore can't be all bad. The stone pillars outside—made of polished granite and as cool to the touch as marble—and the curved glass windows in front allude to the store's origins in 1909 as a bastion of the Royal Bank of Canada. Several ill-advised renovations had robbed the building of much of its charm by the time the bank closed down in the early 1980s, but fortunately it was rescued and restored to its former glory by bookseller Jim Munro, a dishevelled Louis XIV figure (if a Louis XIV figure can be described as "dishevelled"), who peeled back the linoleum and peered behind the false ceilings and the drywall and realized what lay hidden beneath.

Today, a series of tapestries by Victoria artist Carol Sabiston—literary cyphers alluding to classic works of fiction—hang like medieval banners around the interior. The shelves are heavy with words, and Munro's has laid a rightful claim to being the finest seller of books in Canada. (And yes, this is a shameless attempt at getting face-out treatment for my books.) Roy McFarlane and I first met at Munro's, which was where he was working. I'd been spending so much time hanging around the store that the staff began to suspect I was casing the joint. At one point I asked Roy the same question I'd posed at the other shops.

"The most expensive book?" he said, a bit baffled.

"Yes," I say. "The best."

He looked perturbed. "With books, there is no connection between price and quality. You do know that, right?"

So the parallels are not absolute. But still. Tobacco, chocolate and the written word: three great indulgences, three great luxuries. Three great addictions. Between them, they hearken back to a time when life was slower, to an era only half-remembered and largely imagined. In a word: Victoria.

The city of Victoria began as a pre-emptive move, a strategic ploy designed to thwart the territorial designs of the United States. In 1843, the Hudson's Bay Company built a trading post at the southernmost tip of Vancouver's Island, as it was then known, in order to pin down the western border and secure the entire island for Great Britain. It worked. When the 49th parallel was extended across the mountains three years later in a razor-straight line, the border had to jog south around Vancouver's Island just to keep Fort Victoria within British territory. Fish and furs fuelled Fort Victoria, but without the HBC post there, Canada, as a nation stretching "from sea to sea," might never have existed.

Having succeeded in keeping Vancouver's Island, the British then faced a thorny question: what to do with it? The island was massive, almost unmanageably so. Several proposals had been floated over the years, everything from a prison colony to a Mormon homeland—from sinners to saints, so to speak. But the HBC was the only established European presence in the area, and in 1849 Great Britain leased the entire island to the company for a token sum of "seven shillings a year." The HBC was granted complete control over resources, minerals and land sales. (No one thought to consult the thousands upon thousands of Native people already living there.) In exchange, the HBC was required to (a) encourage colonization and (b) operate under the authority of an independent British governor. It would do neither.

Because most of the Hudson's Bay Company employees were from French Canada, the language at Fort Victoria was predominantly French. But that was about to change. In 1849, the same year that it was "rented" to the HBC, Vancouver Island was proclaimed an official Crown colony. *Huzzah!* A grand total of one (1) colonist showed up. And he wasn't even a very good colonist. He was Captain Walter Colquhoun Grant, a former officer in the British Army, and he came adorned with all the essentials for life as a "gentleman farmer": cricket bats, wickets, ornamental brass cannons and an entire library of leather-bound volumes. Captain Grant came ashore and immediately shot a cow, thinking it was a buffalo. Not an auspicious start.

Walter Grant is also credited, or rather blamed, for introducing Scotch broom to Vancouver Island. The homesick captain planted seeds from this flowering bush to remind him of Britain. Unfortunately, the transplanted weed quickly spread beyond his garden and took over entire swaths of countryside, choking out native plants. Today the yellow flowers are thick along the roads, and programs aimed at uprooting the noisome weed continue, to no avail. (There's a moral here somewhere. . . .)

Walter Grant cleared land in a remote section west of the fort and built a lonely cabin, little more than a shanty, which he grandly named "Mullachard" after his ancestral estate in the Old Country. He planted his Scotch broom and polished his cannons and considered suicide.

The colony's first governor, Richard Blanshard, arrived the following year to a rousing round of indifference. The promised official residence wasn't ready, and no one at the HBC seemed in a hurry to complete it, so the hapless Blanshard was forced to live on board his ship instead. Even worse, he discovered that he was governor of a colony consisting of a single morose colonist, giving the colony a citizen-to-administration ratio of precisely 1:1. Blanshard wasn't even receiving a salary. He had expected to fund the costs of enacting legislation, holding councils, and recruiting a militia through revenues generated by the colony (i.e., Walter).

As Blanshard soon learned, Vancouver Island was a Crown colony in name only. The HBC still called the shots. Racked with malaria and lost in a haze of opium, Blanshard resigned eight months after he arrived, and was replaced the following year by James Douglas. Douglas, of the HBC, was the very person who had chosen the site of Fort Victoria, near a Songhee village in a spot Douglas had dubbed "a perfect Eden." (The outline of Fort Victoria can still be seen in Bastion Square, as a double line of bricks in the sidewalk tracing the original boundaries of the garrison.) With the appointment of James Douglas as governor, any pretext of separate domains, one commercial and one imperial, ended. Douglas, a great smouldering mountain of a man, served both empires with an equally autocratic hand.

In spite of the HBC's best efforts, settlers continued to arrive, and a small community grew up around the fort. (Captain Walter Grant, however, left Vancouver Island and rejoined the British Army. He died of dysentery during an imperial adventure in India.) In 1858, a recently arrived colonist described Victoria in his journal as "a quiet village of about 800 inhabitants. No noise, no bustle, no gamblers, no speculators. . . . A few quiet, gentlemanly-behaved inhabitants, chiefly Scotchmen, secluded as it were from the whole world. As to business there was none, the streets were grown over with grass."

Just six weeks later, that same settler would write of how "Victoria was assailed by an indescribable array of Polish Jews, Italian fishermen, French cooks, jobbers, speculators of every kind, land agents, auctioneers, bummers, bankrupts, and brokers of every description."

What happened? *Gold.* Not on the island but on the mainland, along the tumult of the Fraser River. Victoria was the nearest supply depot to the goldfields, and by the end of the year more than 20,000 people had poured in. This wasn't an influx; it was an invasion.

Prior to the gold rush, Vancouver Island had been referred to as "the back of the world." With the first boatload of miners— "between 400 and 500 Yankees, armed with revolvers and bowie knives," in the words of one passenger—that would change forever. (Today they come armed with camcorders and chewing gum, but the Yankee deluge continues.) Victoria was overrun with rough-knuckled prospectors and a motley assortment of mountebanks and ne'er-do-wells. Hotels and brothels appeared like mushrooms after a downpour. In the first six weeks, more than 200 new buildings went up. When it rained, the streets became a gumbo of mud. Local wags took to posting signs advising "No bottom obtainable" and "Two men in this hole."

Even worse was the ungodly stench that hung over the city. Sewage, overflowing cesspools, the scummy runoff from a bathhouse and the sickly-sweet smell of horse manure and pigsties combined to create a "putrescent filth," in the words of the local newspaper. Add to that the stink emanating from the city's opium factories—like the smell of rotting potatoes boiled in their own skins, it was said—and you start to realize that today's wretched aroma of potpourri and gift-shop soap is not so bad.

Victoria was on the brink of the lawless, wild-west anarchy that had plagued earlier gold rushes in California. In the Oregon Territory, a very similar scenario to Victoria's had played out. American settlers had swarmed in and taken de facto control; by the time the British realized what was going on, it was too late. James Douglas was determined not to let that happen again. Moving quickly, he annexed the mainland, proclaiming that the gold in the Fraser Valley was now Crown property; anyone removing said gold without authorization would be arrested and prosecuted. He had no authority to do any of this, of course, but the Americans didn't know that. Douglas then began issuing permits and collecting mining fees. When word reached London that their man in Victoria had single-handedly claimed a region larger than France, nobody blinked. A new colony was created on the mainland with a name chosen personally by Queen Victoria: British Columbia. Douglas retired from the HBC entirely and took firm hold of the reins of both colonies. The island and the mainland would be united in 1866, two years after Douglas—now Sir Douglas—retired.

The gold rush years also saw the first large-scale arrival of Chinese immigrants. Men mainly, they came first as independent miners and then as railway workers. Thousands settled in Victoria. Some ran laundries; others became gardeners and houseboys to the city's monied class. Victoria's Chinatown is the oldest in Canada, and a good deal of the nation's Chinese population can trace their roots back to this city. Today's Chinatown is small, contained in a few square blocks of recessed balconies and parapets. But appearances are deceiving, and in its day Victoria's Chinese community was second only to San Francisco's. As they did in other cities, the Chinese in Victoria formed a community within a community. Or more accurately, in this case, an enclave within an outpost.

Chinatown was also home to the city's infamous and very profitable drug trade. Victoria was the closest port to Asia, and the opium flowed in. With it came the usual sordid sideshows of crime and exploitation. Everything from tattoos to opera could be found in Chinatown after dark, but vice was by far the biggest-selling commodity. By the 1880s, Victoria's red-light district would be the largest on the Pacific Northwest. The city's reputation eventually became so bad that newspapers in Montreal denounced Victoria as a "sin den." (And you know things are bad when *Montreal* clucks its tongue at you.)

Victoria's Chinatown was a neighbourhood of Escherlike dimensions. A network of hidden lanes and secret passageways led from building to building, courtyard to courtyard. In this shadowy world, any number of escape routes might be conjured up. Wooden doors would swing aside, iron gates would slide into place. A closet might open into the next building; a washroom might offer access to a back alley. When the police charged in, full of fury and might, the raids quickly became exercises in futility. It was like trying to storm a labyrinth.

This is not to imply that the opium trade was illegal. On the contrary, it was heavily taxed and provided a healthy income for the government. The raids in Chinatown were meant to catch tax dodgers and snare unlicensed opium dealers. (Later, when the government brought in an exclusionary head tax that singled out Chinese immigrants, the secret corridors and hidden warrens of Chinatown became means for illegal workers to elude capture.)

Today, stone lions and the glazed tiles of the Gate of Harmonious Interest mark the entrance to Victoria's Chinatown. The fleshpots and narcotics are long gone. But for a peek into the past, and what was once Victoria's "Forbidden Town," you need only slip into Fan Tan Alley.

This alley is the narrowest commercial street in North America. It was once the heart of Chinatown's gambling world, where rival gangs roamed Little Canton, where the clatter of fan-tan tiles and the celestial scent of opiates drifted out from behind doors and down stairways. Fan Tan Alley leads off Pandora Street, whose name evokes images of dark urges unleashed. The entrance to the alley is a small gap between buildings; if it weren't signposted you would miss it.

I have visited Fan Tan Alley many times: in the early dawn, when it is still half-asleep; at dusk, when the gates at either end are about to creak shut; and at midday, when the passageway becomes a jostling parade of shoppers. Brick walls squeeze in so close that in places you can run your hands along both sides of the alley at the same time. Today, herbal-infused oils and scented candles have replaced opium as the narcotics of choice. The shops offer up a confusion of cultures—everything from Balinese cat carvings to Navajo blankets, with no rhyme and very little reason. The Fan Tan Chinese Café provides a back-door alleyway special: steaming broths and slithering noodles. For the most part, though, Fan Tan has been colonized by New Age clutter: yogic centres and tarot-card readers, sitars and bongo drums, wicker and wind chimes, "healing crystals" and polished moonstones. Tie-dyed apparel lines the racks. And yet, halfway down, a Chinese barber shop, miraculously untouched by time, exists in its own quiet side pocket. In an unadorned wooden room, a barber slowly strops a razor as an elderly gentleman waits his turn. If the police were to storm through, the walls of Chinatown might fold in upon themselves even now.

Victoria's founding families often fretted over the "menace" posed by the Chinese, but the real threat came from the Anglo-Americans, who had established an economic beach-head here. The first major businesses in the city were opened as northern branches of San Francisco interests. The building components of Victoria's boom years—the lumber, the fix-tures, even the architects—were imported from San Francisco too. And the city's population had become heavily American. In Victoria they celebrated the Fourth of July with disconcert-ing vigour, as American moneymen plotted pie-eyed republi-can takeovers in places with names like the California Saloon, the American Hotel and the Sacramento Restaurant. By 1867, the U.S. government had purchased Alaska from the Russians for $7.2 million, and the Americans bragged that they had British Columbia sandwiched on either side and "could eat her up at any time."

So why isn't Victoria an American city? *Gold*—or, more precisely, the lack thereof. As first one gold rush and then another dwindled and died, as the claims fizzled and caved, the Americans began to leave. Those who remained urged the colony to surrender and "join the U.S.A.!" with increasingly inflammatory rhetoric, but the pro-British faction was now in control, and the movement failed. In 1871, British Columbia joined the Canadian confederation. Bitterly disappointed, Victoria's last American holdouts began selling their property and packing up.

The American departure left a vacuum in its wake. By the 1880s, the Chinese made up half of Victoria's population, but they had been systematically marginalized, and immigration from China was now blocked by quotas, exorbitant fees and restrictive entry requirements. The Songhee had relocated, first across the bay and then onto a reserve, where a smallpox epidemic swept through, decimating their ranks. So it was by attrition, as much as anything, that those of British background rose to prominence in Victoria. It would be their duty, they declared, to lay the foundation of a second England, to "reproduce in the west a facsimile of the civilization" they had left behind in the east. Not the real deal—a reproduction, a facsimile. Many of them had never even been to England, but that was irrelevant. To be a colonial is to be born into exile.

In the 1860s, Victoria was described as a "little San Francisco." Just ten years later, a visitor from the U.S. would comment that "the English character of this place is particularly noticeable." Not in appearance, perhaps, but certainly in mood. The presence of the Royal Naval base in nearby Esquimalt played a crucial role in setting the tone, entrenching as it did the notions of rank and position, as well as supplying officer husbands for Victoria's socially ascendant daughters. The mild climate helped, too; many colonial officers and wealthy British ex-pats retired to Victoria, bringing their titles and presumptions with them. Families that would never have risen above middle-class stature in Britain were suddenly able to assume the mantle of aristocracy.

The English nature of Victoria became a point of pride—
and identity. Wedgwood and Harris tweed took on totemistic
qualities. Tea and crumpets became an act of cultural communion. Croquet and cricket were suddenly the sports of
choice. The city's wealthier set began playing to the stereo-
type, building houses in an appealing mishmash of styles
meant to evoke what they thought a proper English manor
home should be: Queen Anne eclectic, Tudor interiors, even
a castle or two.

In 1880, a traveller from New York commented that, in
Victoria, "everything is intensely English," and that is truer
today than ever. Not simply English but *intensely* English,
self-consciously English. As early as 1904, the city's Tourist
Association was selling Victoria with the tagline "An
Outpost of Empire." But it was Charles Warren, the head of
the city's publicity bureau in the 1920s, who cemented
Victoria's image in the public imagination. *"Cities need personality!"* This was Warren's great insight—and his battle
cry. And what was Victoria's personality? In an early example
of product branding, Warren cast Victoria as "a little bit of
old England." It was a relentless campaign. Victoria became
a theme park. Fake half-panelling was thrown up. Thatched
cottages appeared. Everything English was elevated to
fetish-like levels. Everything else was downplayed or
ignored. Ironically, as popular historian Terry Reksten has
noted, "George Warren, the man most responsible for
Victoria's belief that it somehow really *was* like old England,
was born in San Francisco and had never ventured off the
American continent when he began to insist that Victoria
was so recognizably English."

More than tourists, it was the retirees who shaped Victoria's character—many of them coming from the Canadian prairies, but all of them attracted by the Englishness of the city. The first to arrive was John Tod, described in the records of the time as "an antiquarian pensioner," who retired to Fort Victoria in 1850. By the late 1920s, Victoria had the oldest average population of any major city in Canada. It still does today.

The form is American, the content is English. Architecturally San Francisco, emotionally British—decidedly Canadian. In a word: Victoria.

In Victoria, metaphors abound. You can pluck them from the vine at your leisure. The wax-museum royalty. The Scotch broom choking the landscape. The Bengal Lounge at the Empress, with its palm fronds and tiger skin stretched above the fireplace. Even the petrified dinosaur tracks outside the main doors of the Royal British Columbia Museum. Real tracks of real dinosaurs, cut from the rock and carefully preserved. But my favourite symbol of Victoria is a clock: a *colonial* clock.

I first hear about the clock from Ross Crockford, the former editor of *Monday Magazine*, Victoria's arts-and-activism weekly. Having listened to me gush about the city one too many times—tossing out words like "languid" and "dreamlike" even as I blissfully ignore the crouching queues of teenage panhandlers along Douglas Street—Ross takes me on a walking tour. Our first stop is the clock, located in a downtown shopping mall hidden behind the façades of older buildings. (This parlour trick of hiding modern shopping centres behind a veneer of history is something Canadians are particularly good at. Calgary has done it; so have Charlottetown, Halifax, Montreal and Saint John.) Inside the mall, suspended from the highest part of the ceiling, the clock is a hefty bronze cube of polished imperial sentiments. "Westward the Course of Empire Goes Forth," reads the message emblazoned across it. The clock also tells us the time in Bombay, Singapore, London, Zanzibar and Kowloon, which seems very strange. Why would shoppers in Victoria need to know what time it is in Bombay? Or Singapore? Or London, for that matter? Ah, but this clock is a historical artifact, no? A treasured heirloom of the city's past. A reminder of a time when imperialism was not a dirty word. Except that it isn't. Victoria's colonial clock wasn't built in 1890, but in 1990. It is a reminder that, for colonization to become truly successful, it must at some point become self-inflicted.

"This clock represents the Disneyfication of Victoria," says Ross, warming to his role as unofficial tour guide. "A sort of half-assed attempt at preserving the trappings of Empire, while catering to American expectations of quaintness. It wasn't put up to honour the past, it was put up to fool the tourists."

Like Roy McFarlane, Ross Crockford assures me that there is another Victoria, one very different from the officially packaged version. It's like a Zen paradox—*The Victoria you see is not the real Victoria.* "On weekends, loggers and pulp-mill workers blow into town with money to burn. Nothing genteel about it." There is also, apparently, a writhing underground in Victoria, one filled with Wicca-worshipping covens, drug-fuelled raves, sado-masochistic sex clubs and weed-smoking lesbian bikers. Even opium dens, I imagine.

"Did you know," says Ross, "that there are more practising witches per capita in Victoria than anywhere else in Canada?"

No. But I might have guessed. There's no shortage of odd-ball societies here, everything from the Coronation Street Fan Club to the Near Death Experience Society (surely one and the same!).

You could argue that this tradition of nurturing eccentrics is part of the city's English inheritance. "The illusion of Victoria *is* the real Victoria," I venture. "And what's so bad about that?"

Ross has something else up his sleeve. The next stop on his slightly jaded tour is "what's generally agreed upon as the worst mural in Victoria."

We stroll over to take a look. "You've seen the beautiful killer whales painted on the building down on Wharf Street?" he asks. "This is its counterpart."

Ross is being unduly modest. This isn't simply the worst mural in Victoria. It may very well be the worst mural in Canada, perhaps even the world. I have walked by it several times earlier without really noticing it, but now that I do— *man, oh man*. This mural, an ode to "the perfect Eden," has everything crammed into it: angelic children, wise Indians, a sunset on the beach, city domes, a totem pole, frolicking animals. It is schmaltz. And not even adept schmaltz. The arms of the Indian princess are too short, giving her a weirdly disproportionate appearance. The Thunderbird atop the totem pole looks like Woody the Woodpecker in war paint, and the female fiddle player has impossibly HUGE hands. The crowning glory is the cherubic little boy in the lower corner. Holding a maple leaf. With a teddy bear. In his pocket.

I stagger back like someone overcome by fumes. "Point taken," I say. The weight of that mural cannot be underestimated. *The unbearable lightness of being Victoria.*

The city's historic shift from outpost of America to colony of Great Britain is embodied in the life of one man: an architect from England named Francis Rattenbury. Rattenbury rose to prominence when he was awarded the contract for the new Parliament Buildings at the age of twenty-five. He did a grand job. Part cathedral, part U.S. state capitol, with just a hint of Taj Mahal, Victoria's parliament, completed in 1898, is truly magnificent—even if the acoustics were poor and rumours were rife that young Ratz had copied the plan from that of a maharajah's palace in India—though not the actual Taj Mahal. The Parliament Buildings anchored the city of Victoria as the province's capital, in the face of the young upstart railway burg of Vancouver that had sprung up on the mainland.

Rattenbury went on to resculpt the city's inner harbour, designing both the Empress Hotel and the "Temple of Neptune" steamship terminal. But like a Victorian-era penny dreadful, the tale of Francis Rattenbury ends in a lurid tangle of madness, murder and suicide. In 1923, at the age of fifty-six, Rattenbury, now a respected if flamboyant member of Victoria's high society, met a young flapper named Alma at a soiree held in his honour at the Empress. (He had just been awarded a contract to build the Crystal Gardens.) Alma was pouty, sensuous, daring—a divorcee in a time when that term could still make people blush—and she was thirty years younger than Rattenbury. The aging architect was smitten. He hounded his poor wife, Florrie, until she granted him a divorce, and he then married the younger lady. The upper classes of Victoria were not amused, and after a few years of icy receptions and cold shoulders, Rattenbury was forced to leave. He moved to England with Alma and soon fell into disrepair. He lost a fortune in bad deals, began to drink heavily, grew old and impotent and increasingly deaf. His restless bride, now thirty-eight and bored to tears, hired a seventeen-year-old boy to be her "chauffeur and handyman." She seduced the lad within weeks of his arrival, then moved him into a spare bedroom near hers. And one night, the young chauffeur smashed in the architect's head with a mallet. Rattenbury died three days later. There were whispers that it was Alma, high on drugs and laughing, who had dealt the death blow.

In the trial that followed, Alma first confessed to the killing and then retracted her statement. Although she was acquitted, her young lover was sentenced to hang. Distraught, Alma stabbed herself in the chest repeatedly, hitting her heart three times before flinging herself into the River Avon. The chauffeur's death sentence was commuted, and the young man was eventually set free following a public outcry about this innocent English boy who had been "ensnared" by an immoral older woman. From Canada.

In Rattenbury's downfall and death we catch a glimpse of the city's underbelly, pallid and soft and aching with appetites.

Sunday night. James Bay Inn. It's a long way from High Tea at the Empress. Not physically; if I bolt now I can make it to the Empress in one quick sprint—*too late*. Roy has returned from the bar, armed with beer, and pulled up a chair.

The host and ringmaster for tonight's event is a local poet named Cliff Syringe, which I'm assuming is some sort of subtle pseudonym. (I mean, who names their kids *Cliff* these days?) Cliff is bald, with a goatee and tattooed forearms—tattoos, of course, being *de rigueur* among the poetry set. In his role as host, he has been asked to choose five key words that the participants must incorporate into the poetry they will be writing and then reading to the crowd. "The five words Cliff chooses will set the tone for tonight's event," Roy tells me.

Here is the list of words that Monsieur Syringe provides:

(1) hangover
(2) penis
(3) vulva
(4) inject
(5) death

Yup. "Listen, Roy," I say. "It's been fun, but it is getting late and I do have to catch a train to Nanaimo tomorrow morning"—fake yawn—"so I really should be—"

"No, stay, don't go. Give it a chance." Roy concedes that he's not thrilled with the words Cliff Syringe has come up with, a list he describes, with diplomatic understatement, as being "a bit obvious, a bit contrived." Roy prefers words that present more of a challenge. "When I was hosting, I gave them one word they didn't even know. They had to look it up. 'Phrenology,' or something like that. A different night, a different list of words, and you have a very different experience. This event is a work-in-progress, and always will be, I hope." For Roy, the process was always as important as the final product.

"And besides," he adds, a sly smile surfacing as he plays the predictable but always effective Authorial Ego Card, "we're giving away one of your books as a prize."

"Really? Which one? The tart irreverence of *Why I Hate Canadians*? The hip satire of *Happiness™*? The cutting political commentary of *Bastards & Boneheads*?"

"No, the, ah, the idiot's guide."

"Dummies," I say, with a sigh. "I'm a dummy, Roy. I'm not an idiot."

They are giving away a copy of *Canadian History for Dummies*, possibly the least hip book I have ever written. And it gets worse. My dummies' guide isn't even first prize. That honour goes to a Curious George T-shirt.

As the poets scribble furiously away, Roy takes me around to meet some of them, on the assumption that they will be delighted at having their train of thought interrupted by a guy who was trumped by a monkey. At one point, Roy introduces me to a woman named Donna Li. She is one of the featured poets. She is captivatingly beautiful. And there's me with a mouth full of onion rings.

"My God, she's gorgeous," I whisper to Roy, once I manage to swallow and Donna has gone back to her pen and paper.

"Yes," he says, as though only just noticing it. "She is, isn't she? She's a fantastic poet as well."

The people on hand tonight are neither black-garbed artistes nor flower-adorned nature nymphs; most are of the sweatpants-and-cheap-running-shoes variety. "We're not even successful enough to be poor," is how one participant puts it. "We all have day jobs. And not exotic day jobs. Just day jobs."

But that is not entirely true. "Did I mention," says Roy, "that Donna is a physician?"

"A doctor? But she looks so young."

His voice lowers. "Actually, the first time I met her, I didn't think she was of age to come into a bar." He looks down, sees me jotting this information into my notepad. "But don't publish that. I think she likes to keep her two worlds separate."

"Wouldn't dream of it," I say, graciously closing my pad. "Her secret's safe with me."

Usually, one would boast about being a doctor and hesitate before admitting one wrote poetry. Not here. Not in Victoria, and not at the James Bay Inn.

The first poet up is a man named M.C., who produces a container of Chinese medicine labelled "Happy Brain Pills." He swallows a handful of them right there on stage to, you know, get his brain revving. Then he starts popping something called "Saliva Pills," designed to treat dry mouth. He asks the crowd, "How many should I take?" *Seven,* they yell. *Eight! All of them!* The chants and cheers grow louder as he stuffs his mouth with pills. "Uh-oh, I'm feeling kind of funny," he says, drool spilling over. He barely manages to get (wetly) through his poem.

Next up is an angry young rebel—from the suburbs, it would seem—who recites a long, ranting monologue about being angry. Though "recites" is perhaps not the proper word. "Inflicts" would be more accurate. His poetic recital contains the following references, which I jot down for posterity: "sliced thumbs," "vomit," "blood," "fists to the face" and "a novelist living alone."

Next!! A heavy-set young man with short-cropped hair and a spiderweb tattoo on his elbow strides up to the microphone. The shirt he's wearing reads PART ANIMAL. PART MACHINE on the front and SEARCH & DESTROY on the back.

And it dawns on me what they are doing, these poets. They are raging against Victoria. They are *fighting the mural*. It must be suffocating to be young and restless in Victoria. Growing up here must feel, at times, like living in a diorama.

The poet with the spiderweb elbow reads a piece entitled "Gotta Piss," which describes in loving detail the smell of urine in Victoria's Douglas Street McDonald's restroom, and which contains the following words, more or less at random: "spit," "vomit," "blood," "semen," "yellow urine stains" and, as he has evidently run out of bodily excretions to reference, "a strange mysterious liquid." As this young man waxes euphoric about the "bright orange piss" that erupts from the body "like battery acid," I look over at Roy. This isn't poetry, this is Tourette's syndrome in need of medication. He smiles wanly and gives me a shrug as if to say, "What can you do?"

Next up is a woman Cliff Syringe dubs Maximum Cleavage, who reads a poem about "mainlining smack" in the "urban neon jungle." Or maybe it's a real jungle. It's hard to say. Following her is a thin young man who takes a deep breath, pauses, and begins: "I know that I'm a junkie hooked on my addiction." And I think, *Lou Reed has a lot to answer for.*

The procession continues. It can be funny at times, but tiring. Someone reads a staccato poem about "injecting" a "vulva" with a "hangover" of "death." (He must have worked his penis into the mix too, because he eventually runs out of air and—having hit all the stops—sits down, not to jeers and thrown chairs, but to applause. Incredible.) Another poet mumbles into the microphone about smack and mescaline. Another howls like a coyote with his nuts caught on an electric fence.

"Death is always an option," he sombrely intones.

Yes, I think to myself, *it certainly is*.

But then, well, hell. Donna Li gets up on stage and everything else dissolves. Not because she is beautiful, there are other beautiful women in the room, but because she actually has something to say—no, that's not it. It's not just that she has something to say, it's that she appreciates language. She enjoys the roll and rhythm of words.

In dealing with the five terms that have been lobbed her way, Donna combines the clinical detachment of scientific terminology with a lonely sense of the lyrical. For Donna, the word "inject" brings back memories of medical school, of a fellow student learning how to give an IV by practising on himself. The rubber tourniquet, blue veins and poised needle creating an uncomfortable image of a junkie, but not on a street corner—in a lab coat. Her poem evokes the gnawing doubts of future doctors, the "fear-driven hangovers" and the "formaldehyde preserve" of an early-morning anatomy class in which students peer into the darkness of cadavers. "There were the love affairs, the skipped classes, and remembering this: *Do no harm*."

It is like a quiet implosion in the room. And then it is gone, replaced by more boozy burlesque, more open-mike banter. I stagger over on drunken legs as Donna returns to her seat. "Really good," I keep saying. "Really good."

Roy leads me gently back to my table as Mr. Syringe

bounds on stage to say something about—well, I'm not sure. The beer is working its way down my body. My legs are numb, and the room is a half-stop out of focus.

The girl at the next table leans over and says, "I know him."

"Who?"

"Syringe. I know *of* him."

Her name is Clara. It's her first time at the poetry slam, and she's a little disappointed. "I heard sometimes there were fights on stage." Her ears have been pierced, in a frenzy apparently, and the rings run right up the edge, as on one of those spiral notebooks. She thinks I'm a reporter, and she wants to talk about the "fetish scene" in Victoria. "I have a tattoo," she says. "You'll never guess where."

Fetish scene? I thought this city already *was* one extended fetish scene. I fumble with my notepad and pen, but I can't get past the sight of her multiple piercings.

"Yeah, it did hurt," she says, running her finger along the metal coil of her ear. "But not as much as you'd think."

Think, I write in my notepad. *Hurt.*

At the end of the night—after the lights go up and the tabs have been tallied and the darts have been pulled from the walls and from the stage (figuratively, in the second case)—Roy comes over and says to me, "Well?"

"It didn't hurt," I reply, slurring my words slightly. "Not as much as you'd think." No longer able to take coherent notes, I wave a tape recorder in his general direction. "Roy McFarlane, age—"

"Forty-five."

"Tell me, Roy McFarlane. What the hell was that all about?"

Roy laughs.

"No, really. I want to know. Why d'you think people come here?"

"To celebrate."

"Celebrate what?"

"Language," he says. "The simple fact that we can make sounds that communicate—*something*. The same reason people write books."

"A celebration?"

"That's right. And like any celebration, it can get raucous, crude even, boisterous. That's what poetry is about."

Roy has a way of saying unusual things as though they are the most obvious statements possible. He talks about art and life and literature the way some people tell you the time. "I'll get you up on stage one of these days," he says.

"Like hell you will."

He laughs. "Until next time."

I nod my goodbye and grapple with the door.

So it was smoke and mirrors all along, this city by the sea. Still reeling, I stumble out of the James Bay Inn and back into Victoria. "Where have you been?" I ask the city pointedly. It is a moonless night, and I weave slightly as I go, walking along the high edge of the harbour wall. Sailboats are rising and falling on slow waves, sleeping creatures by the bay, their sails pulled in.

Adorned with prima-donna stage lights, the Parliament Buildings are reduced to a shimmering connect-the-dots outline. For a moment, it feels as though Victoria is retreating into its own outline, the buildings vanishing one by one.

MISSING: Roy McFarlane, 45 years of age. Height 5'6," weight 175 pounds. Last seen May 14, 2001, heading south on Store Street near Swans Pub on a dark blue mountain bike with black fenders. Anyone having information on Mr. McFarlane's whereabouts please call . . .

Just eight days after I leave Victoria, Roy disappears. Friends and family search for weeks, then months. No one knows where he has gone or what has happened to him. He has simply vanished. One moment he is riding his bike through the dusk, putting up posters for the local Green Party candidate, and then . . . nothing. He has become a voice on my tape recorder.

In mid-July, Roy McFarlane's body surfaces in the harbour. He may have had an accident or suffered a trauma and fallen in, but no one is sure of that. No one is sure of anything, except that he is gone. And that he is missed.

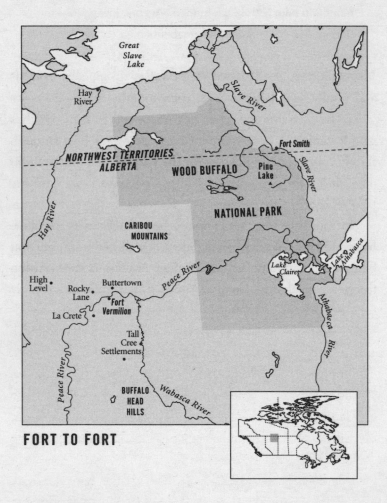

Great
Slave
Lake

Hay
River

Slave River

NORTHWEST TERRITORIES
ALBERTA

Fort Smith

WOOD BUFFALO

Pine
Lake

Slave River

NATIONAL PARK

CARIBOU
MOUNTAINS

Hay River

Peace River

Lake
Claire

Lake Athabasca

High
Level

Buttertown

Rocky
Lane

Fort
Vermilion

La Crete

Tall
Cree
Settlements

Athabasca River

BUFFALO
HEAD
HILLS

Wabasca River

Peace River

FORT TO FORT

chapter two

LEAVING THE FORT

WHEN I WAS SIXTEEN YEARS OLD, I dropped out of school and set off to see the world. I got as far as Saskatoon. . . .

This is where the tale would normally begin, but there is more to it than that. Our stories don't start when we leave home; they start much, much earlier. I was born in Fort Vermilion, Alberta, a fur-trapping community in the northern reaches of Canada's boreal forest, "closer to the Arctic Circle than the American border," as we liked to say. These woodlands form a tangled garden of jack pine and fir; of black spruce and white birch, peeling like papyrus, and the dark lichen-licked bark of the tamarack tree. In Fort Vermilion, stands of lodgepole pine, tall and scraggly, grew in battalions beside the river. Trembling aspen filled our yard with motion, the silvery-grey undersides of their leaves riffling on the slightest of breezes.

The boreal forests of Canada, named after Boreas, Greek God of the North Wind, seem to spend one half of the year frozen and the other half on fire. Summer forest fires burn through, leaving charred animal bones and smouldering stumps behind, and in winter a Nordic cold moves in, heavy and still.

It is an area larger than the imagination, a mixed-bag wood-land salad of mossy bogs and countless nameless lakes. And yet, even though it covers more than a third of the country, Canada's boreal forest barely registers in the national con-sciousness. It is as though the mental map of Canada drops off a few miles north of Edmonton and then re-emerges in the High Arctic. When Canadians speak of "the North!" they mean igloos and Inuit, yet more than a million people live in this mid-range northern forest—many of them in small communities not unlike Fort Vermilion. A sense of disconnectedness comes with living inside such a large swath of missing geography.

Canada? That was just a name on a map.

When I was growing up, the rest of the country seemed so far away it might as well have been an imaginary place. Canada lay far to the south, beyond the curve of horizon. Canada was where the radio signals came from—distant distress calls, strange music, the echoes of faint voices in a far room. I knew Canada existed in the way I knew gravity existed: I could feel its effect, even if it seemed more like a theoretical construct than a real thing. But where Canada was situated, exactly, I couldn't tell you. It was just out there, somewhere.

Fort Vermilion, however, was all too real. *Life was elsewhere,* I knew that instinctively, and yet trying to construct a narrative beyond "the Fort" was akin to running in deep snow. You could grow exhausted just thinking about it.

The town was old. The original fort had been founded in 1788 by Charles Boyer, at the farthest reaches of the north-west fur trade. Boyer was with the North West Company, and the men of the NWC were sworn enemies of the Hudson's Bay traders. The two companies waged a running guerrilla war across almost 5000 kilometres of frontier before the rough, wild, ruthless Nor'Westers were swallowed up by their competitor. The Hudson's Bay Company was ruthless too, but it was a British-run enterprise, staid and explicitly class-conscious. By contrast, the NWC was almost defiantly Canadian: an undisciplined mix of French, Scots and Metis. What was dubbed a "merger" in 1821 was in effect a corporate takeover, and with it the HBC at last became the undisputed lord and proprietor of a vast transcontinental trade empire, one spanning the land from the St. Lawrence to Vancouver Island and up into the Far North. Free traders and renegades still skulked along the fringes, but for the most part the HBC now held a monopoly on the fur trade. From 1821 on, Fort Vermilion was essentially a one-company town. The HBC's motto, it was said, was "We screwed your grandfather, we screwed your father, and we're going to screw you."

The Hudson's Bay Company was still trading in furs right up till the 1980s, and one of my formative memories is of being measured for a pair of winter boots in the Bay store in Fort Vermilion while trappers unloaded bound stacks of pelts at the back counter. (I was surprised to discover that in the cities the Hudson's Bay is a department store, not a grocery/hardware/ fur-trading post.)

Fort Vermilion was named for the reddish-brown clay found along the banks of the Peace River. This colour, it was said, came from the blood of the Cree and Beaver people, which had seeped into the ground during the pitched battles they fought against each other hundreds of years prior to the arrival of Europeans. The beautifully named Peace, flowing wide between the Caribou Mountains and the Buffalo Head

Hills, drew its name not from the river's calm, strong currents but from the fact that it was once a line of demarcation drawn between two nations who had fought each other to a standstill. The Peace River was once an international border.

When I was there, Fort Vermilion (pop. 840) was mainly Metis and white, the language was Bush Cree and English, and the surnames French, with a few Scottish McThises and McThats thrown into the mix. It was a ragtag, hodgepodge sort of place, and even though I was born there, I never belonged, nor did any of my siblings. Not really. You see, my parents came From Out. We had no extended web of relatives, no cousins or in-laws or (as was often the case in Fort Vermilion) cousins who were also in-laws. We were neither "us" nor "them"; we were "none of the above."

Fort Vermilion was a forgotten outpost; if the entire community had vanished from the face of the earth one night, no one would have noticed. Located at the northernmost edge of commercially viable agricultural land in the world—where the cash crop was, predictably enough, winter wheat—the Fort was surrounded by a clutch of smaller communities, each with its own distinct ethnic stamp, each one an outpost unto itself. Buttertown, across the river, was a last bastion of Metis trappers. Rocky Lane, little more than a crossroads and a school, was predominantly Ukrainian. The Tall Cree settlements were treaty-status Indian. And the town of La Crete— in spite of the French label—was the German-speaking home of Old Order Mennonites who were fighting a doomed rearguard action against the inevitable. (When La Crete's isolation began to crumble, and the modernizing taint of the outside world started to seep in, several Mennonite families packed up and left. It tells you something when you have to go all the way to Belize to find a place as remote as the forests and farmlands of northern Alberta.)

We could place people by their surname, whether it was Metis (Lizotte, McAteer, McCarthy/Mercredi), Ukrainian (Pylypiw, Chomiak, Sarapuk), Cree (Courtoreille, Meneen, Habitant) or Mennonite (Dyck, Friesen, Wiebe).

Fort Vermilion and the communities around it were located inside the slipstream of the *auroral oval,* a band of intense solar activity that circles the magnetic pole like a lopsided ring toss. Go farther north and the northern lights actually diminish. Go all the way to the North Pole and you will look south in vain for auroral displays equal to those within this surging atmospheric loop. The Fort was in the most active auroral zone in the world. Which is to say, I grew up with the northern lights as a backdrop: great shimmering curtains of green, soft glowing blues, serpentine streaks of purple, rare undulations of pink. They moved like phantoms across the winter skies of my youth.

I thought it was boring.

I couldn't wait to get out. I was sick of forests, sick of auroras. As the snow lay in thick comfort over the landscape, I would stare at my reflection in the bedroom window and dream of escape. I wanted to travel to distant, exotic locales. To South America. Europe. Asia. Anywhere but here.

My parents first came to Fort Vermilion because my father had been offered a job in nearby Rocky Lane. My mother was a child of Canada's warm West Coast, and she was unprepared for the Fort. "I came straight from Vancouver to fifty-below weather," she told us. "I felt like I had dropped off the edge of the world." It was a hard courtship, to be sure, but by springtime my mother had been won over. "I think it was that first *green day*, that was what did it—when the leaves on all the poplar trees opened on a single day in spring. That was when I fell in love with the North."

Not so my father. His family was from Cape Breton, but he was raised on the open prairie southeast of Regina, and he never settled into Fort Vermilion. The North made him feel small, and a few years after I was born, he dragged the entire family out to Saskatchewan, where we lived on Standing Buffalo Indian Reserve for a while and then, later, in a Regina ghetto. My memories of the prairies are vague: older brothers and younger sisters, rolling hills, open grassland, city squalor. When my parents' marriage collapsed, for good this time, my mother packed up the kids—there were six of us by then—and returned to the Fort.

I always suspected that she was secretly hoping Dad would follow her back, that they would start anew, but she laughs when I suggest this. "We went back to Fort Vermilion because by then it was our home," she says.

As if that weren't enough, when Mom took us on a "vacation," she would take us even *farther* up, into the Northwest Territories and then down to Fort Smith. It was a long trip on a maddeningly indirect route. Although Fort Smith lay almost exactly on the 60th parallel, just a nudge north of the provincial/territorial boundary, the only way to get there was to drive up and then over, past the thundering Alexander and Louise Falls and then veering suddenly southeast, on gravel for much of the way. It took a full day of driving, Fort to Fort, with Mom at the wheel and seven or eight kids (as often as not, foster children and a couple of the town's castoffs had joined our ranks) and a dog—a large dog, usually with some sort of gastrointestinal condition—plus provisions, all folded into a station wagon built for six. We would leave Fort Vermilion in the early hours and arrive in Fort Smith well after midnight. We made that trip in the darkness of winter and during the long, lingering twilights of summer, and it never got any shorter.

To give you an idea of how remote and empty this stretch of road is, we once managed to take a wrong turn at one of the only intersections along the way and we drove for almost *an hour and a half* before we noticed. Hell, we had almost reached the Mackenzie River before Mom would finally admit something was wrong. (Mom was like that.)

"Well," she said chirpily, as she turned the car around to a chorus of groans, "we got to see a new part of the world."

"Yeah, trees," I said. "Wouldn't want to miss that."

Sometimes, because of a three-hour "detour" or simply a late start, we would be forced to drive to Great Slave Lake instead and spend the night in the town of Hay River. This was memorable if only because a developer had seen fit to build an actual apartment building up there, giving the town the rarest of things in the North: a skyline. True, the vaunted "skyline of Hay River" consisted of this one single incongruous building sticking up above the trees, but for us it might as well have been Manhattan glimmering on the horizon.

Unfortunately, Hay River was only halfway to Fort Smith; we still had a long, lonely road ahead of us. But when we finally arrived—exhausted, hallucinatory—good cheer and revelry awaited. We had friends who lived in Fort Smith, just outside of town: Mary Hewson and Martin Barford, who were usually referred to in one breath as "*mary'n'martin*." They had been travelling the North in a converted schoolbus the first time we

met them, which may make them sound like hippies, but they
weren't. Their work ethic was too strong, for one thing. They
both had jobs in Fort Smith, they didn't grow marijuana (at
least, none that I could find), and Martin was building a house
at Salt River—alone, and with his bare hands. Martin, all
Adam's apple and grinning moustache, was one of those manly
men who can fix a diesel engine with a piece of binder twine
and a clothes peg; he set the bar fairly high, male-wise. Mary
and Martin have long since moved away, but The House That
Martin Built is still something of a landmark at Salt River.

"How was the trip!" Mary would say, rushing out as we
pulled into their yard.

"Wonderful!" our mother would reply.

"Tea?" Mary would ask, redundantly. Mom was of Ulster
Irish stock—tea was a given.

"Oh, yes," came the reply. "Tea would be wonderful.
You're lovely tell your mother." This was some sort of weird
Irish greeting, perplexing to the uninitiated, a vestigial rem-
nant of the Old Country.

Historically, the two Forts were rivals. Fort Vermilion was
founded by the Nor'Westers, Fort Smith by the HBC. Fort
Vermilion at that time was largely Cree, Fort Smith predominantly Chipewyan. Fort Vermilion was in Alberta, Fort Smith
was in the Territories. But any hatchets had long since been
buried, and we were never chased out of town or anything.

The original HBC trading post at Fort Smith was built at the
site of a portage route that bypassed a series of dangerous rapids.
(The Chipewyan name for the area was Tthebacha, "below the
currents.") But the city's greatest claim to fame is as a gateway
to Wood Buffalo National Park, the largest national park in

North America and one that covers a vast flat forest the size of, oh, some European country or other. Belgium, maybe. The boundaries are expansive for a reason: they enclose the range of what was once the world's last free-roaming herd of buffalo. These buffalo (or bison, as they are more correctly known) numbered in the thousands when we were there as kids, and the park, although thickly forested, always felt more horizontal than vertical, a sort of northern savannah. With trees. The park is also the only known nesting ground of the whooping crane, a bird so endangered that there were once barely two dozen of them left.

On one of our trips to Fort Smith, when I was eleven or twelve, Martin decided to lead us on an expedition deep into Wood Buffalo National Park, on a road that looped south to Pine Lake. The bison were in rutting season at the time, which meant they had dispersed throughout the woods, privacy being preferred during mating. On the drive down, we passed several lone males rolling around on their backs, scratching an itch they couldn't quite reach, in sandy patches beside the road— legs up, fur fountaining dust. It was slightly undignified, and the bulls would roll to their feet and glare at us as we went by.

At Pine Lake we unloaded and launched our kayaks onto impossibly clear water. We looked in vain for whooping cranes, faced a disappointment of ducks instead and watched the summertime sun not quite fully set. A loon dove under one of our kayaks, and we watched it the entire way as it swam below us and then resurfaced on the other side.

When it came time to make a fire, I was sent out to gather kindling with my little sister, Lorna Joan (a.k.a. "Pruney," a.k.a. "The Prune," a childhood nickname which I have sworn never to reveal and which I will take to my grave). As luck would have it,

Pruney and I found a nicely tramped trail that ran straight through the willows, and we followed it merrily. Of course, the reason the path was so well-trod was that it was a buffalo track. Sure enough, a giant shaggy head appeared, all hump and fur, grunting and snorting as it approached. In a panic, Pruney and I crouched behind the biggest willow we could find—which is to say, a very *small* willow. (If you are in the bush and scrambling to avoid a large rutting animal, willow trees provide woefully scant cover. We looked like a pair of belugas trying to hide behind a chopstick.) The bison shouldered his way past as Pruney and I watched, eyes wide. It was like a landscape moving by.

Back at the campfire, Martin pointed out that if we launched a canoe or kayak above the rapids at Fort Smith, we could paddle to Fort Vermilion with only a portage or two along the way, and be spared the long drive back. Physically, Fort Vermilion wasn't that far from Wood Buffalo National Park, by river, anyway. Small bands of bison would occasionally wander away from the park and follow the north shore of the Peace River all the way down to the edge of Fort Vermilion. Many years earlier, a young Anglican minister (From Out, I should note) had been zipping along the gravel in his new and highly inappropriate luxury sedan when—*wham*—he was slammed by a charging bison. The bison was fine. The pastor's car, not so much. They say a bison will charge only once, but in this case once was plenty. The side of the vehicle was completely caved in.

When word got out that some bison had left the protective boundaries of the national park, several of the local treaty-status Indian men—invoking ancestral hunting rights—drove out in a pickup truck and shot 'em all. It was like hunting cows in an open field. Mind you, those bison did fill the smokehouses with meat that winter and did provide several warm robes. The priest didn't fare as well as the local families. When he went to collect insurance on the damages wrought to his beloved sedan, his claim was rejected. "Buffalo," he was informed, "are considered an Act of God."

"An Act of God?" the priest sputtered. (You'd think, of all people, he would recognize one when he saw it.)

When I was growing up, the tale of the priest, the buffalo and the Act of God was still being told, usually over tea and with much accompanying laughter. But I have to say, after watching that bison move by Pruney and me at Pine Lake, I'm inclined to agree with the ruling.

One by one, my older siblings left Fort Vermilion, and the family photos grew smaller and smaller.

No one ever "moved away." They "left the Fort." That was how it was always worded: *they left the Fort*. The outside world was a scary place; it ate souls whole. The Fort was where your family and feuds and dysfunctional friendships lay. The Fort was home. But we were From Out, and one by one we left until our mother left as well. And after that, there was no reason to go back. I would spend years trying to shake myself free of where I had come from; I would spend years trying to shed myself of the North. But it was like trying to slip free of my own shadow. I left the Fort, but the Fort never really left me.

So. I turn sixteen. I quit school. I pack my bags, set off to see the world—and I end up in Canada's seventeenth largest city.

Now, I'm not knocking Saskatoon; it's a fine place. But when you're a kid from Alberta, well, Saskatchewan just isn't

that exotic. Even less so when you're sixteen and full of nervous energy. My future was spread out before me, with endless
possibilities. I could go anywhere, be anyone. *The world was my
oyster!* Alas, the image was more accurate than I realized. It was
indeed an oyster: slippery, unappetizing and hard to grasp.

I didn't leave northern Alberta; I escaped. Escaped not in
the sense of "prison," though there was certainly that aspect
to it. But escaped in the sense of centripetal forces defeated
and inertia denied. I felt as though I had broken free from the
gravity well of a decaying star. I felt as though I were free-
falling upwards into a liberating buoyancy. It was heady and
exhilarating and sexy—but the triumph was short-lived. As I
soon learned, getting out of Fort Vermilion was the easy part.
Getting out of Canada was far trickier. Somehow, I'd thought
that Canada would simply dissolve before me as I travelled
through it—that I would find myself overseas, in a small café
in Paris or a seaside village in Southeast Asia, in one smooth,
effortless motion. With a single ellipsis, I would sling my
dufflebag over my shoulder, jump onto a Greyhound . . . and
reappear in a distant foreign locale.

I landed with a thud in Saskatoon. I had an older sister
living there—Margaret, from my father's first marriage—and
one of the benefits of being a younger sibling in a large family
is that you inherit a network of couches to crash upon and
refrigerators from which to mooch. Margaret was going
through a messy divorce at the time, so I'm not sure how
much she appreciated having her wee brother Billy show up
at her front door. Even worse, I had—with impeccable timing—arrived just in time for winter. But no matter. I wouldn't
be staying long. Only a few days. Saskatoon was a temporary

way station on the road to Somewhere Else. It would act as a catapult, one that would slingshot me far away, into strange new orbits.

Mind you, Saskatoon was strange enough. That should be its civic motto: "Welcome to Saskatoon! We're a little bit loopy!"

The berry or the city? In case you're wondering, in a chicken-and-egg sort of way, which came first, I am happy to report that the city was named in honour of the berry, and not vice versa. It happened back in the 1880s, when John Lake, the town's pioneer founder, asked the Plains Cree in the area what they called the sweet purply fruit growing in such thick abundance along the banks of the Saskatchewan River. It is said that, upon being told, he leapt to his feet and exclaimed, "Arise, Saskatoon, Queen of the North!"

It was a silly way to name a town, and Lake couldn't even use the excuse that he was drunk at the time. John Lake was the leader of a religious temperance group funded by the Methodist Church, and he had come west with a mission: to establish a New Jerusalem, free from the corrupting influence of "the city." Any berries consumed here would most assuredly *not* be fermented, thank you very much. In a nation of political, cultural and linguistic outposts, the teetotalling colony of Saskatoon was destined to be a "moral bastion" in the wilderness. Or at least, that was the idea, before the Law of Lowest Common Denominators kicked in. Today, Saskatoon has some of the roughest saloons and booziest bars in Canada, and the only surviving reminder of the city's crusading start is a single residential street called Temperance. Still, the anti-whisky zealots did give the city its name, and with the province that was later formed around it the result was "Saskatoon,

Saskatchewan," the place name most often followed by *Gesundheit!* (and the place name most often baked in a pie).

I settled into the City That Sounds Like a Sneeze in fits and starts. My sister was a sculptor, and she often worked with castaway marble, creating fluid figures and haunting human faces that seemed to be emerging from the stone. Although everything else about my sojourn in Saskatoon has taken on an aura of unreality, I still remember the impact one of Margaret's portraits had on me. It was a sculpture of a weeping woman I dubbed the White Lady. The marble my sister used was taken from a discounted headstone, marked down because there was a flaw running through it, an imperfect ripple in the stone. Margaret turned that flaw into a defining trait, carving around it, shaping and cutting and polishing until the ripple became the faint trail of a teardrop.

When I arrived in Saskatoon, the only condition Margaret attached was that I write something every day, whether a journal entry or a short story or even a snippet of poetry. Yes, that's right, *poems*. I admit it. Margaret was working the night shift with campus security at the University of Saskatchewan. When she left for work, I would sit at the kitchen table as the White Lady—eyes shut, tear frozen—looked down. And I would write.

The days turned to weeks, the weeks turned to months. My sojourn became a siege. Winter winds rattled the city, sweeping through like an army of Cossacks, and gradually, almost imperceptibly, my money bled away. It was remarkable, it truly was, the ease with which my funds slipped free of me. I had left home with hundreds of dollars in my pocket—scrimped, borrowed and saved—*hundreds, I tell you!* Now, suddenly, I was flat broke and looking for work.

Instead of wandering the streets of Paris or lounging on a tropical beach beneath gently swaying fronds of palm, I found myself marooned in Saskatoon, where I was hired out like a rented mule by a temporary manpower office. I spent my days lugging heavy machinery across construction sites whilst being yelled at by beetle-browed, knuckle-dragging, hygienically challenged mouth-breathers in hard hats. And yes, yes, yes, I realize that most construction workers are upstanding citizens, salt of the earth and all that, but not the crew I ended up with. They were a living challenge to the theories of Darwinian improvement—at times I could see them de-evolving right before my eyes. The pay was meagre, the mud was thick, and the piercing back pain chronic.

> Come to Saskatoon! where, of all places, your success is most fully assured; where no deserving man has ever yet failed; where there are no poorhouses because there are no poor, where there is comfort, happiness and prosperity and an unlimited field for your intelligence and energy.
>
> —*Saskatoon Board of Trade pamphlet,* 1911

I eventually left the rewarding field of manual labour and, with spirit suitably broken, found work as a dishwasher at a twenty-four-hour restaurant on Idylwyld Drive, downtown, where I spent my nights scrubbing banged-up pots and queasy grease-traps whilst being yelled at by beetle-browed, hygienically challenged line cooks.

At least I was indoors. Having proven my prowess in the dish pits, I was even promoted to the position of short-order cook, where I regularly sweated over—and oftentimes into—the deep fryer: "Extra salt with your fries?" (If you ate at the Fuller's on Idylwyld sometime between December 1981 and March 1982, the odds are you have trace elements of Will still in your system.) The real trouble began when my shift ended, usually at some godforsaken hour, and I had to make the long slog home. My sister's apartment was on the west side of town, on one of Saskatoon's alphabetically arranged avenues: Avenue M, I believe. Which was, as you may have guessed, a fair distance from "A" (better known as Idylwyld).

I have visited Saskatoon many times since, and I am always taken aback by what an attractive place it is, its green valley and wide river, with its scenic bridges, and its handsome greystone campus. I can't reconcile this with the Saskatoon of my youth: the stacks of festering, food-encrusted plates; the drooping garbage bags heavy with wet refuse, dragged out and dumped like corpses at the end of each shift; and that long, soul-destroying trudge back to Avenue M as the alphabet *slooowllly* ticked off, one barren, ice-ridden block after another.

> Come to Saskatoon! IF YOU ARE STEADY, HONEST, INTELLIGENT AND HARDWORKING, YOU CAN-NOT FAIL. Each year your condition will improve. From the moment you arrive with us, you can pluck from your heart all dread of the future and cast it forever from you into the hopelessness of other days. Cling to this truth. Let it cheer you to forgetfulness of whatever little difficulties you may at first encounter.
>
> —*Ibid.*

I don't know if Hell exists, but I know exactly where
Purgatory is located: it lies between Idylwyld and Avenue M
in Saskatoon, Saskatchewan, mid-winter.

Sometimes a word or place becomes symbolic of a larger
event; the literary term for this is *metonymy*: "He met his
Waterloo." "We don't want this turning into another Vietnam."
But as we go through life we collect our own private vocabu-
lary, our own list of place names, our own personal metonymy.
To this day, whenever I hear of a young person struggling and
adrift, I think to myself, *Ah, she's facing her Saskatoon.*

> If you have stagnated, have no brighter prospects for the
> future and are consequently dissatisfied and discouraged, and
> if you feel able for better things, desire them and are willing to
> strive for them,—then, as an intelligent man, you have no
> excuse for indecisions,—Come West! Come to Saskatoon. . . .
>
> —*Ibid.*

As soon as I had scraped together enough money, I escaped.
I fled my prairie Waterloo, bowed and beaten, on a slow train
heading east. The winds were howling, the snow blew across
empty fields, and the sky was grey and cold. That's right. It
was now springtime.

My ongoing journey took me only as far as Manitoba and
my next familial connection. If I am restless, unsettled and ill-
defined, I like to think I came by it honestly. I inherited it from
my father. My dad was hardly ever around when I was growing
up; he would disappear for months, even years, at a time, with
nary a word of warning or a forwarding address, usually just
ahead of a posse of collection agents. He'd reappear in the oddest

locations, as often as not with a new wife in tow. *"Qu'Appelle? What the hell is he doing in Qu'Appelle?"* As luck would have it, my father had recently resurfaced. At one point we'd lost track of him entirely, but he was now in Manitoba, in a place called Dauphin. *"Dauphin? What the hell is he doing in Dauphin?"*

I got off the train at a forlorn little station north of Brandon, on the old Canadian National line, and my father was waiting for me. That in itself was something of a miracle.

"You'll like Dauphin," he said as we loaded my dufflebag into the back of his rust-inflicted Chevy. "Named by the French, founded by the Scots, settled by Ukrainians. It's the damnedest place."

We drove north from the train station, through rolling farm- lands and into Riding Mountain National Park. The skies began to clear and the highway rose like a slow ocean swell, taking us up and over the Manitoba Escarpment, a dramatic rise of forested hills in the middle of the plains. The wooded heights teemed with predators and prey. Three separate ecological zones converge at Riding Mountain: the lakes and marshes of the boreal forest; the scrub meadows and poplar stands of aspen parkland; and, along the crumbling shale of the escarpment itself, hardwood stands of elm and oak, maple and ash that mark the farthest reach of Canada's eastern deciduous woods. I know this because my father told me. He was the only person I ever knew who used words like "deciduous" in casual conversation.

"Riding Mountain is Canada condensed," said Dad. "It's like an ark."

It was as though the nation's wildlife had been squeezed into this one plateau: everything from bogland moose to large herds of elk, from coyotes to Arctic shrews, from snowy owls to tawny grassland gophers. Bears—black, blond, brown and cinnamon—wuffled their way among the trees, the highest concentration in North America. Plains bison were being reintroduced in a fenced range near Lake Audy. Lynx and foxes and even a few cougars were prowling about. Bald eagles and peregrine falcons turned lazy, lethal circles in the sky; ring-necked pheasants scuttled about in the underbrush. Timber wolves loped through the shadows.

It was the most dramatic way possible to enter a prairie town: from the wooded highlands of Riding Mountain, the land in front of us dropped away and we descended onto a checkerboard of farm fields so quickly our ears popped. And there, in a wide flat valley, unexpectedly, improbably, lay a city: Dauphin. The lost prince.

Dauphin is in the middle of nowhere and the centre of everything. Although located at the crosshairs of the continent, in the geographic centre of North America, it still seemed remote and far-flung. A self-anointed "City of Sunshine," Dauphin hosts the annual National Ukrainian Festival, the largest such gathering anywhere outside of the actual Ukraine, and an event that causes the local population to swell to four times its normal size.

I found work at a local pizza parlour, where the community's rich cultural heritage was honoured with a special "Ukrainian pizza" featuring (a) sauerkraut and (b) kolbassa.

"You're kidding, right?" I said, when it was first explained to me what went into a Ukrainian pizza—surely an ethnic oxymoron of the first order.

The guy who was training me wiped his hands on his apron. "You should have been here in February. We have this

Valentine's Day pizza, made in the shape of a heart, right? But the crust sort of loses its shape when it's cooked, and with the tomato paste and cheese and everything, it looks like a *real* heart."

"And this is romantic?" I said.

He shrugged. "Apparently."

My initiation into the world of fine cuisine continued. An influx of Ukrainian Canadians flooded into town for the festival, with much leaping of *shumkas* and painting of *pysankas* and ordering of pizzas. I became something of a hero with the rest of the staff when I developed a subtle new technique for dealing with particularly obnoxious patrons. Whenever a group of young, liquored-up yahoos came stumbling in and started giving the waitresses a hard time, I would carefully cut *only the cheese* on top of their pizza, leaving the crust below as one solid disk. Watching a table of yobs cursing each other as they tried, in vain, to tear a pizza apart along nonexistent lines—why, it was great fun.

Summer bloomed and life was good. The canola fields around Dauphin flowered in a deep intensity of yellow. It was the yellow of highlighter pens, the yellow of glow-in-the-dark Post-it Notes, a yellow so pure, so elemental, it hurt your eyes to look at it. It was a colour you could almost taste.

Dauphin could be beguiling at times. The wide main street angled through the city from Market Mall at one end to leafy green streets and the red brick of the courthouse at the other. The round domed towers of Dauphin's historic Ukrainian Catholic Church, a "prairie cathedral"; the angular rise of grain elevators; the slow, winding river; the warm feathery feel to the air. The days were long and drowsy in Dauphin, the homes were tidy and clean, the yards unnaturally trim. Pink flamingos and garden gnomes adorned the lawns like snapshots of an archetypal suburb circa 1953, and pride of ownership was everywhere in evidence. "A Ukrainian trait," my dad insisted. "It's one of the more annoying aspects of living here."

My dad was renting a boxy little bungalow, and he wasn't much of a groundskeeper. True, he owned an old push mower, more rumour than real, that was lost somewhere in the overgrowth, but it would have taken a machete to get to it. I suppose I should have tried—cutting grass being a sonly duty, after all—but Dad didn't seem to care.

"It's just grass," he'd say. "You can cut it or not. Doesn't matter to me one way or the other."

It did, alas, matter to his neighbours. The people next door had two high-strung Doberman pinschers that ran rampant, and yet they considered my father's unkempt lawn to be an affront.

How shall I put this? Dad was a bit of a crank. When the neighbours came striding over in full snit, hammering on our screen door and demanding to know "just exactly why" Dad had allowed the grass to get so long, my father drew himself up to his full height—well over six feet—and peered down at them through his glasses. "I let it grow to hide the dog shit your friggin' mutts leave behind," he said. Except he didn't say "friggin'."

Dad then sat back down and poured himself a glass of Boodles gin while they stood, mouths open, on the front porch.

Did I mention that my father was a teacher, entrusted with the shaping of young minds? He was a lot of things—a would-be importer/exporter, a salesman, a part-time grifter, a vanity-press publisher—but teaching was what he did best.

It was his default position. When all else failed, he could find a job teaching *somewhere;* in this case, at a small rural school outside of the city.

In my memory, it is always summer in Dauphin, and the grass is always overgrown and green. Often, after an evening spent shovelling pizzas in and out of ovens, the cooks would tumble from the restaurant, reeking of cooked dough and mozzarella, and drive the streets of Dauphin, up and down, shouting our youth from the windows, shouting ourselves hoarse. With waitresses along for the ride, we would roar up the escarpment for a full view: a sky full of stars, the dark forests at our back, a prairie city glowing below. We could hear the passenger trains as they rattled through, could see the windows like the illuminated squares of a film strip unspooling into the night.

It was an interlude, my stay in Dauphin; I knew that even then. It was a detour, not a destination, and it came to an abrupt end when my brother Sean phoned to say, "What the hell are you doing?"

"I'm working in the very demanding field of food-preparation services," I replied, somewhat defensively.

"You're making pizzas. Listen, Billy. I'm living in Red Deer now. Come back to Alberta, stay with me, finish high school. I'll cover your costs."

There are, as noted, advantages to being a younger sibling in a large family. Everyone has to take care of you; it's part of the social contract. So back to Alberta I went, having never made it out of the prairie provinces, let alone to Paris or Tahiti or the Spice Islands of Sumatra. There was no Northwest rite of passage, no shortcut to a more exotic me. I think at some level my dad was relieved to see me go. I had been good company,

I suppose, and if he was expecting a dramatic *"J'accuse!"* moment, when I would thrust a damning forefinger at his chest and denounce his dismal abilities as a father, it never came.

I stayed with my brother in Red Deer. Finished high school. Got my diploma. Lindsay Thurber Comprehensive, class of '83. Grad theme song: "We Are Tomorrow." And the following January, I left again. I joined a cross-Canada volunteer youth corps—a government-funded social experiment that pitted confused young Canadians from every region against one another to see how long they could share communal living conditions before someone snapped and went on a rampage. Paid "a dollar a day and all the granola you can eat," I travelled with my group to the Okanagan Valley of British Columbia, to the tobacco fields of southern Ontario and to the dairy farms of rural Quebec. We cut wilderness trails, worked on museum restorations, and sat with seniors in the terminal ward of a nursing home.

I returned to Saskatoon after my tour of duty as a volunteer ended—again broke, still restless—and stayed at the home of Kay Parley, a family friend known affectionately as Auntie Kay, where I shuffled my notes and wrote out my nineteen-year-old cross-Canada journal in longhand. The following year, I travelled to South America, where I lived in a mountain village in southern Ecuador not far from the Peruvian border. I came back, went to university and got a degree in Fine Arts. Yes, that's right, Fine Arts, I admit it. At some point I wound up in Japan and stayed there for five years.

My sister Margaret continued to work with castaway stone. She continued walking the beat for a few more years as well, and she was awarded a plaque from the Saskatoon

Police Force for a campus crime-prevention program she researched and implemented. (My youngest sister, meanwhile, now works as a prison guard. This attraction to law enforcement among female Fergusons remains a mystery. Perhaps it has something to do with an absentee father who was, if not lawless, at the very least *creative* in his interpretation of what the law allowed.)

My father had been itching to move on, and soon after I left Dauphin he did, leaving a trail of unpaid bills and unanswered questions about his teaching accreditation behind him. He had been teaching French while in Dauphin, a language that he did not technically speak.

Dad kept chasing one scheme after another, and years later he disappeared again. But this time he would not be re-emerging. This time he was gone for good.

Margaret works as a teacher in adult education now, and in one of those odd little coincidences, she left Saskatoon recently and moved to a small town just west of . . . Dauphin. She goes by her middle name now, Gena, just as I have left "Billy" behind—or tried to.

Gena laughs when I tell her that, for me, Saskatoon will always be a synonym for winter, and that Dauphin will always mean summer and second chances.

"Try Dauphin when it's minus 32 and a blizzard is blowing through," she says. "You'll change your mind."

I am connected to my sister by a thin filament of fibre optics and a tenuous string of satellite relay stations that reaches across the prairies. We share anecdotes about Dad, mainly—or Fayther, as my sister always called him in a mock Scottish accent. We know the stories, have heard them many times, have polished them until they glisten. But here's the funny part. My father may have had a wayfarer's soul—restless and eternally thirsty—but in the end, the amount of ground he covered was very small; his life's story stretches from Radville, Saskatchewan, where he was born, to Brandon, Manitoba, where he died. An afternoon's drive across open prairie.

"Gena," I ask. "Whatever happened to the crying woman? I loved that sculpture."

She is surprised I still remember. "That was so long ago," Gena says. "I'm not even sure where she is any more."

But a few weeks later a wooden crate arrives, and when I unscrew the slats, there she is: the White Lady, with her single tear. Imperfect marble, and figures defined by their flaws.

I remember something Dad brought up as we drove through Riding Mountain and towards the train station, out of the forests and into open air. It was a comment made in passing, as unsettling truths inevitably are. "Why this constant urge to be on the road?" he asked me.

With the certainty of teenage wisdom, I replied, "Because I need to find myself, that's why."

"I see. Well," he said, "in my experience people never really travel to find themselves. They travel to *lose* themselves. To leave something behind, some part of them. Either way, they're incomplete."

I think perhaps that was the closest my father ever came to self-awareness. It came and went, there and then gone, the way unsettling truths sometimes do.

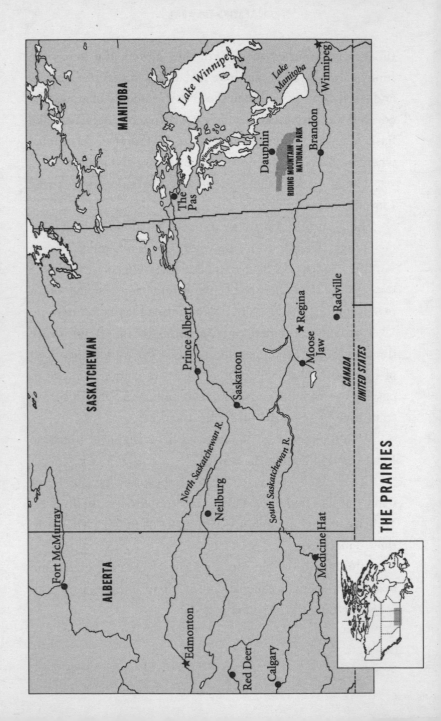

THE PRAIRIES

chapter three

BEAUTY TIPS FROM MOOSE JAW

THE FIRE STARTED ON NEW YEAR'S DAY, 2004, with an electrical short in the Chow Building, on the corner of River Street and Main. It spread quickly, crawling up walls and curling along ceilings, heating windows until the glass blackened, then shattered, sending buckets of dark smoke out into the cold air.

On that first day of January, the wind chill stood at minus 22 degrees Celsius. Firefighters, their gear sheathed in ice, fought the flames for fifty hours straight, working in shifts. Water, pumped in from three ladder trucks, formed thick fountains of ice; it hung from the rafters and fallen timbers in icicles as heavy as stalactites. When the floor of the first building began to give way, the men fell back, and soon after that the front wall collapsed, taking the ceiling down with it. The fire then burned its way into the next historic structure, taking out businesses one by one.

In the end, the fire gutted seven shops and destroyed the city's two oldest commercial buildings. Police managed to evacuate people from its path and, aside from the frostbite and smoke inhalation suffered by the firefighters, no one was injured. But the damage was in the millions. Even harder than the monetary loss was the historic one; the buildings consumed in that fire were irreplaceable. Built in 1892, they were the heart of Moose Jaw's downtown district and a key to its revitalization. Shopkeepers surveyed the wreckage with hollow dismay.

"In twenty-eight years," the fire chief said, "this is one of the worst I've ever seen. It's catastrophic."

• • •

Late summer. Early autumn. That in-between season.

We are collecting Large Objects by the Side of the Highway, posing for photographs in front of the Vegreville Easter Egg. Cut Knife's Giant Tomahawk and Concrete Teepee. The Fibreglass Snowman in Kenaston ("Blizzard Capital of Saskatchewan!"). The Leaning Coffee Pot of Davidson.

It's a long, slow boomerang up to Edmonton, across to Regina, and then back home to Calgary. A rite of citizenship, I believe: the Long Drive.

My wife, Terumi, is from southern Japan, a land of narrow lanes and ancient hot springs, where cherry blossom petals fall across temple ponds. I, however, am from the land of enormous objects and big-ass highways. A land of fibreglass landmarks and open skies.

Our son, Alex, age three and a half, is surprisingly serene, all things considered, strapped into his seat back there as the prairie floats by on either side. Partly, this comes from being an only child (his brother-to-be is just a flutter in his mother's stomach at this stage); he has no one to battle or feud with, no one to stake back-seat territorial claims against, no one to goad. But Alex's quiet demeanour is also due largely to the video pack slung over the seat in front of him. This does help whittle down the hours. At a cost, though. To me. I fear the neurological damage has already been done before we reach the Saskatchewan border, with the theme song from Tele-tubbies burned forever into the CD of my mind.

If you had asked me at age twenty who I thought I'd be at thirty-seven, the answer most definitely would *not* have been "someone who knows all of the Teletubbies by name and can also identify each of their favourite things." (Dipsy, green; likes to dance; favourite thing: hat. Po, red; enjoys hopping up and down; favourite thing: scooter.)

With Tinky-Winky and Laa-laa echoing in my ears, I pull off the highway and into the town of Neilburg. It's the sort of place not normally worth a detour, but Neilburg is where my father once turned up, many years ago. My brother Sean and I spent a Christmas here, in a small rented house with our father, as he tried to convince us of the many great things he was going to do. Someday. After he died, memories of that winter in Neilburg kept surfacing like a message in a Magic 8 Ball.

Terumi stays in the car, drowsy with prenatal lullabies. I walk the town's quiet streets with Alex on my shoulders, trying to recognize something—anything—about the place. It is familiar in only the most nebulous of ways. I'm not even sure the house I've found is the one Dad lived in; I stand looking at it for a long while but can't decide. My shoulders are aching and the winds are picking up, com-ing at us from all sides, staggering me this way and that, threatening to topple Alex from his perch and harrying us back to the car.

"Did you find your dad?" Terumi asks, half-asleep, as we climb in.

I look in the mirror, smooth down my wind-addled hair. "Maybe. I'm not sure."

Saskatchewan is a study in light and texture. The fields are laid out like swaths of fabric: coarse canvas, creased linen. Cumulus clouds throw lakes of dark shadow upon the hills. The road rolls on. Geese tumble across the sky, heading south to warmer climes: countless black flecks against the thickening blue. Terumi wants to know why they don't spell out stuff. Messages, like "Happy Birthday" or "Hello!"

"Seems like a waste," she murmurs, head against the window. Terumi has been in the car too long.

So have I. Cows are gathered in the corner of a field, having some sort of cow meeting, and I try to imagine what the agenda might be as we drift by at 120 kilometres an hour.

We drive on, into the night and out again, sleeping in motels, interchangeable, and small towns, likewise. Names on grain elevators mark the places that we pass. We can always see the next town approaching, even from a great distance; the elevators move towards us as though carried on a conveyor belt. As dusk falls, the lights of the next community are already beaded along the horizon—the nighttime version of a prairie mirage.

"Are we here?" Alex asks.

"Well, yes," I say pedantically. "We are always *here*, Alex. It doesn't matter where we go. We're always 'here.'"

He looks out the window. "Too bad."

Are we here? It starts to gnaw at me. At its core, Alex's query is a philosophical conundrum, and one not readily answered. Are we ever truly here? And what *were* those cows discussing back there? Why the big secretive meeting in the corner of the field?

I am caught in the vertigo of a prairie highway, pinned between competing points of perspective, one diverging, one converging. In the rearview mirror, the road is moving away. Through the windshield, the same road is coming right at me. Two views of a relentless Morse-code message, dash-dash-dash, moving simultaneously in opposite directions into two different vanishing points.

I feel woozy, and I am about to pull over when Alex puts forth another query, this one more easily resolved. "Can we stop? I have to pee."

"Yes!" I say, glad to have an answer. "Yes, we can stop."

Things I learned while standing on the side of the highway in the middle of the night, trying not to get peed on as I hold a three-year-old so that he doesn't trip or fall down a ditch as he looks up at the night sky and asks questions about the moon while he pees (invariably) into the wind:

(1) Although warm initially, pee very soon becomes cold.

(2) If you get pee on your shoelaces, there is nothing you can do. Your shoelaces will never dry, and you will never get the odour out. Best to throw them away and start anew.

(3) There are a lot of stars. Man, are there a lot of stars. Out here, beyond the refractive fog of city streetlights, the sky is awash with them. The Milky Way—it's like a river of rhinestones; it spills across from horizon to horizon. Thousands and thousands of stars.

(4) Cars on the highway travel *really* fast. You can hear the rising pitch of Doppler-effect waves pushed in front of them as they come nearer, nearer, then blast past, rattling the air. When we are inside our cars, hurtling across a landscape, we don't realize how quickly we are moving—until we stop.

Walking back to the car, shoelaces damp, son on shoulders, I say in my wise and fatherly way, "You know, son, long ago, sailors and sea captains could guide their ships by using the stars."

"Really?" he says. "How?"

I stop. Think about this for a moment. "I have no idea."

By day three of our Long Drive, I feel as though I am somehow to blame for the landscape, as though I am personally responsible, as though I should apologize for it.

"This is Regina," I say. "I'm sorry."

But there's no need, because Terumi, raised in the semitropics, finds the open space of the prairies fascinating. Sleep-inducing, but fascinating. She approaches Regina without preconceptions, without bias or baggage, and her response to the city is instructive. She likes Regina. She likes the wide streets and the clear skies and the beauty of the legislative grounds. It's not that she sees the city differently; it's that she sees a different city entirely. The Regina I experience will always be filtered through memories of childhood poverty and urban ghettos. Regina is where my parents' marriage broke apart. Regina is the city my mother fled; it is why we ended up back in the Fort.

I slingshot out of the Queen City, trailing ghosts as we head west on the Trans-Canada. We're on our way to Moose Jaw, which has been our roundabout destination all along.

Now, about the name. "Moose Jaw." An odd name, that one. Sounds more like a punchline than a real place, and I've had people from other countries express surprise when they find out that Moose Jaw actually exists. "I thought it was like Timbuktu or Xanadu," a British friend said. "Sort of made up." But no. Like Timbuktu, Moose Jaw is real. And as with the city of Medicine Hat, farther west on this same highway, there are all sorts of fanciful explanations for how Moose Jaw got its name. Many of these involve English aristocrats ingeniously fixing broken wagon wheels with—aha!—the jawbone from a moose. But the more likely explanation is that the name was derived from the Cree word *moosgaw*, meaning "warm breeze." Which is to say, chances are the name Moose Jaw really has nothing to do with moose (mooses? meese?) or their jawbones. But that hasn't stopped the town from adopting the noble ungulate as its civic symbol.

Large Objects by the Side of the Highway are often visual puns. In Alberta, the town of Black Diamond has on display an enormous tin diamond painted black. Pincher Creek has a gigantic pair of pincers. In Saskatchewan, the town of Turtleford has the world's largest turtle, and—this may be the most groan-inducing example of all—the Manitoba community of Gladstone has erected a giant smiling boulder they've dubbed "Happy Rock." Indian Head, east of Regina, has a huge head of, well, an Indian: a Sioux chief in full headdress. Moose Jaw stopped short of having a gigantic jawbone built, but they do have a moose, a big clunky concrete mascot named Mac, and Terumi and I dutifully pull over for one of those photos that mark us as the sophisticated world travellers we are. "Here's us at the giant cowboy boot, and here we are at the world's biggest hockey stick and here—here we are beside the Moose Jaw moose." Then, as a knowing aside, casually dropped, "Goes by the name of Mac."

The city of Moose Jaw lies south of the highway, in a valley that hides below the horizon. A river runs through it, and a creek.

Here in the dry belt, where water is more than simply sustenance—it quenches thirst, settles dust, offers hope—the word "oasis" has an almost mystical resonance. The oasis, as an idea, stands in opposition to the garrison. Garrisons represent an essentially defensive position, both threatened and threatening, but an oasis is idyllic. Soothing. An oasis cures parched throats and provides a haven in a harsh world. And that is why we are here. Moose Jaw, Saskatchewan, is the home of the Temple Gardens Mineral Spa, and my wife, a connoisseur of hot springs, has come to submerge herself in this self-described "oasis on the prairies."

"You have to wear a swimsuit," I remind her as we turn off the highway. "Public nudity is still frowned on in Canada."

She shakes her head in disbelief. "I know."

Driving into Moose Jaw is an object lesson in city planning. The usual franchise-and-chain-store clutter greets you on the hill leading into town—the inevitable shopping mall, the Wal-Mart, the Burger King. But through luck and a bit of foresight, Moose Jaw has managed to keep the worst of this at bay. As you descend into the valley along Main Street, the generic franchises thin out and a tree-lined town comes into view. True, a few franchise outlets have begun to creep down the hill, dangerously close to the heart of town, but so far they have been held back. (Caribou Street seems to be the dividing line. When you go for an aimless stroll in Moose Jaw, Caribou is where you slow down, pause, look across at the Pizza Hut and the 7-Eleven and then—quite sensibly—turn around.)

Dribbling ice cream, Terumi, Alex and I wander up one side of Main and down the other. The handsome city hall, sandstone on brick, with its domed roof and stolid presence; the wide, optimistic main street; the loose, ambly feel—Moose Jaw has always struck me as a prairie town in the *best* sense of the term.

"So much space," says Terumi.

The Victory Church of Moose Jaw (fun-filled marquee: "If You Were to Die Today, Where Would You Spend Eternity?!") shares its venue with the Discount Plumbing and Heating Company. Cobb's Cobblery, meanwhile, advertises "Saddles, Custom Belts and Hockey Equipment Repairs." Right here on Main Street you can still ride up on a horse and get your saddle fixed.

Chinese restaurants line the streets of Moose Jaw, and in addition to the usual won-ton and chicken balls they

offer something called "Canadian cuisine." The sweet-
and-sour Chinese café can be found across Canada, but
nowhere is it as venerable a tradition as on the prairies.
Every little town from Duck Lake to Bienfait has its own
formica and vinyl-seat version of the Lucky Phoenix
Golden Oriental Silver Dragon Café (mix and match those
six words, and maybe throw in a "Peking" and a "Jade Tiger"
or two, and you can come up with the name of pretty much
any Chinese restaurant in any given prairie town), and every
one of them will also offer "Canadian cuisine." And what is
Canadian cuisine? To judge by the menus, grilled cheese
sandwiches, mainly.

We eat at a restaurant called Nit's, because how often can
you dine in a place named for the larval eggs of head lice?
Nit's offers Thai food and Canadian cuisine—and the food is
delicious. I've ordered Alex the grilled cheese sandwich,
telling him, "It's part of your heritage, son."

"The thing is," the man at the next table is saying to his
friend. "The thing is, Regina isn't big enough to be a *real* city.
And it's not small enough to feel like a small town. No sense
of community, that's the thing. Now, Moose Jaw—Moose Jaw
has it just right."

Down from Nit's and inside a drugstore, modern and
bland (not a knock on this particular drugstore; all pharma-
cies are blandly modern these days), I stumble upon an
antique coin-operated weigh scale that promises HONEST
WEIGHT—though I'm not sure how much of a draw this truly
is. I suspect a machine offering "the weight you wish you
were" or "the weight you honestly believe you should be"
would do much better. Still, it's a wonderful contraption.

History as knick-knack. *Put coin in slot, push plunger,* read the instructions, and on the front, an advertisement: *Insist on Feen-a-mint, the chewing gum laxative!*

"Honey," I say to my wife, who is filling a basket with such non-essentials as band-aids, aspirin and the like. "Do you think we should stock up on chewing-gum laxatives? I mean, for the drive back to Calgary?"

She knows me well enough by this point not even to break her stride. "You need new shoelaces," she says. "Laxatives can wait."

The Hutterites are in town today, families dressed in dour dark wool, self-contained enclaves speaking in Low German. They eschew technology, but not—I note happily—ice cream. It is a golden afternoon, and we drift with the crowds across a footbridge and into Crescent Park. A faint chill hangs in the air. The leaves are starting to scatter, raked from the branches by dry autumn winds, but the feeling is still summery and green, and the park is contoured with water. A cascade. An amphitheatre. The whiteness of swans. Above the trees, the sandstone crown of St. Andrew's Church. And in the park a cross of stone, marking the memory of those "who died for King and Country." Embedded in the cross, like an X-ray of its skeleton, is a sword. I can't decide if this is an example of honesty or of unintentional irony.

The hotel and spa are across the street from the park. We check in, dump our bags, change into our swimming apparel—*oh, those prudish Canadians!*—and then hurry down the hall to the mineral bath, where we slip into the earth-warmed waters of Moose Jaw.

The geothermal springs here gurgle up at 42 degrees Celsius, replete with such intoxicating substances as sodium sulphate, Epsom salts, potassium, calcium, magnesium, bicarbonate, fluoride, boron, bromine and strontium (which is radioactive, no?). It's a regular molecular stew, and Terumi nods her approval. After the scalding hot springs of Japan, the waters here feel almost tepid, but it is still very soothing. Even if we can't jump in buck naked.

Terumi soaks awhile and then heads for the Oasis Beauty Spa, as Alex and I float along, under a walkway, into the outdoor thermal pool. Night is falling, and the air is growing cooler. We are snug up to our necks in the water, noses cold but bodies enveloped in heat. Steam is rising from the surface, and softly, almost imperceptibly, it begins to snow: loose flakes wafting down, melting in mid-air from the heat. We watch the snowflakes disappearing one by one, like tiny lights blinking off.

If you were to die today, where would you spend eternity? You could do worse than Moose Jaw.

The Moose Jaw hot springs were discovered by happenstance back in 1910, and not without a certain rueful disappointment; they were drilling for natural gas, you see, when up pumped a flood of geothermal water. In the 1930s, a "natatorium" was built, and people came from across the prairies to bathe in its salubrious waters, in a pool lined with white marble and illuminated by underwater lights. The natatorium was a fixture in Moose Jaw for twenty-five years, but by the 1950s the original wooden shafts had rotted away and the baths eventually closed. Today's Temple Gardens spa, opened in 1995, represents a revival.

For the record, I am a health spa neophyte. I have never had my cuticles buffed or my eyebrows plucked. I have never been wrapped in seaweed or dunked in herbal tea, and the last time I had mousse in my hair was when I passed out in the Denny's dessert tray at two in the morning. I always thought toner was something you put into a Xerox machine.

Normally, this wouldn't matter. There are many things I still haven't done: skydive, learn to whistle a recognizable tune, snorkel, my 1989 taxes. But I have made the mistake of mentioning my lack of beauty spa experience, my virginability, if you will, to Kim Izzo, an editor at *Flare* magazine. And Kim, in her gleeful way, has decided it would be an absolute riot to send someone as clued out as me to a spa.

I've told Terumi about this on the faint hope that she may veto the idea. Instead, she all but pushes me through the spa's doors the next morning (assuming, I suppose, that I will emerge from the other end squeaky clean and looking not unlike, say, a young Pierce Brosnan. Talk about yer faint hopes).

"But I've never been to a spa before," I protest. "I don't know what to do—I don't know the etiquette involved."

"Nothing to worry about," she says. "Just relax and you'll be fine." I've heard that before—usually prior to a bungee jump or a dentist's drill.

So I slink into the Temple Gardens spa, bathrobe pulled tight, eyes darting, and am taken to a small room where a reclining chair awaits. They are going to start at my feet and presumably work their way up. My reflexologist, I am told, will be with me shortly. A few minutes later the door opens and in walks . . . a guy.

This is not exactly what I'd expected. If anyone is going to fondle my feet, I'd prefer it wasn't someone with a moustache.

"Brad Moffatt," he says. I shake his hand in a gruff but friendly fashion. My voice has mysteriously dropped a few octaves.

"How about them Leafs?" I say.

Brad dims the lights and puts on soft music. It's like being on a date. He begins rubbing mint lavender oil onto my feet, at which point I start dropping subtle hints that I am married. To a woman.

"I'm married," I say. "To a woman."

He nods and continues to rub. "You seem tense," he says.

You don't know the half of it.

As he works on my feet, Brad speaks in a calm, scientific manner about "energy meridians" and "ancient Chinese techniques" and the importance of "removing toxins from your system." I have always been dubious about reflexology, and the notion that your liver and pancreas can be "cleansed" by tweaking your big toe. What if your problem is not your pancreas? What if you have a sore foot? How does reflexology deal with *that?* Do they have to massage your liver?

Still, there's no denying that Mr. Moffatt has worked magic on my toes, and the soles of my feet are still tingling as I'm taken to another room to receive my first-ever facial. The aesthetician who's been asked to take care of me (I'm assuming she drew the short straw) is a young woman named Jackie Hill, who examines my skin like an Amsterdam diamond dealer. Having trained a magnifying glass on me at close range, she begins to speak, not coincidentally perhaps, about clogged pores and damaged capillaries. And what would cause such things? "Oh," she says. "Too much alcohol or caffeine, or too much sun and not enough sunscreen."

Guilty on all counts.

Who knew that beauty was so complicated? When I heard the word "facial" I imagined some sort of mud pack, maybe, with cucumbers over the eyes, like you see in the movies. It turns out to be far more complex than that. Ms. Hill goes through a dozen steps at least: cleanser, toner, moisturizer, "enzyme peel" (who knew I had enzymes, let alone that they needed peeling?), more cleanser, more goop, more moisturizer, lots of gel under the eyes and finally a Zorro-style eye mask to help "reduce wrinkles."

The focus on wrinkles around the eyes—at least three of the steps seem to deal with these—is revealing. Temple Gardens, like spas everywhere, is aimed primarily at women. When it comes to aging, wrinkles aren't something men worry about. Baldness, love handles, rampant and inexplicable ear hair: *yes*. But wrinkles? It's one of the few remaining advantages of being a man that the creases around your eyes make you look distinguished, not old.

Jackie massages my scalp and temples, and even my earlobes (which is nice, but honestly, my earlobes hardly ever get fatigued). She then works on my arms and fingers until they become jellied boneless limbs.

It's not over yet. I am passed on next to a soft-spoken but determined young masseuse named Damara Brown, who has powerfully strong hands for someone so small. A couple of times I glance over my shoulder to make sure it isn't a trick, half-expecting to discover that Damara has tiptoed away and I am now being kneaded by a burly lumberjack named Carl.

The only memories I have of sore-muscle treatments prior to visiting Moose Jaw involve no-neck coaches knuckling out charley horses and telling us to "Walk it off. It's just a bruise." *But there's a bone protruding from the*—"It's just a bruise, walk it off!" As a result, I suppose, I have always associated massages with twisted ankles and cruel sporting events. This, however, is different.

The full-body massage Damara gives me is almost hypnotic. At one point, as she unravels knots I didn't even know I had, I nod off and end up snoring in that "strangled seagull" fashion of mine that women find so appealing. I wake with a start—tongue lolling, eyes unfocused, a large pool of saliva spreading across the table—and immediately ask Damara to marry me.

Well, not quite. But I want to. I want to ask Jackie to marry me, as well. Hell, after the way he worked on my feet, I wanted to ask Brad to marry me.

My session ends with a rosehip body wrap. Oiled down and bound in layers of plastic, I soon discover how much heat the human body generates. It is prickly and itchy under there, and a tad claustrophobic, but the wrap does make my skin supple and soft. Why, I am positively glowing afterwards! Not Pierce Brosnan, exactly, but still, the difference is remarkable, and Terumi is pleased. Indeed, I will now be able to speak knowledgeably, and at great length if you let me, about the state of my pores and the maintenance said pores require.

I am pleased, also, to think I pulled it off. I didn't do anything too stupid or gauche, and even though it was my first time at a spa, I managed to bluff my way through in a suitably suave, urbane fashion without any embarrassing social gaffes.

"So," Terumi asks. "How much did you tip?"

"Tip?" I say. "You're supposed to *tip?*"

Young men on horseback storming Main Street. The first steam locomotive pulling into town. The vanishing tracks of buffalo. The history of Moose Jaw is a series of tableaux on the sides of buildings.

Inspired by a similar project in the Vancouver Island community of Chemainus, the murals of Moose Jaw have transformed this prairie city into an open-air art gallery. It's true that some of Moose Jaw's murals are cornball—complete with teddy bears, snow angels and sunsets—but none is as exquisitely bad as the one I marvelled at in Victoria. In Moose Jaw, the murals vary from New Yorker–style illustrations of flappers and the jazz era to depictions of settlers on ox carts, from ceramic-tile mosaics to Soviet-realism depictions of hearty, sun-kissed pioneers breaking the sod.

Moose Jaw began in 1882 as a Canadian Pacific Railway town, settled by land speculators who arrived one step ahead of the railway to stake out the townsite and claim the best property. The valley had water, woods and shelter, which made it an ideal choice for a CPR divisional point. With a roundhouse and a regional office and a flurry of sidetracks, Moose Jaw was the main transfer site for passengers travelling east or west. In its day, it was the most important rail junction between Winnipeg and the Rockies.

Moose Jaw was also the northern terminus for the celebrated Soo Line, which linked up with the CPR line in 1893

and ran south across the border, into the States. The Soo
Line connected Moose Jaw to Chicago, which would prove
both a godsend and a curse during the Prohibition years of
the 1920s.

The city of Victoria, founded by the HBC, was built by
gold. Moose Jaw, founded by the CPR, was also built by gold—
liquid gold, in this case. Hoo-ha! Whisky was to Moose Jaw
what temperance was to Saskatoon—it defined the city in its
formative years. I doubt that any community in Canada owes
as much to the illegal whisky trade.

They called it "Loose Jaw" and "Little Chicago," and in
Moose Jaw, unlike most places in Canada, the twenties really
did roar. Perhaps only Montreal had a more exciting run
during those freewheeling years between one great war and
the next. Moose Jaw's River Street was an all-night carnival of
brothels and bootleg joints, of poolrooms and faro games, jazz
bands and poker brawls and girls who waved at you from the
windows. "You came out of the Moose Jaw station, turned left
on River Street, and you could have been in New Orleans,"
one visitor noted. It was denounced from the pulpit and in
the press as the "sin city of Saskatchewan" and "the Sodom
and Gomorrah of the prairies." And with the provincial capital just down the line, Moose Jaw quickly became Regina's
red-light district.

"Moose Jaw isn't a city or a municipality or even a geographic location," one newspaper editor steamed. "Moose Jaw
is a goddamn virus that has permanently afflicted Regina and
for which there is no known cure!"

The funny thing is, Saskatchewan had voted in favour of
Prohibition, and the province was officially "dry" when the 1920s

rolled round. Ah, but there was a loophole, you see. The act banned only the *consumption* of alcohol. It did not prohibit the manufacture of alcohol, nor its export or storage, and Moose Jaw soon had warehouses full of the stuff. The barrels in these warehouses proved unusually leaky, and the hotels and back-room bars of Moose Jaw were practically floating on whisky— warm, amber, tongue-numbing, inhibition-loosening whisky.

The Soo Line became a "Prohibition pipeline," as did the many dusty unmarked roads that ran south, across the vast and porous border, into the United States. Even better, although Saskatchewan repealed Prohibition in 1924, the States did not. It was still "dry"—and very, very thirsty. Moose Jaw thrived.

There had been whispers of bootlegger hideaways and passageways beneath the streets of Moose Jaw for years: a network of tunnels, it was said, that ran from the railyards to River Street, and from the warehouses to the hotels and gambling dens. These tales were dismissed as rumours— until 1985, that is, when a manhole collapsed, revealing a brick-lined chamber below. Was it a water cistern? An old sewage tank? Or was it part of a long-lost clandestine world, one rife with good-time girls and gangsters, tommy guns and rum-runners? In the absence of evidence, the imagination soars.

Today, visitors can tour the Tunnels of Moose Jaw™. But let's be upfront about this: fun though they may be, the tun-nels of Moose Jaw are, ahem, "creative reconstructions." Which is a nice way of saying "fake." That doesn't mean the legends are without merit, though. Booze *was* smuggled out of Moose Jaw warehouses. Bootleggers and gangsters *did* make Moose Jaw their base—the scrawny Pittsburgh Kid came here and was duly captured. The post office *was* robbed in broad daylight, and the local chief of police, the irascibly charming Walter Johnson, *was* corrupt—or, at the very least, indulgent. (During one federal sting operation, pretty much the entire Moose Jaw police department ended up behind bars.) The whisky trade in Saskatchewan involved shootouts and ambushes and unsolved murders and even a car chase or two, usually across bald prairie in the middle of the night. And there were indeed tunnels below Moose Jaw's city streets.

In several buildings downtown there are sealed passageways and mysterious doorways that lead from one basement to the next. Were these the lairs of gangsters and gamblers? Are they simply old utility corridors, built to allow access by maintenance workers? Or were they both: utility corridors later used for illicit purposes? When the tourist tunnels were being built, the owners of these real passageways declined to have them incorporated into the official tour. Which is a shame, because they would have added a hint of authenticity to the enterprise.

Did Al Capone ever visit Moose Jaw? The evidence is mainly anecdotal, and the odds are slim. But that hasn't stopped the good people at the Tunnels of Moose Jaw™ from promoting the disconcerting image of American mobsters ruling the town as though it were their personal fiefdom. (Hello? International border?) Nor has it stopped one enterprising innkeeper from opening Capone's Hideaway!, a theme motel complete with a Chicago-style getaway car impaled on a signpost out front and a selection of rooms decked out in what can only be described, charitably, as sort-of-1920s bric-a-brac.

For the life of me, I can't understand why we need to import American lore when the real story is so much more fascinating. The Bronfman empire was built here, on the bootlegged whisky of the Canadian West. River Street was a raucous place on its own, without inventing dubious connections to the toadlike Al Capone. Why not celebrate someone like Annie Hoburg instead? Annie blew into town in 1883 under the cover of opening Moose Jaw's first restaurant, catering to the rail crews, but her true trade was in whisky, and she soon established herself as the most ingenious bootlegger west of Winnipeg.

Annie Hoburg was a legend in her own time. She had special rubber containers sewn into her petticoats; after all, it would be quite improper for a police officer to search beneath a lady's skirt! Young Annie and her baby carriage were a common site in Moose Jaw; she could often be seen pushing her buggy down to the station. The fact that she didn't have any actual children was a minor detail. So what if her baby, swaddled in blankets, tended to clink when the buggy hit a bump? Annie is sometimes credited with establishing Moose Jaw's first brothel, as well, though she was more realtor than madam. Either way, it can be argued that, indirectly, she was the true founder of Moose Jaw's original red-light district.

The swirling tilt-a-whirl world of Moose Jaw in the 1920s came to an end in the Great Depression of the 1930s. The Promised Land turned to dust and the creeks ran dry. The southern prairies were already facing a devastating drought when the stock market collapsed. Everything came up snake eyes, and no one talked about easy wealth and good times any more, as the champagne days of flappers and jazz faded first into memory and then into myth.

The tour company likes to suggest that the original tunnels were built by Moose Jaw's Chinese community. Supposedly, Chinese families were driven underground by relentless persecution. After the Chinese were pushed out, the bootleggers moved in. Supposedly.

This was all news to Moose Jaw's Chinese community.

A separate tunnel tour takes visitors underground into these "Chinese" passages. It depicts a world of workers forced to scurry from the lye vats of laundry rooms to their crowded sleeping quarters ("rat-infested" sleeping quarters, as the guides unfailingly point out). But this is pure bunk. There's not a shred of evidence to support it, and the notion that Moose Jaw's Chinese community raised its children in underground squalor is, if you think about, an insult to them—and a libel on the people of Moose Jaw and their ancestors. (Columnist Allan Fotheringham, who grew up south of the city, is particularly enamoured with these images. Back when Fotheringham was still writing for *Maclean's*, I counted at least three occasions on which he referred to the Chinese in Moose Jaw as raising their children in dark "rat-infested" tunnels.)

Bruce Fairman, owner of a computer shop off Main Street, is a local historian with an in-depth knowledge of Moose Jaw. True to his surname, he tries to be balanced, even if he is, in his own words, "a naysayer."

"It's folklore," he tells me. "Which is fine—folklore gives

a town character. The problem is, they're presenting it as fact. As for the Chinese community here, it was very small up until the twenties. There was no need to live underground."

It's true there were angry confrontations between railworkers and the Chinese men—all of them here without families, it should be noted—who were brought in during a strike, but that was more labour-related than racial. A Chinese restaurant owner, Quong Wing, was once charged and fined for employing "white women" in his establishment. He fought the decision all the way to the Supreme Court, and lost. But there were no "rat-infested" tunnels with families cowering inside. The Chinese community has been operating businesses in Moose Jaw since 1889 (within seven years of the town's founding), and some of the city's finest buildings were erected by businesspeople like Yip Foo, Chin Foon and the Chow family. They thrived precisely because they did *not* face widespread persecution. In spite of the attitudes prevalent at the time, the Chinese were welcomed here to a degree that does credit to Moose Jaw, and to have that turned on its head is strange indeed. It's an odd way to promote a city.

At the other end of the fact-fiction spectrum were the miniature "cash cars" of Joyner's Department Store, built in 1892. For my money, this was one of the best attractions in Moose Jaw. And unlike the tunnels, the cash cars were authentic.

Installed by Walter Joyner in 1915, in the days before pneumatic tubes, the system resembled a mini–Victorian railway, the cars suspended in midair by pulleys and wires and moved along on cables. It was an elaborate network, over 300 metres long, running between three floors and two buildings, zipping around corners and disappearing through passageways. Whenever a customer made a purchase, the Joyner's clerk would tuck the bill and the payment into a small money box that was then clamped onto a cable that whisked the car away to a central cashier. Like a switchboard operator, the cashier sat at the back of the store where the cables converged, taking in the money and sending back change.

There were once hundreds of these cash cars in service across Canada; Eaton's and Woolworths both used them. The Moose Jaw cash cars were the only ones left in North America, and one of only two systems remaining in the world. The cash cars were in use right up until the store closed in 1994. Not a bad run. And although Joyner's Department Store became an old-fashioned candy shoppe, the cash cars still hummed with life. The original electric motor (never rebuilt, never replaced) still turned the belt that ran the pulleys, which turned the cables that moved the cars.

Demonstrations of the cash cars were held throughout the day, and whenever I passed through Moose Jaw, I always stopped by Joyner's to marvel at this ingenious system. I took Alex to see them. He called it the "railway show." And on New Year's Day, 2004, the Joyner's Building would be destroyed by the fire that gutted the city's most historic block—taking with it the cash car system. History, up in flames.

It's our last day in Moose Jaw, and Alex asks to see the train show one more time. But there's a lot of highway to cover, and I tell him, "Next time, okay? We'll be back next year, don't worry. We'll stop by and see it then. I promise."

• • •

I'm south of the city on Highway Two, alone this time, on a dry day in August in a summer without rain. Up from the valley, the fields are the colour of scorched paper; the sky is a blistering blue. The heat rises in wavering sheets from the road. Telephone poles file past. A train trestle spans a coulee in a cat's cradle of lumber as Moose Jaw recedes in the rearview mirror.

Overhead, military planes streak by—Snowbirds on manoeuvres in a clean and empty sky. The air base south of Moose Jaw has been the training ground of fighter pilots since the 1940s, and it is also home to Canada's premier aerial acrobatic team. They are drawn here by the clear views, the wide horizon and the almost unlimited airspace. But open skies can be deceptive. On April 8, 1954, a student pilot on a solo training flight above Moose Jaw collided in mid-air with a Vancouver-bound commercial airliner that had thirty-five people on board. The airliner split open and the burning wreckage plunged into the city, narrowly missing a school with 300 children inside and destroying a nearby house, killing a woman and setting two more homes ablaze. Bodies fell from the sky.

With so much horizon and so little shade, a single figure can cast a far shadow out here, and I am chasing one such shadow across the fields, a shadow thrown by a solitary man long gone, and the strange artifact he left behind. And even

though I've been watching for it—scanning every hill, every
crest, every small rise—it still comes as a surprise when I
spot it coming up quickly on my right: a deep-keeled ship
moored on the open prairie, an ocean-going vessel, held in
place by steel support beams. The name on the side reads
DONTIANEN, but this is a mistake, an error made during
restoration, when the first letter, faded and cracked, was mis-
read. It is the *Sontianen,* the "little dung beetle," and it's a
testament to the will of one man: Tom Sukanen, the Noah of
the grasslands.

Tom Sukanen was a shipbuilder from Finland who
arrived in Saskatchewan in 1911. He had migrated to the
New World at the age of twenty, settled in Minnesota and
tried his hand at farming. He married a Finnish girl and they
had four children—three daughters and a son—but life was
difficult and they struggled to get by. The soil was poor, the
work was hard.

So Tom went north to Saskatchewan, where free land still
beckoned. Promising his family that he would return for them,
he set out on foot. Tom Sukanen *walked* to Saskatchewan,
almost 1000 kilometres across the sun-baked plains. (His
strength was legendary; they say he stood over six feet tall and
weighed 280 pounds.) He settled in the Macrorie district,
north of Moose Jaw. He worked hard, saved his money, and
in 1918, after a seven-year absence, he walked *back* to
Minnesota to get his family. He arrived to find the farm abandoned and the fields overgrown. His wife had died in a flu
epidemic, and his children had been scattered, sent into foster homes and government care. In the eyes of the law,
Sukanen had deserted his family.

He was able to locate only one of his children, his son, John. Together they slipped away and started walking towards Saskatchewan, but just five kilometres from the Canadian border, Tom and his son were intercepted by U.S. authorities, and John was taken back into custody. Sukanen was nothing if not stubborn, and almost immediately he set out on a second attempt to get his son. This time, though, he was stopped before he could make contact. He was deported from the United States and threatened with jail if he ever returned. He never saw his son again.

The crops had failed on Sukanen's farm, and the fields were parched. Sukanen formulated a plan. He purchased a set of maps from the Regina Archives and over the next several years charted his course: up the Saskatchewan River, into the deep waters of the Nelson and then onward to Hudson Bay, around the northern tip of Ungava and back to Finland. He spent his savings on steel and oak, on sheets of brass and iron cables, and in the depths of the Great Depression, Tom Sukanen began work on the *Sontianen*.

The topsoil crumbled into black dust and was carried away in towering storms that darkened the skies. Then came the grasshoppers, in waves, like an Old Testament plague. Sukanen's neighbours could hear his hammer echoing across the hills, could see the glow of his forge burning against the night sky. They whispered in disapproving terms about the "crazy Finlander" who thought he could sail a ship out of the prairies and across the ocean.

Month after month, year after year, Sukanen refused to yield. He rolled the steel for his boiler by hand and forged his own rivets. Slowly, in sections, the ship began to take shape: an oak cabin, an iron hull, a deep tapered keel. By now he was a wild figure, emaciated, blackened with soot, living on gopher meat and raw grain. Still he pushed on, even though his health was fading. When he went into town for supplies, the shopkeepers would ask him what he was doing, and why. "There is a great flood coming," Sukanen would reply. "And when it does, I will be ready. I will sail away and return to my home in Finland."

By 1941, the iron ship was done. Sukanen had only to move the sections across open prairie to the Saskatchewan River to reassemble them and sail free. But the hull alone weighed twenty tons, and he spent two years pulling it forward, first with his horses and then, when they had all died, alone, by hand. He was winching the hull and keel towards the river when they finally came for him. In 1943, the shipbuilder was committed to the psychiatric asylum in North Battleford, where he died that same year. They say he was still holding his hammer when they brought him in.

For more than thirty years, Tom Sukanen's ship lay in pieces in a farmer's field. It might have been forgotten entirely had it not been for a farmer named Lawrence Mullin. Moon Mullin, as he is better known, had heard about Sukanen's ship, and he chased down the wisps of rumour until he finally found the abandoned sections of the vessel. In 1973, Mullin had the keel, hull and boiler of the *Sontianen* hauled to a pioneer village south of Moose Jaw, where it was reassembled and restored.

If Tom Sukanen was obsessed with his ship, Moon Mullin was just as obsessed with Sukanen. Not only did he find a home for the *Sontianen*, he even had Tom Sukanen's body exhumed and moved from North Battleford to be reinterred next to the ship. Burial regulations required that the land be designated a cemetery, and for that a church or chapel needed to be on the site, so Mullin had a small Finnish chapel built beside the ship. Sukanen's grave is marked with a simple white cross, the date he died and an epitaph that reads:

Tom Sukanen
Shipbuilder

The *Sontianen* is propped up on dry grass, its bow pointed towards Finland. I walk along the loose-rattle ribs of a weathered boardwalk, down to the ship, as grasshoppers flit in and out of the stubble. The size of Sukanen's ship doesn't become apparent until you reach the hull and lay your hand upon it, until you look towards the deck from below the waterline. My forehead is hot with sweat, and the salt is burning my eyes. Overhead, planes fly past in tight formation into a sea of blue.

To see the *Sontianen* against the Saskatchewan sky is to confront something deep in the heart of who we are. Beyond the rosy-cheeked images of immigration-board posters touting the promise of a Last Best West, Canada was founded as much on heartbreak as on sunshine. There is an ache—deeper than nostalgia, stronger than regret—that underscores the Canadian experience and informs so much of our immigrant past. It is the dream of escape, the dream of flight. Of return.

Tom Sukanen died on April 23, 1943. By then, the drought had ended and the rains had returned. The skies opened, the streams rose and the Saskatchewan River ran high, brimming with water, flowing towards the sea.

The closest I come to meeting Tom Sukanen face to face is an encounter in a nursing home in Port Alberni, B.C.

Her name is Aili Jowsey. Eighty-eight years old, hair snowy white but memory still clear. There is a gentle firmness to what she says. I meet Mrs. Jowsey in an unexpected way, through an e-mail sent from Victoria. I have been on the trail of Sukanen for some time when I receive the following message: "Dear Mr. Ferguson: My name is Brian Dodsworth. My mother-in-law, Aili Jowsey, is originally from Saskatchewan and she knew Tom Sukanen. Some of the things written about him are not true."

Do I want to meet Mrs. Jowsey? Yes, yes, of course. It has never occurred to me that there may still be people alive who knew Sukanen and remember his strange quest first-hand. Mrs. Jowsey was born and raised in the Finnish community of Macrorie. Her maiden name was Markkula, and Tom Sukanen was her neighbour.

"He lived on a farm next to ours," she says, her voice as soft as a whisper.

"You knew Tom," I say, amazed by the thought of this.

"*Tomiamus*," she replies, using his Finnish name. "Yes, I knew him. And he was not the hermit people say he was. He was well known among the Finnish families, not antisocial. He would come by, use the sauna, visit my parents."

"A big man?"

"No, not really. He was an ordinary man, of ordinary size. But he was strong, that part is true. Prairie stoves are

by no means light, and he could carry one on his back,
I know that."

"Was he crazy, in the end?"

"No, no, I wouldn't say he was crazy. Eccentric. He had
his own calendar, had it written on his ceiling using all these
calculations, and he would show up at our house on a
Tuesday, and that would be his Sabbath. And he would ask,
'Why aren't you in church? Why are you working on the
Sabbath? Your calendar is all wrong,' that's what he'd tell us."
She smiles at the memory.

"Was he teasing?"

"I suppose he might have been."

"And the *Sontianen?*" I ask. "Did you ever see it, before. . . ."

"A friend of mine—we would have been in high school
then—she came by and said, 'You have to see this ship your
neighbour is building!' So we walked over, it was just a mile and
a half down, and stopped in for a visit. It was very impressive,
what he was doing. He was almost shy about it. He made us coffee and boiled eggs, as I recall. That was before his food ran out."

"Do you think—Would he have made it? Back to Finland?"

"Might have. The Vikings made it over on little boats.
Tomiamus might have made it as well."

We speak for some time about Saskatchewan and her
memories of the prairies, before she married and moved away.
She has been very gracious, and I thank her for this. Then, as
I am gathering up my things, she says, "His son came back,
you know."

"His son?"

"His son, he came to Macrorie—came from Minnesota,
looking for his father."

I sit down. "And?"

"Tomiamus wouldn't even go into town, wouldn't meet with the young man. He turned his back when they told him—when they said someone was looking for him. Tomiamus wouldn't listen, he refused, he said, 'I have no family.' It was after that, I think, that the ship took over his life."

I track down Moon Mullin in a Moose Jaw seniors' residence, where he lives with his wife, Hazel. At ninety-one, Mr. Mullin's voice wavers, and he moves with the slow consideration of someone whose world has become a low-level obstacle course. But his mind is sharp, and he is filled with enthusiasm and vigour. A small man, but strong. You can see that even now.

Mr. Mullin, a one-time newspaper boy, claims to have been a "tunnel crawler" during Prohibition. "Oh, there were tunnels all right," he says. "There were tunnels, but you wouldn't have been able to have tours. They were only two or three feet high, most of them. Me and the other four boys the rum-runners recruited, we were small enough we could crawl through."

As a tunnel crawler, Mr. Mullin says, he ran messages and warnings of imminent police raids up and down the mazelike passages, from one gambling den to the next. For the next hour or so, Moon Mullin tells tales, tall and otherwise, of his youth among the bootleggers, the bagmen and what he refers to as the "strong arms" and the "soiled doves" (the thugs and call girls of River Street). And then I change tack.

"Why Tom Sukanen?" I ask. Why did it matter so much? Someone Mr. Mullin didn't know, had never met. "Why was it so important to you that the *Sontianen* be saved?"

"Well," Mr. Mullin says, "I have always hated to see a fellow run down like that. I heard the stories, couldn't get it out of my mind. That man built a ship—by his own hands. A man puts his life into building this, and there it is, just laying on the side of a hill? Didn't seem right. We had to restore his ship, we owed him that, to make amends for how he was treated—to give him back some of his reputation. He was a great man, a giant of a man. I didn't want to see him condemned like that." Mr. Mullin leans forward. His eyes are rheumy but his gaze is clear. "Tom Sukanen didn't do anything wrong. He wasn't crazy, he wasn't a lunatic. He just wanted to go home." He repeats this last point slowly, emphasizing every word: "He just . . . wanted . . . to go . . . home."

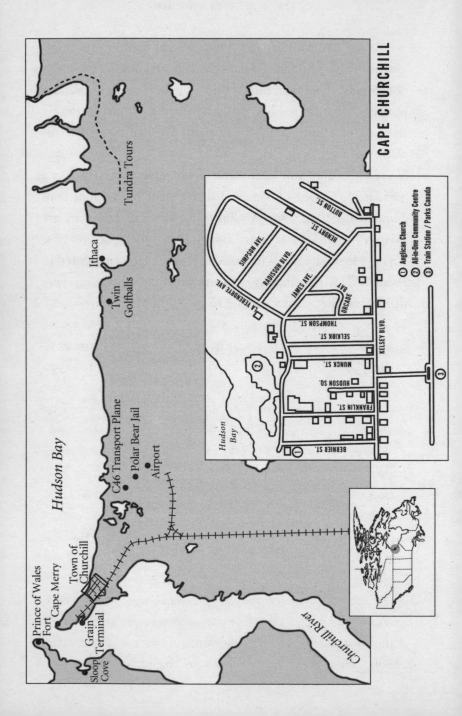

CAPE CHURCHILL

Hudson Bay

Tundra Tours

Ithaca

Twin
Golfballs

C46 Transport Plane

Polar Bear Jail

Airport

Prince of Wales
Fort

Cape Merry

Town of
Churchill

Grain
Terminal

Sloop
Cove

Churchill River

Hudson Bay

BUTTON ST.

HENDRY ST.

SIMPSON AVE.

RADISSON BLVD.

JAMES AVE.

LA VERENDRYE AVE.

ORCADE
BAY

THOMPSON ST.

SELKIRK ST.

MUNCK ST.

HUDSON SQ.

FRANKLIN ST.

BERNIER ST.

KELSEY BLVD.

① Anglican Church

② All-in-One Community Centre

③ Train Station / Parks Canada

chapter four

POLAR BEAR SEASON

IT'S A STRANGE SENSATION: it feels not so much that we have lifted off, but that the ground has dropped away.

The helicopter tilts forward, into its own momentum, and we sweep out across the tundra. Along the shores of Hudson Bay, slushy saline ice formations are taking hold. Winter is setting in. On the expansive emptiness below, spectral shapes are on the move, creamy gold against the white. *Ursus maritimus*, the bear of the sea. *Wapusk* to the Cree. *Nanuk* to the Inuit. The world's largest land carnivore.

Our flight path takes us high above several oversized man-made structures. Odes to past follies, they are arranged like board-game tokens on an empty field: the rusting hull of the *MV Ithaca,* a vermilion silhouette marooned in shallow waters just offshore; the twin domes of an abandoned radar station, teed up like giant golf balls; and—most unsettling of all—a C-46 transport plane lodged in the landscape.

"Went down about twenty-five years ago," says Scott deWindt, our young pilot, speaking through the static-crack of the headphones. "One of her engines gave out just after takeoff. They tried circling back to the airport, but they didn't make it. Lucky no one was hurt." And then, almost as an afterthought: "Great place for parties in the summer, though."

Beyond the airplane and the shipwreck, past the giant golf balls and the abandoned rocket launch sites, are the streets of Churchill, Manitoba, coming in quickly towards us—as incongruous an image as any marooned ship or crashed plane. Looking almost suburban, the houses of the town pass beneath us. Just beyond lies the harbour, where Churchill's grain terminal rises up in a sudden slab of cement. Visible for forty miles in all directions, the terminal is a bookmark above the horizon line, indicating both the town's location and its reason for existing.

At Churchill, a northern railway meets saltwater tides. A suture line of train tracks runs to the terminal docks, where ships slide in, hungry for cargo. Churchill is the narrow end of the funnel: wheat from across the Canadian prairies flows through, into container holds and cargo bays, to be hauled away in ocean-going convoys, bound for Europe via the arctic shortcut of Hudson Bay.

"Last ship of the season," says Scott, indicating a lonely vessel ploughing its way towards the port.

These three elements—the port, the railway and the grain terminal—converged in the 1930s to create the modern town of Churchill. A small trading settlement had taken shape on the far side of the river, but when the rail line reached the bay on the more convenient eastern shore, the community simply . . . decamped. Over the next few years, several buildings, including two churches, were taken apart and skidded across the ice by dogsled and tractor, then reassembled on the other side. If Churchill today looks as though it dropped out of the sky, it's because, in a sense, it did.

The helicopter swings out, blades thumping the air, as we cross the Churchill River. There, on an exposed knuckle of rock on the other side, sits an even greater folly, and the most incongruous icon of all: a sprawling stone fortress, its walls arranged in the classic star formation of British imperial defence. Prince of Wales Fort, Canada's northern Gibraltar. A geometric presence amid the rounded contours of a subarctic shore.

Scott dragonflies down for a closer look. "We may not be landing after all," he shouts. He points to the snow in front of the fortress. "Bear tracks."

Every summer, as the ice melts on Hudson Bay, more than 1200 polar bears are forced ashore east of Churchill, where they wait, hungry and ill-tempered, for the waters to freeze again.

Given the choice, most polar bears would stay on the pack ice year-round, feasting on plump seals. Farther up, in the High Arctic, they do. But in the Hudson Bay lowlands around Churchill, that isn't an option. This is the world's southernmost range of polar bears, and as the ice crumbles beneath them the bears retreat, begrudgingly, onto land. With its scarcity of seals, land represents a seasonal purgatory. In summer, temperatures can reach 30 degrees Celsius and the bears stumble about in a state of walking hibernation. Many of them will go weeks, even months, without eating, living off the fat stores they have built up over winter. When the ice begins to form again in November, the area around Cape Churchill, jutting out as it does into the bay, is the first to freeze over. The stranded bruins make their way there, in one of the greatest concentrations of polar bears in the world.

They are aquatic animals, powerful swimmers, expert hunters. As soon as the ice surface is thick enough to support their weight, they disappear once again into the long twilights and dark nights of a Hudson Bay winter.

If a metaphor exists for the Canadian collective unconscious, it is this: Hudson Bay, that cold-water inland sea, so central to our history and our geography, so rarely glimpsed first-hand. For most Canadians, Hudson Bay exists only on maps: the cartographic emptiness in the middle of who we are. Our route into the interior. *That part of one's mental life of which one is not ordinarily aware, but which influences one's behaviour nonetheless, and which is revealed in one's dreams*: this definition of the subconscious mind can be applied directly to the bay's position within Canada. If Joseph Conrad had been Canadian, he would have set *Heart of Darkness* on Hudson Bay.

Canada, as Northrop Frye observed, has no Atlantic seaboard, and during much of our history there were only two trade routes in: one down the St. Lawrence and the other through Hudson Bay. Both involved being surrounded and then slowly engulfed, as Frye puts it, "like a tiny Jonah entering an inconceivably large whale:"

> To enter the United States is a matter of crossing an ocean;
> to enter Canada is a matter of being silently swallowed by
> an alien continent.

The very name of the bay aches with loss, echoing as it does the voyage of Henry Hudson, who sailed his ship, the

Discovery, into these waters in 1610. Hudson was chasing the chimera of a Northwest Passage, that sea route to China and the East Indies. Having fought his way through the "furious overfall" that separates northern Quebec and Baffin Island— a churning 700-kilometre bottleneck of ice floes and treacherous tidal currents—Hudson and his men broke free into "a great and whirling sea."

Hudson was convinced that he had conquered the passage, and that he had made it through to the far side of the world. But he and his men were not at the gateway to Asia; they were trapped in the heart of an almighty and unforgiving continent. Turning towards warmer climes, they sailed south—and into a dead end. After a harrowing winter frozen in at the bottom of James Bay, Hudson's cutthroat gang of sailors—"a devil's brew of malcontents," in author Peter Newman's words—boiled over in mutiny. They seized Hudson and set him adrift, arms bound, in a small boat with his young son and a handful of other crew members, some loyal, some ill, some just plain unpopular. Henry Hudson vanished into history.

Hudson never reached the western edge of the bay that bears his name. The first Europeans to land at what is now Churchill arrived in 1619, under the leadership of Jens Munk, illegitimate son of a disgraced Danish nobleman. Munk was in a race to the Orient against another sea captain—a nobleman of higher rank, who had a larger fleet and several hundred men. But while his competitor took the slow, warmwater route south, around Africa and the Cape of Good Hope, Munk turned his gaze west. What if the rumours were true? What if a northern passage did exist? What if you could reach the East by sailing *west*—"seek the sunrise through the sunset," as they said?

With two ships, the *Unicorn* and the *Lamprey*, and a crew of sixty-three, Munk fought his way into Hudson's desolate bay through "storm and squall, hail and mist." He sought shelter at the mouth of a nameless river and took possession of the interior—akin to a flea claiming ownership of the elephant it happens to land upon. He named this land "Nova Dania": New Denmark.

Jens Munk shot a polar bear that was feeding on the carcass of a white whale, and his men fared well on whale blubber and bear meat. But the weather soon turned, and the bay was blasted by "fearsome snow and storm." The Danes pulled their ships aground, built small hunting huts on shore and hunkered down on the *Unicorn* to wait out winter. In spring, they would sail on to China.

The land along the river was eerily quiet, though when Munk scouted the area he came upon evidence of human habitation: firepits, stone rings, the bones of animals that had been cooked and eaten. A strange sickness swept through his crew, and the men began to die. The food ran out; the arctic cold descended. Scurvy took its toll. A hunting party that went ashore was lost in a blizzard. With the ship's surgeons dead and the priest dying, Munk was helpless.

I feel like a lost and lonely bird. These words, written in Munk's journal, are among the most poignant lines ever penned in the history of early exploration. (I've also seen the words translated as "wild and forsaken," but the meaning is the same: untethered, unfettered, tossed to the wind.) By June, only Munk was still alive on board the ship. He wrote his last will and testament, bidding "Good night to all the world and my soul into the hand of God," then crawled into his bed to die. But after a few days he found the stench of rotting bodies unbearable, and he staggered out onto the deck.

And there, on shore, were two of his men, emaciated but still alive. They helped Munk ashore and built a small fire. Green shoots had begun to appear through the snow, and the men clawed at the stalks, sucking on the roots for sustenance. Two weeks later the ice opened in the river, and they were able to net several trout. They made a broth with the fish and drank it. Slowly they regained their strength. Still malnourished and badly frostbitten, they managed to refloat the *Lamprey* on the spring tide. The wind caught their sails and they slipped free of the bay. This crew of three, skeleton in every sense, manoeuvred their vessel through the churning Hudson Strait, past Greenland and on to Europe, through a hurricane and with a damaged rudder, no less. It's a feat that still stands in the annals of seafaring history.

It had long been assumed that the men of the ill-fated Munk expedition died of scurvy, but clues in the captain's journal tell a different story. The culprit? Tainted polar-bear meat. Call it a case of post-mortem revenge. Jens Munk, as captain and commander, splurged on fuel and had *his* meat well roasted. The rest of the crew, however, ate theirs parboiled in vinegar. Polar bears are often riddled with roundworms from eating infected seals, and the men on the Lamprey almost certainly died from trichinosis. It was a particularly nasty way to go, as the symptoms described by Munk attest. Partially boiled bear meat is not to everyone's liking, and the two seamen who survived had passed on the meal.

Not long after Munk and the two crewmen departed, the northern Chipewyan returned to their summer camps nearby. After walking among the crosses, and the decaying bodies of strange men on the eerily empty *Unicorn*, they renamed the waterway "The Strangers' River." Two worlds had passed each other in silence and mystery, but the strangers would be back.

Canada's binary code of French/English, either/or, was played out distinctly in the colonization of the Northwest fur trade: France had claimed the St. Lawrence, England took the bay. The Hudson's Bay Company, founded in 1670 by a "Company of Adventurers," was given dominion over all lands that flowed into the bay, an area so large no one even knew its boundaries. It was like casting a net into the ocean and claiming Atlantis. At its peak, the company's territory would encompass nearly five million square kilometres, an area ten times the size of the Holy Roman Empire, making the HBC the largest commercial landowner on earth and the biggest private company—in terms of real estate—in human history.

In fact, the HBC was a small-scale enterprise at first. The company built a string of trading posts along the coast of Hudson Bay and James Bay. The French responded with a daring overland attack launched from the rivers of New France, in what has been described as "the first commando raid in history." The battle for Hudson Bay raged for years, and trading posts changed hands so often the officials back in Europe had trouble keeping track of which outpost was under which king's rule.

The HBC failed in its first attempt at establishing a fort on Jens Munk's wintering site, along the river named in honour of the company's new governor, John Churchill, Duke of Marlborough. The territorial boundaries of three warring nations converged dramatically at the mouth of the Churchill River: to the north, the Inuit; to the west, the Chipewyan; and to the south, the Woodland Cree. The Churchill River was, in effect, a war zone.

The Cree, armed by white traders, held the upper hand. If the HBC wanted the Chipewyan to bring their furs to Churchill, it would have to broker a deal between the two groups. And so, in 1715, a company spokesman named William Stuart ventured deep into Chipewyan territory with a large delegation of Cree in tow. Travelling with them was a Chipewyan woman named Thanadelthur. Captured and held as a slave by the Cree, Thanadelthur had escaped to the safety of an HBC post on the Nelson River, and she had now offered her services as ambassador, translator and envoy. It was not an easy undertaking. The Chipewyan melted away into the barrenlands as the Cree trudged in. Food was scarce, and after months in the wilderness the HBC party was living on moss and facing starvation. A desperate Stuart sent word to the post at Churchill, to no avail. Thanadelthur finally struck off on her own, returning ten days later with more than 150 of her countrymen. In the negotiations that followed, she cajoled, exhorted and scolded the Cree and Chipewyan leaders until they finally hammered out a truce. (Predictably, perhaps, one of the first things the Chipewyan did after their peace treaty with the Cree was to turn their newly acquired firearms on the Inuit.)

Sadly, Thanadelthur was to die that winter after contracting a European-borne disease. William Stuart became unhinged by the hardships he had faced on the barrenlands; he ended his days a lunatic, tied to his bed while he raved wild-eyed at invisible demons. He died in 1719, aged forty-one. The HBC built its post at the Churchill River among the bones of the doomed Munk expedition. With so little shelter available, the main building was set directly on top of several Danish graves.

This original post would later be replaced by a fortress on an exposed outcrop at the river's mouth. The French were building Louisbourg on Cape Breton Island to guard the entrance to the St. Lawrence; Britain would have its own northern Louisbourg, on the edge of Hudson Bay.

Work began in 1731, with the cornerstone laid the following year. The fortress was made from grey-green Precambrian quartz, blasted out of the bedrock with gunpowder and bonded with ground limestone cement. Prince of Wales Fort would be a bastion of Britain's mercantile empire, and one of the most magnificent stone structures in North America. It took forty years to build. And it would fall without a single shot being fired.

Our helicopter circles the fortress, noise echoing off stone walls. The danger is real; finding polar-bear paw prints is like finding tiger tracks around a campfire. But there are no bears prowling the perimeter—or at least none we can spot from the air—and Scott brings us down.

Accompanying me are Stacey Jack, Parks Canada's communications manager for the region, and Jackie Schollie, also with Parks Canada, who is our designated "polar-bear monitor." I have to admit, Jackie's title makes me jumpy.

I would have preferred "polar-bear wrangler" or "polar-bear fighter." But *monitor?* Monitor seems too passive, as in: "Here comes the polar bear. And there goes Mr. Ferguson. The bear has now caught up to Mr. Ferguson and appears to be eating him. We will continue to monitor this situation as it unfolds."

Happily, Ms. Schollie comes armed with a rifle and a suitably steely gaze. "A warning shot first. Then we run like hell for the chopper" is how I interpret the Important Safety Information I receive.

The three of us make our way, heads hunched, from under helicopter blades that are only now spinning into view.

Jackie stops to examine the bear tracks we spotted earlier, and I swallow hard. Footprints in the wild are somehow more unnerving than the real thing, hinting as they do of menaces unseen. Even in my heavy polar trek boots, I can fit both feet into a single paw print.

"That's, ah—that's a big bear," I say.

Jackie nods, scans the horizon.

"So," I say. "Polar bear comes, you'll leap in front of me, right? Take a bullet, so to speak."

"Nope."

Jackie slings the rifle over her shoulder as we trudge through the snow towards the fort. The doors are hidden by a ravelin—a free-standing defensive wall, perfect for a polar bear to hide behind. Chivalrous to a fault, I step back and let the ladies go first, but no ambush awaits. So far.

I look at the snowbanks that slope right to the top of the fortress wall. "Do polar bears ever get *inside?*" I ask Stacey.

"When the drifts get high enough, I suppose they could," she says.

The lock turns, the doors open with an obligatory moan, and we enter into history. The cold snap of a Union Jack. Arctic lichen frozen on stone walls. The maze of walls inside forms an open-air plan, the rooftops and upper floors long gone.

"This would have been the stonemason's shop," says Stacey, stopping to point out a cryptic insignia. "Freemason. And these would have been the tailor's shop, the carpenter's shop and, finally, a combined blacksmith shop and bakery." Odd combination. They both require a firepit, I suppose, but still. Imagine getting your daily bread from the local blacksmith. "So, boys. How're the biscuits and assorted fresh-baked goods?" "Gritty." "Manure-scented." "By eighteenth-century standards, just fine!"

Across from the courtyard are the men's barracks, and in front of these, the governor's quarters. "Samuel Hearne slept here," I say with a wonderment that surprises even me.

"Actually, it would have been in mid-air," Stacey says. "The sleeping quarters were most likely on the second floor."

I stare up into the middle distance and picture Samuel Hearne as a ghostly afterglow, pacing the floors as he tries to decide what to do about the French warships anchored offshore. Time, as they say, is nature's way of preventing everything from happening at once. If we could collapse the centuries, he would appear: Samuel Hearne, the sailor who walked to the Arctic Ocean. The man, according to biographer Ken McGoogan, who was the inspiration for Coleridge's "Rime of the Ancient Mariner."

Samuel Hearne was a traveller, a trader, a sailor, an explorer, an author and a gifted amateur naturalist. A humane voice in a harsh time. If Tom Sukanen was a Noah-like figure of the grasslands, then Samuel Hearne was the Arctic Moses. Indeed, McGoogan himself has made the comparison.

In 1770, after two previous attempts, Hearne struck out overland from Prince of Wales Fort towards the Arctic Ocean—a distance, out and back, of more than 5600 kilometres. The thought of it is staggering. Hearne made his trek on foot the entire way, across the barrenlands and through two howling arctic winters, and the only reason he survived was because he adopted Native dress and diet. He travelled light and lived off the land. More important, his expedition was led by the legendary Chipewyan chieftain Matonabbee, a towering figure in every sense.

Matonabbee led the expedition west, along the treeline—feasting and fasting as they went, depending on the game they encountered—before turning north across the barrens. Their numbers increased as more and more Chipewyan hunters joined them, until—with a sense of horror—Hearne realized that he was now part of a war party. The Chipewyan were intent on killing Inuit. As they drew near the Arctic Ocean, Matonabbee and his men fell upon a band of Inuit sleeping by the side of a river and massacred them. One young girl wrapped herself around Hearne's legs, pleading for mercy while the Chipewyan speared her. Hearne was helpless to intervene, and his account of the attack is difficult to read even now. It haunted him for the rest of his life, and he was never able to recount the events of that day without weeping.

Samuel Hearne walked from Hudson Bay to the Arctic Ocean. He went in search of fabled copper mines and an equally fabled passage to the Orient; he found neither. The copper fields were little more than a sparse jumble of rocks.

And no passage existed; if it had, Hearne would have crossed it. Wiser but by no means richer, he turned and made the long trek back to Prince of Wales Fort, with Matonabbee once again leading the way.

In his combined attempts, Samuel Hearne spent two years, seven months and twenty-four days on the tundra. But his hard-won lessons in survival were mostly lost on later explorers, who continued to sail blithely into the Arctic archipelago. Among them: Sir John Franklin, who came with ships filled with champagne and fine china and even a grand piano. The Franklin expedition left the North strewn with bodies— Franklin is, in fact, credited with killing more of his crewmen than all other Arctic explorers combined. Hearne and Franklin are, in many ways, archetypal figures. They represent starkly differing views of how to approach the problem of the North. Do you adapt? Do you learn to live with it—amid it? Or do you try to impose your will upon it? Do you arrive loaded down with baggage? Or do you move lightly across the surface?

On August 8, 1782, Samuel Hearne, now governor of Prince of Wales Fort, watched in dismay as enemy warships appeared off the coast. Hearne had seen battle before. He was courageous, but not foolhardy. He took a quick tally— upwards of 400 seasoned French troops versus forty poorly trained HBC employees—and decided against an Alamo-style last stand. Grand though it was, Prince of Wales Fort was still a commercial fortification, privately owned and manned by fur traders, not soldiers. The great northern Gibraltar was surrendered to the French without a fight.

Samuel Hearne was taken captive, along with his men, as the French looted the fort, spiking the cannons, burning the

wooden buildings inside and breaching the outer walls—
leaving few supplies and little shelter for the Cree and
Chipewyan. Hundreds of them would starve to death that
winter, and with them Hearne's Metis wife, Mary Norton.

By the time Matonabbee arrived at Prince of Wales Fort,
the fortress lay empty and smouldering. Matonabbee's old
friend was gone and—he believed—dead. In the Athabasca
region, a smallpox epidemic had wiped out entire tribes, as
many as 90 percent of the Chipewyan had died, and the
assumed death of Hearne was more than Matonabbee could
face. He hanged himself.

Samuel Hearne was neither executed nor imprisoned.
Released by the French, he returned to the Churchill River
only to learn of Mary's slow death and Matonabbee's suicide.
Hearne abandoned the fallen fortress and built a new post
upriver. Prince of Wales Fort would lie in ruins for more than
150 years.

The wooden structures inside are gone now, but the stone
walls have been restored. We climb the steps to the inner
ramparts and look out across Hudson Bay. "Can we go down,"
I ask, "to the water's edge?"

Jackie shakes her head. It isn't safe out there, beyond the
garrison walls. Cast-iron cannons point outwards in all directions, and when I look down the sightline of one, I find it is
aimed directly at the grain terminal on the far side of the river.

Time to leave. Jackie goes first, making sure no nasty
surprises await. Stacey and I follow, moving through the snow
and back towards the helicopter, where Scott is waiting. As
we walk, the conversation turns to Sloop Cove, several kilometres south of the fort. Sloop Cove is where the HBC used

to dock its boats, and it just may be the only *levitating* heritage site in Canada.

"It's called 'isostatic rebound,'" says Stacey.

During the last Ice Age a continental ice sheet, four kilometres deep in places, covered the region, laying its mammoth weight across the land. When these glaciers retreated 8000 years ago, the melting floodwaters created Hudson Bay. But like a giant sponge filling out after a heavy weight has been lifted, the land began to rise, emerging from the sea.

"It's slowing down," says Stacey. "But the ground around here is still rising about half a centimetre a year."

That's one metre straight up, every 200 years. Sloop Cove, once a harbour, is now a meadow, and the iron mooring rings bolted into the bedrock at water's edge are now hanging high and dry. I've read that Samuel Hearne carved his name in rock at Sloop Cove alongside those of other HBC employees, and since then his chiselled signature has ridden the isostatic rebound upwards. When I mention this to Scott, he takes it as a personal challenge.

"Hang on," he says. And we lift off in a cloud of flying powder.

With Jackie giving directions, Scott locates the cove. We come in low along the water, veering at the last moment to hover directly in front of the rock face. The helicopter blades blow back the snow and suddenly, right in front of us, it appears, etched into the granite: "S^L Hearne, July ye 1, 1767."

Scott lingers as long as he can and then pulls back; we arc up into the sky. And it dawns on me that exactly 100 years after Samuel Hearne carved his name at Sloop Cove—

100 years later to the very day—a new country was called into existence.

Bone-white beluga whales congregate at the mouth of the Churchill River every July, feeding on small fish and calving in the river's warm water. As many as 3000 whales can crowd the estuary at any one time. Sociable, vocal, curious, gentle— the belugas of Churchill are a sharp contrast to the town's other great white icon. Even as the belugas loll in shallow waters, chirping and clicking, enormous paw prints are appearing along the sands of Hudson Bay.

Generally speaking, one comes to Churchill for whales in summer and bears in winter. It is early November, and I am here for the bears.

Churchill's status as the Polar Bear Capital of the World is only the town's most recent incarnation. When the last spike of the CPR was driven home in a mountain pass in British Columbia in 1885, trade routes shifted south, along an east-west axis. After 215 years, the Hudson Bay sea route had been bypassed. The trading post at Churchill was in decline, with one trader noting that "a more dilapidated hamlet could scarcely be found anywhere."

Luckily, the seeds of the town's redemption had already been planted. As early as the 1870s, in a bid to end the Eastern domination of Canada's shipping routes, Western Canadian business developers and agricultural interests began calling for a rail link between Winnipeg and Hudson Bay, a route to transport wheat instead of furs. Which is to say, the town of Churchill was ruined by one railway and saved by another.

The tracks to Hudson Bay had to thread their way through muskeg capable of swallowing entire locomotives, and then cross a field of permafrost whose surface was constantly thawing and refreezing. Hordes of blackflies and mosquitoes tormented the workers. In the end, 3000 men laid tracks across the tundra: an army in the wilderness, trying to achieve the impossible. Construction began in 1908. The project lurched forward, then sputtered and stalled, only to be revived in the 1920s and pushed to completion. In 1929, the end of steel reached Churchill, and a final spike was hammered into place. Just in time for the Great Depression.

Still, the railway helped anchor Churchill. The Dirty Thirties gave way to the horrors of the Second World War, and in 1942 a new invasion began. East of town, a U.S. air base sprang up almost overnight, and thousands of American troops poured in. The base quickly became a community unto itself, with a population of more than 4000 at its peak, and its own hospital, chapel, post office, bowling alley and movie theatre. This at a time when Churchill, with scarcely 200 people, was, in the words of author Mark Fleming, "little more than a frontier trading post with no running water, sewage system or street lights."

Churchill became a colony of the United States, and the people living in the town—Canadian citizens, it should be noted—were forced to carry ID cards, to be presented on demand to the U.S. military police. It was an insult to Canadian sovereignty, but money talks, and the base provided a welcome boom for the community. Shops and cafés opened. Business was good. And though the Canadian government eventually took the base over, the American presence—and influence—remained. In the 1950s, the U.S. Air Force started launching rockets from Cape Churchill, the discarded sections falling like spent shotgun shells to the tundra below. The remains of these rockets are still embedded in the subarctic peat, like debris on a distant planet.

Here's something you may not know: Canada was the third nation in space. But whereas the Soviets and the Americans were locked in an escalating arms race, Canada saw the conquest of space as quite literally that: the conquest of *space*. Space as in *size*. When Canada sent its first exploratory satellite into orbit in 1962, the goal was improving long-distance communications. The satellites Canada sent up, either through NASA or from Churchill, were fuelled by a desire to cross distances, to overcome the sheer scope of our geography. The solar storms of the northern lights often disrupted radio signals, and the Churchill rocket range was ideally located to probe this phenomenon. Canada's National Research Council took control of the rocket range, firing thousands of rockets heavenward.

Cape Churchill was the first rocket research centre in Canada, and the last. The final liftoff came on May 8, 1985. By then the military base was gone, and the homes had been bulldozed out of existence, leaving behind only the faint outline of streets and yards like a blueprint—still visible from the air, they say.

The hubbub of the air base and rocket range east of town had discouraged bears from passing through. Any that did wander in too close were shot on sight. But with the base gone, the polar bears at Cape Churchill pressed their advantage, taking control of the town dump and pushing into

Churchill itself. A local man was mauled to death in the middle of town, and this brought the crisis to a head. Bear traps now ring the community. The dump is off-limits to bears, and a twenty-four-hour polar-bear alert system is in place.

The squalor in Churchill, once described as "the worst in Canada," slowly improved. Streetlights were finally installed, water mains and sewage lines upgraded.

The Hudson Bay railway is running still, as improbable as ever. If nothing else, it is likely the slowest-moving train line in North America. The tracks, laid directly on the permafrost, tend to buckle, pushed ahead like dough under a rolling pin when the trains run too fast or too heavy. Derailments are common.

The docks of Churchill may be closer to Europe than those in Montreal, but what the Hudson Bay route makes up for in distance, it loses in the shortness of its season. At best, the shipping in Churchill lasts eighty-eight days. Even then, the vessels that zigzag through the Hudson Strait have to run a gauntlet of icebergs and half-submerged floes (the dreaded growlers). Ships often arrive in Churchill with crumpled hulls and blanched-looking crews. The motto of Churchill dockworkers: "We load, ship and repair."

Churchill is Canada's only arctic seaport. But the real touchstone of the town's identity, and its central point of pride, are the bears that prowl its borders. It's the polar bears that have made Churchill famous.

I've been invited to Churchill by Cathy Senecal, author of *Pelicans to Polar Bears*, a guidebook to Manitoba wildlife. Through Cathy's work with Travel Manitoba, I will spend three days on the treeless tundra east of Churchill on a

Frontiers North Adventure Tour. Now, normally, when you put the words "frontier," "north" and "adventure" in the same sentence, you are setting yourself up for disappointment. But not this time. This time, the name says it all.

On the flight up from Winnipeg, the cultivated farmlands of the Canadian prairie fall away. The logic of straight lines is transformed into the whorls and curves of the Red River Delta; the Red—the only major river that flows *into* Canada—ends in a swirl of indecision. We fly above the gun-metal glow of Lake Winnipeg, pulling the shadow of our plane across the surface of the water. But this too falls away, and a pockmarked landscape appears. Endless small ponds dot the horizon, unnamed, uncounted—uncountable. Spindly sticks of taiga trees bristle below us like porcupine quills.

The airplane bucks, hitting every patch of turbulence along the way, and I begin to realize that the company's name, Calm Air, is short for "Calm down, we hardly ever crash." Landing a plane in Churchill is a matter of bounces. One bounce: good. Two bounces: bad. And three? Well, if the runway seems unusually lumpy, you may want to scan the area for predators. A few years ago, one of the Churchill ground crew was out on the runway, waving in a plane, when the pilot ignored his signals and veered directly towards him, lights flashing. When the man on the ground looked over his shoulder, he was confronted by a polar bear on its hind legs, just metres away. The pilot revved his engines to keep the bear at bay while the crewman ran for cover.

No bears this afternoon, just a bracing wind like the crack of a whip as we stumble out of the plane and make our way across the tarmac. From the parka-and-snowboot confusion that is the Churchill airport—a turmoil of refugee-camp proportions, with outgoing and incoming passengers boarding through the same door at the same time—I am herded onto a long yellow schoolbus for the ride into town.

Churchill is not connected to the outside world by road; all its cars and trucks—and schoolbuses—have to be shipped in by boat or train. This has fostered a certain genius in the local townspeople when it comes to maintaining their vehicular investments. Whether it's that of a skidoo or a pickup or an ATV, any spark of mechanical life will be painstakingly nurtured, and the lifespan extended well beyond the normal "best before" date. In Churchill, vehicles are kept running at all costs. They are reworked and jerry-built, taken apart and put back together. Constantly.

But before we can rendezvous with our buggy and roll off into the tundra, we first have to get to Churchill—alive, preferably. The odds aren't good. Our driver is a boisterous young bravado boy, unencumbered by normal notions of mortality. He drives his schoolbus as though he were joyriding across moguls, bouncing us off our seats as we more or less snowboard our way towards town. Who knew a schoolbus could be so agile?

Then, as the road curves to the left, there it is. A curve of cold marble: Canada's inland sea. A wall of wind is pushing the waves onto shore, lips of whitecaps folding over. The undulating basalt along the shore is some of the oldest rock on earth. This is part of the planet's original crust, where the age is counted not in millions but in billions of years, and the endless hollows and humps provide perfect hiding spots for slumbering bears.

The few trees we see clinging to the rocks have been cut clean on one side. "Oh, those," says the driver, as he banks from one sliding skid to the next. "Churchill's famous one-sided trees! Unofficial town symbol."

When these stunted spruce trees are hit by prevailing winds, airborne ice crystals act like sandpaper, shearing off any branches on the windward side.

"They make great Christmas trees," the driver says, laughing. "Fit right in the corner and you only have to decorate one side. Stick one in front of a mirror," he says, "and you got yourself a whole tree."

"See that guy?" our driver shouts. He's pointing to a lone tourist who is viewing the bay through the lens of a camera, far from his vehicle, oblivious to everything except what is contained in his viewfinder. "Bear chow," says the driver. "I never want to see any of you doing that! *Ever.* Look how far he is from his rent-a-van—and he has the door closed! A bear pops up? That guy'll be scat before you know it. They might look slow and plodding, but trust me, you can't outrun a polar bear, and you sure as shit can't outwrestle one."

"Have any tourists died in polar-bear encounters?" I ask.

"Not yet," he says. "But with the number of people coming in every year and the number of bears crossing their paths, it's just a matter of time."

The first polar bear I see in Churchill is airborne: a distant tear-shaped drop of milky fur suspended below a helicopter, in a net.

When bears stray too close to town and warning shots don't startle them away, they are darted, tagged and placed in a holding cell until they can be airlifted to safety. The group I'm travelling with is treated in a similar fashion. Having survived the drive into town, we are now fed, weighed, tagged and enumerated before reboarding our bus for the ride out to the tundra-buggy drop-off point.

I have been clumped in with other journalists, photogs and general ne'er-do-wells. Cathy Senecal, unflappable as always, is riding herd on us, which is a bit like trying to rake leaves in a cyclone. Other than Cathy, I am the only Canadian in the group, which may or may not say something about us as a country. The others include: Polly Chevalier, upbeat, funny, an editor with *Child* magazine (she has a French surname, a British accent and a Manhattan gig; does any of that make sense?); Michael Park, originally with Fox News but now on assignment with the *New York Post* ("A lateral move, I know," he says); Candyce Stapen, who writes for several guidebooks and will spend most of her time wrapped in blankets, shivering; and Kerrick James, a travel photographer from Arizona. (*Of course* he's a travel photographer; with a name like Kerrick James, what choice did he have? In the same way that Shania Twain had to become a country-and-western singer. A name like that, what else could she possibly be? Doctor? Investment banker? Philosopher? *Being and Nothingness,* by Shania Twain. It just doesn't scan.)

Also in our group is Larry MacGregor, who—we discover—is a civilian. However, with the arsenal of photography equipment he's lugging and his slightly disreputable albeit gregarious air, we mistake him for a fellow journalist. "Really?" he says. He seems pleased by this. "It's not actually a compliment," Michael says. Finally, there is Jorge Zepeda, author, columnist and publisher from Mexico City, who is wearing a dazed look. (Jorge hasn't read the fine print: "I thought it was like a safari park. You know, we would stay in a nice hotel with fine dining, take a day trip out to look at some bears, go back to the hotel.") Jorge has arrived in the warmest jacket he has, the sort of thing Canadians don in early autumn—a stylish woollen overcoat with a scarf tossed artfully over one shoulder. Not exactly polar-bear scouting outerwear. By the second day, Jorge will be sporting a giant puffy down-filled jacket. By the third day, he'll be cracking jokes with the best of us and keeping the banter rolling with the nimble-footedness of a lumberjack on a spinning log.

It's a good bunch. Relaxed and good-humoured and enjoying life as only expense-account travellers can. Also on board, through no fault of their own, is a family from England: Mr. and Mrs. Evans from Southampton, their daughter Liz and her boyfriend Rob. Now, in my experience, there are only two types of English people in this world (I realize this is a gross generalization, but then, so are the Laws of Thermodynamics). When it comes to the English, they are either absolutely insufferable or disarmingly endearing.

Fortunately, our "English passengers," as they will become known out on the tundra, are of the "disarmingly endearing" variety. The fact that they've been more or less taken hostage by a mob of rowdy reprobates is accepted with unflagging good cheer. They are also very punctual and polite. No one will ever mistake them for journalists.

Our first stop in Churchill after reboarding the bus is not at the Eskimo Museum or the community hall. No. We must first stock up on supplies necessary for the trek ahead of us.

"Booze!" we shout. "Booze!" We're like a gang of orangutans hooting for bananas.

"Liquor store and bank are in the same building," our driver says, as he fishtails the schoolbus around a corner. "Saves time," he shouts. "You take out your money and you walk across the hall. One-stop shopping."

It is very efficient, I must admit. The only improvement I can think of would be if the bank were actually *in* the liquor store.

The afternoon light drains from the sky. Night seeps in as, bottles clinking, we are driven east, far from town, out to the tundra-buggy platform. Finally, we arrive at what looks like a space-station docking site. Buses roll in, passengers tumble off one vehicle and onto another, buggies pull out. This all occurs on a platform high above the ground.

The tundra buggies are a uniquely Canadian approach to arctic exploration. They were invented, and are wholly built, right in Churchill, with the original such vehicle (Buggy #1) patched together back in 1979 by Len Smith, a local handyman, using sections of a snowplough, a gravel truck and the inevitable schoolbus. (Schoolbuses are to Churchill what buffaloes were to the Plains Indians. A schoolbus in Churchill is picked apart as cleanly as any bison, and will inevitably go through several stages—from student transportation to airport limousine to outer shell of a tundra buggy—as it is systematically stripped.) The bodies of the buggies are dropped onto giant car-toon wheels, which raise the vehicles three metres into the air, putting passengers out of polar-bear strike range. In theory.

Not too long ago, a large male bear managed to get up the side of a buggy and forced his head in through a window.

Having just missed a startled passenger, who leapt to one side in the nick of time, the bear tore apart the seat instead. And in 1984, an American tourist was leaning out of a buggy window to take a picture of a bird when a polar bear, which had been hiding beneath the vehicle, lunged up and grabbed the man's arm in its jaws. As the tourist shrieked, the bear began to slowly, methodically tug at him, in an attempt to drag the poor man out the window or, failing that, to chew his arm off. The buggy guide punched the bear repeatedly in the nose (a sensitive spot for bears) until it finally let go, but the tourist almost bled to death. Buggies only go twenty or twenty-five kilometres an hour, so the man was a long time being "whisked" to safety. But here's the part that tells you just how captivating these tours are—this same visitor returned to Churchill *the very next year* for another buggy outing. No word if the bear was waiting for him, like the crocodile in *Peter Pan* who, having gotten a taste of Captain Hook, now wants the rest of him as well. *Tick   tick . . . tick . . .*

On the docking platform, my group is loaded onto lucky Buggy #13. Cathy takes a head count, the buggy rumbles to life, and we roll away into the night.

It's a three-hour ride across the tundra moonscape. Our headlights form tunnels of light in the darkness, catching images of wastelands and scrub willows and Arctic hares that bound away. We can see the distant lights of other buggies passing on the horizon like ships.

Tundra is a spongy carpet—a mantle of peat over bedrock, mossy and layered in lichen—and the oversized buggy wheels allow us to ride across it without damaging the ecosystem. In winter, travelling on tundra is like riding over frozen waves. We pitch and roll, pitch and roll.

"We'll be staying at a lodge," Cathy lied when we first got to Churchill. *Lodge* conjures up images of fireplaces and marshmallows and outdoor hot tubs. The "lodge" we arrive at is essentially a row of retired buggies that have been linked together and towed out like a train into the middle of nowhere. (Another use for schoolbuses: when all is done, you can sleep in them, too.) The Frontiers North "lodge" looks like an Antarctic research post, on wheels. It too sits up above the land, in theoretical safety.

We are assigned bunk beds and shown where the toilets and the cookhouse are, with nary a hot tub or ski lift in sight. No matter. We will spend the next three days meeting bears. Real bears on their own turf.

I crawl up into my bunk bed, stepping on Polly as I do, and then fall backwards into a deep, deep sleep.

When I awake, there is a pre-dawn glow in my bunkside porthole, and when I peer out through the glass, I see a polar bear looking back at me. He sits on his haunches, head turned, silent.

The bears are at their most active early in the morning. During breakfast in the dining car, amid a flurry of camera shutters, a pair of young males gives us a front-row perform-ance as they spar: rearing up, swatting one another and then dropping down to perform the Polar-Bear Tango, nose to nose, as first one bear and then the other advances while his dance partner backs up. Add a Latin guitar and some smoul-dering sexuality, and you could be in La Boca. Eventually, however, the two bears get tired out and wander away, disappearing into nothingness with a disconcerting ease.

"Ready for more beers, are ya? Who's ready for beers?"

Well, it's a bit early in the day, but yes—a beer would be fine.

As it turns out, no. Our buggy guide is an energetic, sun-creased young woman named Hayley Shephard, who happens to be from New Zealand. Which is to say, we will be out on the buggy "lookin' for beers." Polar beers. Of the many accents present in our buggy—Murican, Meheecan, Hoser and Brit—Hayley's is in a league of its own. There's a three-second delay every time she speaks as we silently translate her comments into something that more closely resembles English. This is followed by an "Ah, yes, I see" moment.

When we drag our gear onto the buggy, the English passengers are already in their seats, hands folded on their laps, as the rest of us straggle in. Our moonbuggy pulls away from the "lodge," but we don't have to go very far. Tundra in the daylight is a land of flat planes, of low skies and level horizons. In this freeze-dried world, the animals appear from nowhere; one moment there is only snow and rock, and the next, a fully formed bear has materialized. They move across the landscape with a silence that is both unnerving and exhilarating: gliding footsteps, massive paws turned slightly inward, shoulders rolling, heads low, long necks tapering into nose. It is a fluid gait, one with strength in reserve.

As Mr. Evans, patriarch of the passengers English, notes, the bears exude a sense of confidence; they lack the jittery sadness of animals penned in a zoo. Polar bears in the wild sit at the top of the food chain, at the top of the world. They are without fear and have even been known to rear up and try to swat down high-flying helicopters: a gesture that would be cute if the intent behind it weren't so ominous.

"This is their realm, after all," Cathy says. We are mere interlopers, someone offers. "That, and a potential source of protein," Cathy adds with a laugh.

The average polar bear is bigger than a Bengal tiger, larger than a lion, stronger than a grizzly. They can weigh up to 800 kilograms—as much as a small car—and can reach speeds of fifty kilometres an hour, more than fast enough to overtake an Olympic track star with a generous head start. Polar bears have been known to hunt and kill walruses and even whales. Whales, mind you.

The world population is around 30,000. Of these, more than 16,000 are in Canada. More polar bears live in Canada than in the rest of the world combined, which raises the question, Why the hell did we choose the beaver as our national emblem? We could have had Nanuk of the North, Lord of the Arctic, as our symbol. Instead we get stuck with Squirrelly McTeeth. *Sheesh.*

Our driver, Chris, eases the buggy into gear, and we roll out into a larger emptiness. Chris follows the ragged edge of scrubland willow bush, and Hayley tells us to "keep our eyes peeled for litter crittahs" (i.e., smaller animals). "Attic haze, bads, rabids—tha works." (i.e., Arctic hares, an assortment of birds, and possibly rabbits, as well as other creatures). So. Let me get this straight. We are looking for white rabbits, white ptarmigans and white foxes on a white background. On her first sightings, I suspect Hayley is making it up—"Look! A white rabid— eating vanilla ice cream. And he's juggling golf balls!"

But soon, animals begin to separate themselves from the landscape. An Arctic hare, creamy white, suddenly bolts away—not hopping, running. So many shades of white. Polar bears have a slightly golden tinge. The willow ptarmigan sometimes has a pinkish hue; the birds lift off like cotton balls taking flight as our buggy bounces past. Beneath the scrub of Arctic willow, a reverse silhouette appears against the black-grey background. It is an Arctic fox, all plume and softness. Unlike the bears and the hares and the ptarmigans, the Arctic fox is pure white. They are among the smallest members of the canine family. More feline than canine, really. Dainty even. And, as Hayley tells us, they have the warmest, thickest fur on earth. We watch one female—the aptly named vixen of the animal kingdom—primp in front of us, and Polly whispers, "You just know her name is Fifi and she speaks with a Parisian accent."

The buggy roams as far as Gordon Point, a spike of land driven into the bay. Salt water has glazed the rocks along the shore. The sea here is like mercury: no longer liquid but not quite solid, with a viscosity halfway between water and ice.

The tundra buggies have viewing platforms attached like balconies on the back. The air outside is crisp and cold, and when I inhale I can feel ice crystals forming in my lungs. It's like sucking on a mentholated cough drop. Inhaling crystals, exhaling steam. Even in our fur-ruffed parkas and waddling snow pants, some still bearing price tags, even in our giant ridiculous boots and moist-mouthed balaclavas, we are chilled. The perpetually shivering Candyce has come well stocked with those little gel heatpacks, which she shares selflessly with the rest of us. I stuff my boots with them—was there ever a better use of controlled chemical reactions?—and still I feel the chill.

"I never imagined your *eyeballs* could get cold," someone says with genuine wonder.

We inhale deeply, sinuses anaesthetized.

Hayley bounds to the back of the buggy, happy to point out a smudge of distant carnage. "Move inside; Chris'll get us closer." (The tour operators used to allow passengers to stay out on the viewing platforms while the buggies were in motion, but—get this—the back latch on one of the platform doors? It sprang open as the buggy lurched forward. And one of the passengers? He *fell out*. Now, how fast do you think that tourist clambered back in? Pretty damn quick, I imagine. He probably clawed himself up on air and adrenalin alone.)

"There!" says Hayley as we roll to a stop. "Out past the litter beers."

A smear of blood, rust-coloured against the ice, marks the spot where a seal—caught in a hollow by low tide—has just been killed. Sure enough, a large male is lumbering away, the fur on his face matted red, a look of grim satisfaction in his walk. To one side, a mother and two young cubs watch warily as the male leaves. Soon other scavengers pop into view: a skittish fox, an impatient raven. The seal meat is a rare blessing. Many of the bears have been chewing on kelp to stave off their hunger, and it is a sad sight indeed: carnivores reduced to eating seaweed.

The polar bears of Churchill are on thin ice. With global warming, average annual temperatures are creeping up, and the thickness of the northern pack ice is decreasing every year. The spring thaw that forces the bears ashore happens two weeks earlier now than it did twenty years ago, and those two lost weeks are critical. Polar bears need to pack on as much weight as they can in winter to survive the scarcities of summer, and every week that their seal-hunting season is shortened by translates into ten kilos lost in weight. Less weight on the pregnant females means fewer cubs, and less chance of maintaining the population. If the warming trend doesn't level off, the bears of Cape Churchill, already at the outer edge of polar-bear territory, will be the first to disappear.

On the tundra, man-made structures take on a disproportionate weight. They seem larger, closer, more important than they actually are. Radar domes, watchtowers, telephone lines: anything that rises above the horizon takes on a towering significance.

We ride along on an arctic highway of eskers: raised beds of rubbled rock. These were once the stream bottoms of glacial rivers, which ran through ancient icefields. When the glaciers melted, it was as though the stream beds were flipped inside out; the debris that had collected along the bottom formed raised mounds when the ice beneath them retreated. Today, eskers snake across the tundra like arteries.

The highest elevation in Cape Churchill is one of the mildest swells of land imaginable. It was once a beach ridge, before the bay floor rose in isostatic rebound. Our buggy rolls over this unlikely height of land, a few metres high at best, with ease. We follow an esker inland to the outer fringes of the boreal forest, which is slowly encroaching on the tundra as more and more spruce trees, white and black, stubbornly take root. What look like clumps of separate trees are in fact "clones" growing from a single root system. It's a strategy that increases the odds that at least some offshoots will survive. Like the low tangle of willow bushes, the clustered spruce trees of Cape Churchill are tenacious. Some of the older clumps, stunted though they are, are more than a hundred years old.

That night after our first day, while we are snug inside the lodge, a blizzard blows through. Gale-force winds rock the joined buses and howl in through every seam and crack. On the open platform between cars, Larry and I hold our hands out into the wind, feeling icy granules pincushion into us like sand in a storm. Then we remember the tourist who almost got his arm gnawed off, and we quickly withdraw. All night the wind rocks us; the feeling that we are on a train is stronger than ever. I lie in bed, peering through my porthole, watching bears frolic in the blowing storm.

We wake to skies that are almost painfully blue. They stay clear all day, and that night we watch as the auroras unfold against a field of stars.

We have arrived in Churchill at the peak of an eleven-year cycle of sunspot activity. A massive solar flare—the third-largest in recorded history—has made the news, uncurling from the sun's surface and releasing a fountain of charged atomic particles that is even now washing across the earth's upper atmosphere. As this cosmic stream spirals towards the magnetic poles, it creates one of the greatest displays of northern lights seen in decades. The currents ripple on a distant solar wind like liquid fire, and we stand on the buggy's back deck, heads craned, necks aching. I am hurtled back in time to a childhood spent under these same night skies. These same northern lights. And I am impressed by how much they have improved. Why, they aren't boring at all any more. "This," Jorge says, gesturing to polar bears illuminated in green and blue, "this is a thing that will stay with you until you die."

By the third day, the chemical toilets at the lodge are starting to get, oh, how shall I put this, a wee bit *aromatic*. Nothing is left behind on the tundra; whatever goes out comes back—in whatever form that happens to take. I have, with my usual luck, been assigned one of the berths nearest the washroom stalls. Mere feet away, in fact. Only Polly, in the bunk below, and Jorge, whose pillow butts up to the wall (the exceedingly thin wall) that separates the toilets from our sleeping quarters, have it worse.

In the bunk across from mine, Jorge is lying on his back, looking wistfully at the ceiling. "I think," he says, to no one in particular, "that after this trip, I can write—what is the word, a *dissertation?*—on the many noises the human body can make."

Polly begins dousing both her belongings and herself with heavy fumigating doses of perfume, which might work at close quarters, perhaps, but the effect dissipates as the scent wafts upwards to my bunk. Instead of conquering the cesspool smell, it mingles with it. Perfumed sewage; it is, oddly enough, worse than sewage alone.

"That wasn't snoring," I tell Polly when she comments on the strangled noises I've been making at night. "That was gagging."

On our final day at the "lodge" (and really, there are not quotation marks strong enough to convey what an absolute misnomer that term is), Polly and Michael and I and a few others are taken back, through the kitchen, to meet the Bear Man.

His name is Dennis, and he lives in a buggy docked at the other end of the lodge, separate from everyone else. If Dennis the Bear Man has a surname, no one seems to know it. I suspect it actually is "Bear Man." Certainly, I never hear him referred to in any other way.

If you stop now to imagine what a bear man looks like, you're right, that's him. He is a Grizzly Adams of the polar-bear set, with a thick, full beard and intense, unblinking eyes. He's a physically solid presence, bigger still inside the cramped confines of his buggy. Polly has a crush on Dennis, I can tell. Partly from the way she bats her eyes and partly from the way she says, "I have such a crush on him!"

Dennis the Bear Man lives a semi-nomadic life inside his trapper's shack on wheels. Although linked to the lodge, he can detach himself and roll away whenever he likes. He lives in Buggy #1, in fact, the original rover, which is the equivalent of a historic site out here. With its stovepipes and bunk bed and low ceiling, the inside of Dennis's buggy looks like some-thing out of the Yukon—except that this particular hermit's hut comes equipped with an Acer computer, an Internet link-up and a flat-screen monitor. This is the command centre of *polarbearcam.com,* and Dennis is a bear man of a new era.

"I take live pictures of the bears outside my buggy and I post 'em on my website." He says this in the same way a prospector might say, "I pan the cricks fer gold and then stake my claim in the muck."

Dennis has been watching bears for twenty-five years. He's been running the webcam for three. "Why did I start working with bears?" He casts a hard look at the scrum of journalists now wedged into his cabin. "So I wouldn't have to deal with people." He is kidding. We think.

Dennis was born and raised in Churchill, back before the polar-bear alert system was in place.

"Were you afraid?" someone asks.

"Afraid? Of course I was afraid. Growing up in Churchill with no streetlights, sun barely rising in winter. Walking home from school in the dark, knowing there are bears out there—somewhere. You grow up with respect for 'em. And fear." Then, more to himself than to us: "I don't know, maybe that's why I'm doing this—to get over that fear." And suddenly we can see little Dennis, heart pounding, holding his breath as he hurries home through dark silent streets. Little Dennis confronting the garrison mentality at its most primal.

Is he still afraid? Out here in his small, movable fortress?

"After twenty-five years, I'm past the fear. But I'm still endlessly fascinated by them. I see—*patterns*."

Meaning?

"Well, let's say there is a female *here* and I see a large male approaching from over *there*—and the wind is coming from, say, that direction. I know that when she picks up his scent she will move away, over to *there*, onto that ice floe. I reposition the camera, and sure enough, she comes into frame." He would have made an excellent hunter.

The view outside Dennis's tundra-buggy home is of a treeless expanse of snow filled with hidden predators. Binoculars hang from the wall; computer wires are twisted together in unsuccessful braids, looking like the tubings one

associates with life-support systems. A postcard of a beach in
Spain is tacked above his monitor.

"Over there," someone whispers, *"a bear."*

Dennis looks out. "Dancer," he says.

Dancer—so named because the bear routinely rears up
on his hind legs beside Dennis's buggy and then dances backwards, looking in—has dropped by for a visit. Like Polly,
Dancer has a crush on Dennis.

Dennis scoffs at any notion that he and the bear have a
special rapport. "I'm not his pal; I'm just the guy in the buggy."
But he is unconvincing—even, I suspect, to himself. Dancer
loves Dennis. You can see it in the way the bear hangs around,
forlorn when Dennis is out of sight, playful when he comes
into view.

Dennis can call Dancer, though he is not so much a bear
whisperer as a bear shouter. "You want to meet him? Sure."
He opens the window. *"Dancer! Get over here!!"*

Dancer plods over and stands up against the side of
Dennis's buggy. With a start, I realize that this buggy is much
lower than the others. And the window is open. Dancer's face
fills the frame. He is right beside me, and the group is
stunned into silence by his appearance.

You don't realize how truly large a polar bear is until you
see one close up. Dancer's face fills the entire window of
the converted schoolbus that is Buggy #1. The bear is less
than a foot away from me, a distance measured in inches,
measured in heartbeats. He breathes through his nose, and
I can feel the whuff of warm air on my face. His scarred
muzzle, the long lashes and gentle eyes, every hair—it
stands out in precise detail. I am face to face with the wild,

and—incredibly—my instinct is not to pull away but to move closer. I can feel myself lean forward ever so slightly. The world's largest land carnivore. . . .

"Careful," says Dennis. And the moment is gone. The stillness is broken. I veer back.

Dancer breaks away, walking backwards on his hind legs, looking past me, trying to spot Dennis. After a few seconds, he reels and turns away. I've been holding my breath, and my chest aches, but only when the bear has danced himself into darkness do I exhale.

Later, back in Winnipeg, waiting for my flight home, I will huddle inside a Salisbury House restaurant, my face still chilblained and raw from the winds of Hudson Bay, and I will watch the snows whip along Portage Avenue, and when the waitress comes to fill my coffee and clear my plates I will turn to her and I will say, eyes shining, *"I've seen polar bears."*

In Churchill, after three days on the tundra. A big bed in a warm room. Long showers, very hot. Toilets that flush. Towels, non-communal. It's wonderful.

We decide to go out for drinks. We ask the English passengers if they would like to join us, and—I can only assume some sort of Stockholm Syndrome has taken hold— they do. We order beer and revel in our shared experiences.

On our final day in town, the rest of the group goes dogsledding. I pass. Trappers and dog teams were still a common sight when I was growing up in Fort Vermilion, and Mom raised sled dogs for a while in the belief that money could be made that way. It can't. Sled dogs eat twice their market value in food. (My mother is a wonderful woman, but she lacks certain instincts when it comes to business.)

Instead, I amble about Churchill. The snow squeaks underfoot. Snowmobiles rumble down the main street. Snarling dogs, tethered to run lines, make lunging feints when I wander by too closely. I pass the corrugated tin box that is the Northern Store, heir to the Hudson's Bay empire. It's painted a lovely UPS brown, which is—and this has been scientifically proven—the ugliest shade ever concocted. It is a shade not quite vibrant enough to be described as "dung-coloured."

The winds and ice have sandblasted the buildings of Churchill, leaving the paint faded. As one fellow laments when I comment on the town's pastel hues, "Paint a house in Churchill, and it looks old before the last coat has even dried." In Churchill, function *is* form. The boxy, workmanlike buildings, like crates on a dock, nonetheless enjoy a rich inner life as cafés, shops, dance floors, lounges, homes.

I stop by a café, ask the waitress if they sell slide film. She checks. They don't. No matter. I have taken hundreds of slides already and still have a few frames left.

The only other patrons in the place are locals—Metis and Cree men, mainly, dressed in ski-doo suits rakishly half-zipped, torsos like rain barrels. As is my habit, I elbow my way into the conversation and, with suitably macabre timing, ask them about . . . Halloween. Halloween occurs right in the middle of bear season, and while walking around town I've spotted several jack-o'-lanterns, carved from exotic imported pumpkins, frozen solid on doorsteps, their grins now grimaces.

"Do you really let your kids go out trick-or-treating?" I ask the table of local men. "At night?"

"Sure," they say. "But they go out with armed escorts."

"Well, bear patrols, anyway," someone says.

"There're rifles everywhere, so it's very safe." (A statement that shouldn't make sense but does.)

Others concur. "In Churchill, kids can dress up as anything they like—'cept polar bears. You don't dress up as a polar bear around here on Halloween."

"You don't even want to be a ghost."

"Or anything white."

The woman pouring the coffee laughs at the inadvertent double meaning and turns to one of the men. "Too bad for you, eh, John? You've been trying to be white for years."

The table roars with laughter. "You're cheeky, you," the man in question fires back.

I take my leave—stiffing them for my coffee, I realize later—and walk down towards the train station, where the Parks Canada office is located. I pass more frozen jack-o'-lanterns along the way.

On the helicopter back from Prince of Wales Fort, Stacey Jack offered to show me around Churchill. I've decided to take her up on this, and I arrive at her office unannounced. As is my habit.

"I was wondering when you'd drop by," she says.

Stacey drives a great tank of a truck, a standard-issue Parks Canada vehicle, I assume, and we start off for Cape Merry, at the end of town. The abandoned shacks of dock workers, some tumbledown, some maintained, are huddled on one side, taking the brunt of the Hudson Bay wind. "Bear trap," Stacey points out, and she slows down to check. The gate on the culvert has been sprung, and inside we can see a confused ball of golden-white fur. Farther down, along a pathway tucked out of view among the rocks, are the stone walls and cannons of a British military battery that dates back to the 1740s. But with one bear in the trap and others lurking about, Stacey suggests I skip the walk to the battery, and I do. I'll take her word for it that it's there.

Although she now works in communications (as a "journalist wrangler," essentially), Stacey Jack is trained as an archaeologist. Originally from northern Ontario, she's Ojibwa, but she has clearly found her niche here. And, she lets slip, she was once a licensed private investigator. How stylish is that? *A private eye.*

"That was a long time ago," she says with an embarassed smile. "I was living down in the States, in Chicago, and I was ready to start work when I got a call about a job with the band office back in Ontario. So instead of becoming a private eye, I returned home. Later I studied archaeology, was hired by Parks Canada, transferred to Churchill."

"So you never tailed a dame or pumped a wise guy full a' lead."

"No," she says with a laugh.

"Still," I say. "Working up here with the polar bears and everything. Must be pretty cool."

"It is," she says. *It is.*

Overheard in the Churchill Motel dining room: a group of waitresses from a nearby café, all young, all smoking furiously, are venting about the day's customers. Stacey and I have just finished a late lunch, and I am warming myself with coffee and second-hand smoke. When people talk this loud, it doesn't count as eavesdropping.

"Those fuckin' Australians," one of the girls says, eyes rolling almost audibly. "You know the ones—that whole tableful. If they would listen to what I said the first time, I wouldn'ta had'ta repeat myself fifty million-hundred fuckin' times. Chicken gumbo? What is chicken gumbo? I just fuckin' explained it to the person sitting right fuckin' next to you. It's rice. It's canned tomato. It's gross, don't order it."

I chuckle to myself. Ah yes, the camaraderie of bad jobs. Brings back memories of Saskatoon, it does.

"I know what you mean," one of the other waitresses says. "I know exactly what you mean. Like, what is with that fuckin' idiot asking me about slide film? Do I look like I work in a fuckin' camera shop?"

"Check!" I call, waving across the room to my server.

I say farewell to Stacey outside and then trudge up the almost imperceptible tilt that runs through town to take a look at Churchill's remarkable all-in-one community centre. It's amazing. It really is. This single sprawling complex—big, but not *that* big—somehow manages to contain (a) a hockey arena, (b) a curling rink, (c) a swimming pool, (d) a bowling alley, (e) a movie theatre, (f) a library, (g) a gymnasium and (h), (i), (j), (k) and (1): a high school, a community college, various municipal offices, an indoor playground and a fully equipped medical centre. All under one roof. This is beyond garrison. This is the Canadian equivalent of terraforming.

I tromp through the complex, stewing with envy. As I said, I grew up in a northern town, same latitude as Churchill and

more or less the same size, and we sure as hell had no goddamn bowling alley or swimming pool. We didn't even have
an indoor hockey rink until I was in junior high. Before that,
games were played in crisp minus 40 conditions, with the ice
cracking and splitting.

Outside, still in a funk, I run into Polly. She is beaming,
fresh from the dogsleds and already wistful about leaving.
"You might still see another bear before we leave," I offer.
"They wander right into town sometimes. Never know."

"You think?" she says, clearly pleased at the possibility.

Polly and I stop by the Anglican church to see the Lady
Franklin window. (Lady Franklin, wife of the hapless Sir
John, donated a stained-glass window in her husband's honour to a different church at a different trading post. How it
ended up in Churchill, I couldn't tell you.) As Polly and I step
back outside, into the sudden snap of cold air, we see a sign
just across the road from the church.

POLAR BEAR WARNING
STOP
Do Not Walk in This Area

We exchange glances. Laugh nervously. And it hits us, full
force. We aren't out on the tundra any more. We are in front
of a church. The community centre is, like, just over there.
There are people's homes right behind us.

On the other side of the warning sign lie the hillocks and
gullies of the Hudson Bay coast. The town of Churchill runs
almost to the edge of the bay, but this last stretch is off-
limits. It is right there, the bay, so near—and so far away. The

opportunity to walk down and touch the water, to dip my hand into the nation's collective unconscious, to feel it, to taste it, is all but irresistible.

Less than the length of a city block. I have only to follow the path past the rocks, past the rolling, innumerable hiding places.

I look at Polly. She looks at me. "You want to go?" I say, casting an eye to the shore. Polly is done up in heavy parka and wuffling snow pants. Worst-case scenario, I know I won't have to outrun a polar bear. I will only have to outrun Polly.

"I don't know," she says, but you can tell the answer is yes. All it takes is the gentlest of prods.

"Think of it," I say, voice furtive. "It's like the source of the Nile or the Elephants' Graveyard. Hudson Bay. Do you know how few people have ever seen it—let alone *touched* it?"

So we do. We walk down, wuffle, wuffle, wuffle, trying not to make a sound and failing miserably. And you know, that bay seemed to get farther and farther away the more we walked towards it. It was as though we were trapped in a funhouse illusion, as though the ground were rolling away from us on a treadmill. In horror films, there's a cheesy but surprisingly effective technique in which the camera dollies forward and zooms out at the same time. The lines of perspective shift but the actor's position doesn't change. It creates in the viewer a vaguely nauseating sensation, and it is usually done right before the chainsaw-wielding maniac appears. That's what this feels like now.

I am reminded of the moronic tourists our bus driver was always pointing out, and I think, with a perverse sort of pride, "We have entered their ranks."

It's the longest three-minute walk of my life. But finally Polly and I reach the water's edge. In front of us, Hudson Bay arcs into the distance with the earth's curvature. We tug off our gloves, plunge our hands into the interior of the continent. It's so cold it feels as though the water has grabbed hold of us. We cup our hands, taste the bay. It is salty and green. Ice floes float past, looking an awful lot like aquatic bears. I know that in southern swamps crocodiles will often drift in, pretending to be logs. And polar bears? Of all the questions I should have asked earlier. . . .

"This is fantastic," says Polly. She is whispering—and so am I, just in case a bear, having missed our clumsy, plump presences and delectable body odours, happens to overhear our conversation.

"Quick," I whisper, oddly out of breath, fumbling the camera to Polly. "Take my picture."

When she steps back to frame the shot, I strike a comic pose for posterity—eyes gaping, jaw open, hand pointing wildly to one side. Polly responds with an impressive mid-air pirouette. "What? *What?*"

Things not to do when you're standing in a polar-bear danger zone and someone is kind enough to take your photo: open your eyes wide and point wildly to one side.

"Sorry," I say. And wouldn't it be ironic if the last words Polly heard before she entered the digestive tract of a polar bear were those of a Canadian. Apologizing.

Polly and I head back to the sanctity of the church parking lot, walking at a quick pace. By the time we get past the magic force field just beyond the warning sign, we are giddy with laughter and disproportionately pleased with ourselves.

Jorge is waiting for us when we get to the top of the hillock. He has been watching our antics, and he has the look of a faintly amused but ultimately disappointed parent.

"You didn't see the sign?"

We saw the sign.

"There are bears, you know."

We know.

"Ah," I say. "But we stood at the shore of Hudson Bay. We touched the water. We tasted it. Seawater. It was cold. It was salty."

Jorge is not nearly as impressed by this as I'd hoped. "You risk your life to find this out? That it is cold and salty?" He shrugs. "Maybe if you'd discovered it was warm and tasted of sugar, well, yes, I can see, but. . . ."

Jorge is right. And he is wrong. Because in a weird way it *was* worth the risk. To reach out into that inland sea, to grasp it, taste it, to drink it in. It was worth it. It was. It was.

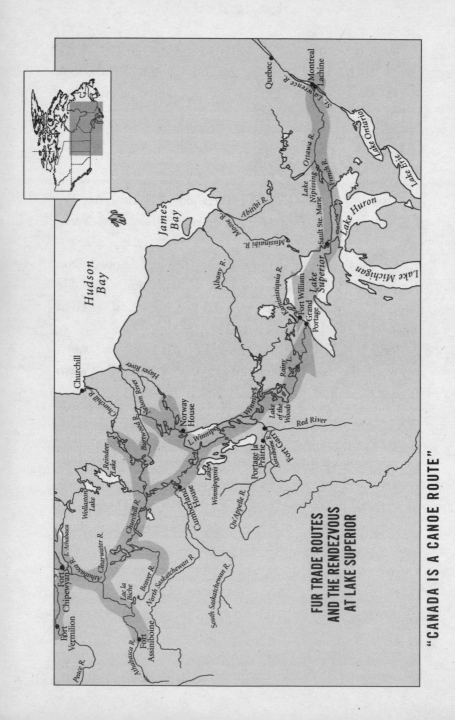

FUR TRADE ROUTES
AND THE RENDEZVOUS
AT LAKE SUPERIOR

"CANADA IS A CANOE ROUTE"

chapter five

SLEEPING GIANT

EVERYWHERE WE GO, PEOPLE TRY to force-feed us pancakes. Alex and I have been in town only two days and what began as a steady refrain has become something closer to a religious mantra. "Have you been to the Hoito? You've got to go to the Hoito."

The Hoito is a Finnish restaurant in the city of Thunder Bay, Ontario, and the meal of choice is apparently pancakes. This suits Alex just fine. A restaurant where pancakes are the main course? What could be better?

Alex is now four and a half (or four and three-quarters, by his calculations), and with a new baby dominating our home life back in Calgary—already four months old and he *still* can't kick a soccer ball or build chesterfield-cushion forts in the rec room—Alex has been feeling sort of down lately. So we have thrown a tent and some sleeping bags into a backpack and flown to Thunder Bay on a father-son camping expedition. If this means missing a week of dirty diapers and 4:00 a.m. feedings, so be it. That's a price I'm willing to pay.

I don't think I have ever been in such a sprawling, undefined place. Thunder Bay is really two cities in one, formed in

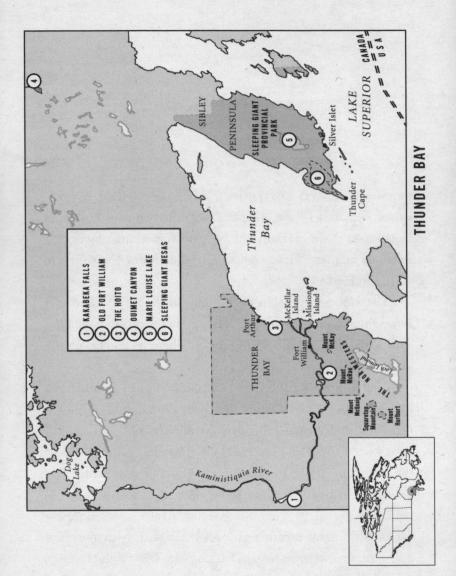

THUNDER BAY

1970 by the amalgamation of Fort William in the south and
Port Arthur above it. It's an uneasy union. Though joined by
bureaucratic fiat, they don't seem to have become a cohesive
whole. They spill into each other, with the outskirts of one
meeting the outskirts of the next in what is, paradoxically, the
inner city; fast-food franchises and big-box stores signal not
the edge of town but a muddled middle ground. The seam
that appears to weld the two of them together is, predictably
enough, a shopping mall—and not just any mall, but the
Inter-City Mall, "the largest regional shopping centre in
northwestern Ontario"! How's that for a string of qualifiers?

More confusing still, in this city without a discernible
centre, the streets change names when they cross old boundaries. Hence May Street becomes Memorial, and Memorial
in turn becomes Algoma. (Though how the merger of two
cities could result in streets with three names is something I
never figured out. And, oh yes. The city's East End? It's in the
south.) Going the other way, Cumberland becomes Water
Street, and Water Street becomes Fort William Road. A single
drive across town to the Hoito and back involves six different
street names. It's a long way to go for pancakes, true, but if
every city has its own distinct dish—battered cod in St.
John's; gravy and cheese curds in Anytown, Quebec; great
slabs of marinated steak in Calgary—then the taste that
defines Thunder Bay is that of Finnish flapjacks.

This city, on the rugged western shore of Lake Superior,
contains the largest Finnish community anywhere outside of
Finland. The Hoito is located on the lower level of the historic Finlandia Club, in a lived-in section of town known as
"Little Finland." Established in 1918, the Hoito was founded

as a community project to supply Finnish loggers with affordable meals, using single-sitting meal tickets purchased at subsidized rates. The diner as socialist collective.

Today the Hoito no longer runs on a meal-ticket system, but the menu still offers salt fish, Finnish sausage, *mojakka* and *karjalan piirakka* (fish-and-potato soup and rice-and-potato pastries) and something called *villi*—which, we are told, is "clabbered milk." The Pelimanni Finnish-Canadian Orchestra is rehearsing upstairs, and they are roaring through a jangly tune reminiscent—to Alex's ears, anyway—of merry-go-round music. It goes well with the *villi* and *mojakka*, not to mention the pancakes and artery-clotting creams.

But here's the thing about pancakes, and I apologize in advance to any Finns, Dutchmen or Smitty's employees out there: no matter what you do to them, whether you heap them with sour cream or pile on layers of pickled halibut, they are still, well, pancakes. And as with Scandinavian food any-where, the problem is that a week later you're hungry again.

Loaded down with Nordic ballast, a pound each at least in a doughy ball in our stomachs, Alex and I stagger out onto the weathered side streets of Bay and Algoma. This intersec-tion, and the neighbourhood around it, is the heart of Thunder Bay's Finnish experience, with Finnish books, bakeries, boutiques and (of course) pancakes. Public saunas, Finnish credit unions, Nordic-style skiing. It's sad, really; Tomiamus Sukanen didn't need to sail across an ocean, he had only to make his way to Thunder Bay.

Alex and I are not here for the pancakes, though. Our final destination lies far from the city, on the peninsula that juts out into Lake Superior, forming the eastern flank of the bay.

Thunder Bay lies at the lakehead of Canada's other historic water route to the interior: the Great Lakes–St. Lawrence. We have come here, rustic father and trusting son, to get in touch with our "inner voyagers." And we are armed with the necessary supplies: a sack full of mini-marshmallows, a compass that lists to the east, a map of downtown Sarnia (wrong map, as it turns out) and an indomitable supply of pluck. (Pluck being defined as "a disorganized clatter thrown into a rucksack almost at random.") Much like the Long Drive, this too is a rite of citizenship: the Ill-Advised Camping Trip.

With the Fall of New France in 1763, the Hudson's Bay Company reigned supreme and unchallenged . . . for about five minutes.

You'd think, with England triumphant and the threat from France removed (for the time being, anyway), the HBC would have had a free hand in the fur trade, but no. Independent traders, together with Scottish merchants recently arrived in Montreal, quickly picked up where the French had left off. Dismissed with a resounding snort by the HBC as "pedlars from Canada," these new players in the fur trade came to constitute a far more serious threat to HBC profits than New France ever had. They pushed farther west and farther north, crossing the height of land beyond the HBC's territorial claims and moving into the Athabasca region, founding Fort Chipewyan and Fort Vermilion. It was a land so rich in furs that it was trumpeted as a "northern El Dorado," and the woods were soon swarming with maverick fur traders intercepting Native suppliers, haggling, harassing, outbidding and generally outflanking the 100-year-old company. "Pilferers!" the

HBC cried. And then it got worse. By 1784 these pilferers, these crass pedlars, had formed an alliance: the North West Company. It would become the greatest transcontinental trade adventure in Canadian history, running a transport and supply system that would span almost 6500 kilometres. The NWC funnelled a fortune in furs through the Great Lakes, down the St. Lawrence and on to Europe, where the beavers and ermine of Canada were reincarnated as top hats and lavish robes. Marten, mink, buffalo, wolf. Fox furs and deerskins. More than a colony, Montreal became a fur transportation centre perched on the edge of an almost unfathomable wilderness.

The Nor'Westers drove the HBC to the brink of bankruptcy, and the venerable English company was forced to improvise, something it did reluctantly at first. After more than a century spent "sleeping on the edge of a frozen sea" (as their critics had described it), the governors of the HBC changed their policy of waiting for Native suppliers to come to them. In 1774, under the direction of our old friend Samuel Hearne, they built Cumberland House in what is now eastern Saskatchewan.

More and more inland trading posts followed—Fort This and Fort That, Fort Here and Fort There—as the two rivals hopscotched down the waterways of the interior. The competition was cutthroat at times, but even though the methods they employed were often indistinguishable, the NWC and the HBC were fundamentally different in character. Historian Daniel Francis notes, "If a Hudson's Bay Company trading house resembled a military barracks, a Nor'Wester establishment had more in common with a rowdy tavern."

The HBC was run out of London; the NWC was based in Montreal. Hudson's Bay Company employees were paid salaries; the Nor'Westers were part of a profit-sharing enterprise.

The birchbark canoe and the French-Canadian voyageur were the mainstays of the North West fur trade; the HBC, still centred for the most part in the Hudson Bay taiga, developed its own distinctive form of transport—the flat-bottomed, slow-moving but effective York boat.

The differences between the two companies extended even to their respective Scottish elements. The HBC was, at its heart, an English enterprise, although Lowlander Scots held prominent positions in the company, and Orkney Islanders made up a large part of the labour force. The NWC was run by Highlanders, and it showed. Clan loyalties and ancient Highland hierarchies, not to mention an almost heroic capacity for whisky: these suited perfectly the tribal nature of the fur trade. The men in charge of the NWC's inland forts were the Canadian equivalent of Highland chieftains, and the outposts they established would help lay the groundwork of a larger national autonomy.

The NWC helped set the contours and boundaries, as well as the east-west axis, of what would one day become Canada. French explorers and Canadian woodsmen opened pathways to European trade, and the Scots built these into a transcontinental network, but they were all relying on routes that predated European arrival by hundreds and even thousands of years. It was Native trading patterns that dictated the course the NWC would follow. Historian Arthur Lower is credited with the satori-inducing aphorism "Canada is a canoe route." But we can take Lower's insight even further: more than anything, Canada is an aboriginal trade map. It was a map traced not with quill and ink, but with birchbark and paddle.

Like the covered wagon in the American West or the Viking longboats of Norse glory, the canoe—an exemplary form of aboriginal adaptive technology—is Canada's founding vessel. More than merely a means of transportation, the canoe has become iconic. You want symbolism? We've got symbolism. Consider this: canoes are held together by internal tension. The sides, running from bow to stern, are forced apart in the middle by wooden thwarts, giving the vessel its defining tautness. It's the deceptive simplicity of the canoe— the elegance, the symmetry, the long clean entry curves at the waterline—that makes it such a perfect blend of function and form. The canoe possesses, in the words of one fur trade officer, "a faultless grace and beauty."

Light, manageable, easily repaired. The canoe could hold staggering amounts of cargo and yet skim lightly through the shallowest of waters—ideal for the many sandbars and shoals along the rivers, streams and deltas of Canada's Northwest. Birchbark canoes were also temporary constructs. Biodegradable. Heroic and yet anonymous. Much like the voyageurs and Natives who paddled them, they easily returned to the forests whence they had come.

Canada's three major drainage systems, from Hudson Bay to the Great Lakes to the Mackenzie Delta, radiate water routes, virtually all of them navigable. It's an incredible system of rivers, with low heights of land and wide basins separated by surprisingly manageable portages, most just a few kilometres long. Even now, if the mood strikes you, you can take a canoe from Montreal to the Rockies or up to the Arctic Ocean.

"You get the feeling," canoeist and filmmaker Bill Mason said, "that God designed the canoe first and then set about creating a country in which it would flourish."

The Nor'Westers may have been livelier and more daring than their HBC counterparts, but they faced a serious obstacle. Unlike their rivals, they had no Hudson Bay shortcut to aid them, no "Get out of the continental interior free" pass. From breakup to freeze-up there were only five months of ice-free navigation, and the NWC was already pushing on towards the Pacific. It was not physically possible for fur traders to make the trip out from Montreal and back again in a single season.

Solution? Brigades of canoes would meet halfway, at Lake Superior, to exchange trade goods from Montreal for furs. The original rendezvous point was at Grand Portage, but when the border between Canada and the United States was finally settled, the NWC found its post on the wrong side of the line. So in 1802, the post packed up and shuffled north a notch, to the mouth of the Kaministiquia River, at what is now Thunder Bay.

Fort William, as the NWC post at Kaministiquia was later named, became both the company's inland headquarters and the central transshipment point in North America. Though located in the wild heart of the continent, it was connected to a wider commercial network, one that spanned the globe. The warehouses at the fort were stocked with nutmeg from the Indies and silks from China, with cotton from India and textiles from England, with Brazilian tobacco and warm Jamaican rum, with Italian violins and beads from Venice. Anticipating the later historic thesis regarding Canada's evolution, trader Ross Cox described Fort William as a "metropolitan post of the interior."

In early spring, two canoe brigades set out from opposite ends of the fur trade: one from the farthest reaches of the Northwest, the other from Lachine, just past the rapids west of Montreal. The voyageurs have been heralded in song and romanticized for their hardy, freewheeling spirit. (A book on Canadian astronauts was subtitled *Canada's Voyageurs in Space*.) But the voyageurs were still, essentially, little more than human mule trains. An army officer observed, "No men in the world are more severely worked than are these Canadian voyageurs. I have known them to work in a canoe twenty hours out of twenty-four, and go at that rate during a fortnight or three weeks without a day of rest." The voyageurs laboured under strict contracts. Most were short and stocky (five-foot four was considered the ideal height), and each was expected to carry two forty-kilogram packs at a time when portaging. It wasn't the scope of the portages but the crippling loads the voyageurs carried that took their toll. The men often suffered hernias. (Those gaily coloured sashes wound tightly around their waists were not just for decoration; they acted as restraints, in the same way a weightlifter's belt does.) They drowned in rapids. They tumbled down embankments. They buried their dead along the trail and marked the graves with rough wooden crosses, and on some portages, it was said, the crosses were as thick as trees.

The large freight canoes from Montreal and the lighter northern ones converged at Fort William with great fanfare and, as often as not, fisticuffs. The *hivernants*, who lived inland and wintered in *le pays d'en haut*, were boastful, tough, rough-edged travellers, and they referred to themselves as the true *hommes du nord*. The Montreal voyageurs, on the other hand, returned to the comforts of home before the snows flew. Their "lavish" diet en route consisted of salt pork and beans, which gave rise to the dismissive nickname *mangeurs de lard*: pork eaters. While the Montreal men dressed like— and indeed often were—habitant farmers, the northern men adopted Native dress, with buckskins and leather trousers and long braided hair. They left the backwoods scattered with broken hearts and French surnames, as I can attest from my years in Fort Vermilion.

At Fort William, goods were exchanged, bills were tallied, brandy was quaffed, songs were sung. And all the while, the *hommes du nord* baited the Montreal men mercilessly. How tough were *les hommes du nord*? They were so tough they thought the regular voyageurs were a bunch of namby-pamby girly-men. They'd swagger over to the Montreal camp and confront them with the boast "*Je suis un . . . HOMME DU NORD!*" To which the Montreal voyageurs responded in a decidedly non-verbal manner. "At every annual rendezvous," historian Ogden Tanner writes, "dozens of men were treated for knife wounds, gouged eyes, torn ears and bitten-off noses."

Although defined by three great cultural divides—Ojibwa suppliers, French Canadian voyageurs, Scots administrators— Fort William was a surprisingly cosmopolitan outpost. In 1817 alone, a tally of nationalities at the fort included free traders and company employees from Germany, Italy, Denmark, Sweden, Switzerland, Holland, Lithuania, the Hawaiian Islands,

Bengal and the Gold Coast of Africa, as well as a small band
of Iroquois from the east and a pair of legendary black
voyageurs, Pierre Bonga and one of his sons, who were
descended from West Indian slaves. Fort William was a
mélange of accents and dialects.

Alas, even with this Great Rendezvous on the shore of
Lake Superior, the NWC was never able to overcome the
advantage the HBC had with its Hudson Bay route. Nor was
the HBC ever able to beat the Nor'Westers at their own game,
though they matched them blow for blow. The rivalry between
the two companies eventually exhausted both sides, and they
collapsed into a merger in 1821. But by then the fur trade era
in the Northwest was already in decline, replaced by settlers,
the timber trade and farming. The habitant was ascendant,
and the voyageur faded into history like woodsmoke.

At some level, I suppose, Canadians will always be caught
between the garden and the forest, the farm and the river, the
settled and the wild. It is a struggle between habitant and
voyageur, between Franklin and Hearne—and if the corpse of
Franklin always seems to win, it is the canoe that glides
effortlessly through our dreams.

After 1821, trade shifted north to Hudson Bay. A visitor
recalled "empty warehouses and useless offices" at Fort
William in 1823 and recorded how, called for the evening
meal, "We were 6 or 8 at a table in a hall that was large
enough to dine 300." By the 1840s, silk hats had begun to
replace beaver as the fashion of choice among Europe's
inbred aristocrats.

The post at Fort William struggled on until 1883, when
the land was turned over to the Canadian Pacific Railway.

The CPR had chosen this strategic site for a grain terminus and shipping depot. It was the same pattern seen at Churchill: from furs to wheat, from river to rail. The last surviving fur trade building at Fort William, a stone warehouse almost a hundred years old, was bulldozed in 1902 to make room for an expanded rail yard. NWC, HBC, CPR. So much of Canada's history is contained in that stark parade of letters. Today, the weed-grown rail yards of Thunder Bay's East End mark the original site of Fort William, but a full-scale reconstruction of the post has been built a few kilometres upriver. The new Fort William (helpfully named Old Fort William) is a faithfully rendered imagining of our past.

It's midsummer, humid but not yet muggy, and Alex is on my shoulders once again. He's one year taller than he was in Moose Jaw and that much heavier. Sure, *les hommes du nord* could pack eighty kilos of beaver pelts at a time, but let's see them navigate the path from the parking lot to the fort with a squirming burden on their shoulders that grabs fistfuls of hair and veers back with a "Whoa Nelly!" lurch every time a tree branch draws near. "Goddammit, stop that!" I yell, just as a group of visitors crosses paths with us, thereby instantly labelling myself as World's Worst Father. (A hard title to win, but one for which I may have a hereditary advantage.)

The scale of Old Fort William is impressive: twenty-five acres and forty-two buildings. The site hosts a re-enactment of the Great Rendezvous every summer, which—with my usual impeccable timing—we have just missed. I'm assuming it was a fun-filled, celebratory event with many a boisterous voyageur stepping out of his canoe and into song, toque at a jaunty angle (minus the broken bones and hernia and bitten-off nose, of course). But what I find most interesting about Old Fort William is not the steeply pitched roofs and reconstructed buildings, nor the painstakingly authentic costumes and personas donned by the interpreters, nor the fine attention to detail—but rather the way in which the forest has been used to separate past from present.

At the interpretive centre, a path winds its way through thick woods of birch and black ash. It's a long hike, and when you finally arrive at the fort it's like bursting out of the undergrowth into the early nineteenth century. Emerging from the forest—"Whoa Nelly!"—we come first to the birchbark wigwams of an Ojibwa encampment, then the sharpened logs of the palisade walls and the broad wharf on the Kaministiquia River.

Once we are past the voyageur encampment and through the main gate, the courtyard opens up. The Great Hall faces us, and to the right are storehouses stocked with furs: bear skins, warm disks of stretched beaver, the windsock shapes of otter pelts. The apothecary, the powder magazine, the jail (or rather, the "gaol"), the naval sheds. It's all here.

"So," I say, slinging Alex from my shoulders and stumbling back a bit. "What do you think?"

"I think," he says, with the solemnity of someone considering a very serious matter, "I have been four and three-quarters for a long time. I think maybe I am four and *four*-quarters by now."

"Well, no," I say, wiping my brow. "Four quarters is equal to one. If you were four and four-quarters, you'd be five."

"Wow," he says softly. "I'm five now?" And for the rest of the trip, this is what he will tell people.

From the observation tower at Old Fort William, you look out across river and trees and restored rooftops and wigwams. The present day is nowhere to be seen. . . but it can be smelled.

The sour aroma of Thunder Bay's pulp mills hangs in the air like a fart in an elevator. No one wants to acknowledge it, but it can't really be ignored, either. Yet this malodorous hint of the nearby city is apt, for it gives evidence—pungent evidence—that the lakehead region is still a crucial trade link.

Thunder Bay is Canada's third great port, after Halifax and Vancouver, and the city's massive banks of grain terminals act as a continental storehouse. The place is still the site of a Great Rendezvous. The freighters of today ply the same Great Lakes–St. Lawrence transportation route opened up by the Nor'Westers, with iron ore, potash, wheat and timber having replaced furs as the trade goods of choice.

Thunder Bay is a working-class place with working-class grit. The glory days of the grain trade may be over, but was there ever an inland city more perfectly situated? The vastness of Superior, the world's largest freshwater lake. The towering presence of Mt. McKay, rising up like an anvil 300 metres above the city. And that deep curve of water, the city's namesake: Animike Wekwid to the Ojibwa and Baie de Tonnerre to the French, with the meaning the same in both languages: *Thunder Bay.*

A canoe, a beaver and a voyageur as standard-bearers: Thunder Bay's coat of arms, displayed on public buildings and welcoming signs, is replete with NWC iconography. The Scots managers and French Canadian canoemen are gone, but the third pillar of the fur trade trinity is still an important presence. More than 6000 Ojibwa live in Thunder Bay today, with their own network of community centres, development corporations, business networks and treaty councils.

It's been popular among certain agenda-touting journalists to come to Thunder Bay, visit a derelict part of town, spot a "drunken Indian" or two and then leave quickly, making grim pronouncements. Yes, there are social problems facing the city's Ojibwa (or Anishinabe, as they increasingly prefer to be known, though not unanimously), just as there are problems facing aboriginal communities elsewhere. The Ojibwa are dealing with them. There is no magic wand you can wave to undo the years of economic and social trauma; it's a slow process, but it is underway. In the meantime, I can go around spotting "drunken Caucasians," if you'd like. ("We drive slowly through the mean streets on the rubby side of town, with our windows up and doors locked, and peer at several inebriated young men—who appear to be white—outside a local bar.")

Thunder Bay's Ojibwa community has been joined by other enclaves. The Finns who first came here to work in the logging industry were followed in the 1930s and 1940s by Italian labourers, who arrived to work on the rails. The Italian Hall is on the same block as the Finlandia Club, and Alex and I wander among shops with names like "Finnport" and "Bambino." The Italians and Finns of Thunder Bay often ceremonially exchange flags—the tricolour of one for the pale blue cross of the other, as they stand beneath the maple leaf of the Canadian. There is also—and here I'm just guessing—a brisk "pancakes for pasta" trade.

The Finns hold their annual St. Urho's Day festivities in March. This is matched by the two-day summertime Festa Italiana and, a week or two later, the Ojibwa Keeshigun, a traditional powwow held at Old Fort William. You've got to love this country. It provides such a wonderful venue for cross-pollination—even if it does mean eating the occasional Ukrainian pizza or pancake Italiano.

My son's Japanese name is Genki, meaning "lively" or "full of life," and he has grown into his name with enthusiasm, though not without moments of pure terror (on his parents' part), such as when, say, with unbridled genkiness, he charges headlong towards a crashing torrent of water. Though I didn't *specifically* promise my wife that I wouldn't let Genki Alex fall off a cliff and be swept away, I'm fairly certain it's the sort of thing of which she would disapprove. I all but tackle Alex at the edge of the gorge surrounding Kakabeka Falls, as Terumi's final instructions come back to me with unusual clarity.

"Just bring him back in one piece," she said. "With sticks in his hair and dirt under his fingers. But in one piece."

Kakabeka Falls, "the Niagara of the North," makes a heart-stopping forty-metre drop. The Kaministiquia River churns over from level to level, pummelling the rocky outcrops below in a rage of gravity. A constant thunder and a billow of cold mist fill the air. The falls here are more rugged, more confined, more crag-ridden than those at Niagara, but there is the same calm slide, the same free fall of water into noisy tumult—the way a roller coaster will pause at the top before plunging downward.

Stairs and viewing platforms run like a game of Snakes and Ladders up and down the edge of the gorge, and Alex bolts this way and that with fearless abandon. Had we only named him "Afraid of Heights."

The falls at Kakabeka are west of Thunder Bay, along the Trans-Canada Highway and just past a gathering of gas stations and motels referred to—ironically, I'm assuming—as "a town." A sharp contrast to the days of the voyageurs, when Kakabeka marked the start of the almost vertical Portage de la Montagne, a true test of mettle.

"Fortunately," I tell Alex, "we won't be riding a canoe over Kakabeka." I can see the disappointment descend on his face.

Having survived our visit to the Niagara of the North, we take the Thunder Bay Expressway and continue to the "Grand Canyon of Northern Ontario"—though the only thing Ouimet shares with the Grand Canyon is a general geological designation. Canyons they both may be, but that is where the comparison ends.

The north shore of Lake Superior marks the southern reach of the boreal forest. Thin topsoil with glimpses of bedrock beneath; stands of tamarack, that odd not-quite-evergreen that drops its needles in the fall; the gnarled, arthritic pine and peeling birch of the Canadian Shield. And at Ouimet Canyon, the bottom falls out of it. It is a startling view: a sudden drop, 100 metres straight down—and I mean straight down. At eye level, 150 metres across this chasm, the forest continues unaltered. Slabs of shale have broken away from the canyon walls, leaving free-standing columns and pillars behind. One such spire of stone, dubbed Indian Head, resembles a human face in profile.

WARNING

Steep Cliffs

Crevices

Unstable Rock

STAY ON THE TRAIL

and this, in red . . .

WARNING

Stay Well Back from Cliff Edge

Parents: Children Are Your Responsibility!

Damn. Just as I suspected, I should have read the fine print before we started having kids.

There is a constant wind at Ouimet, even on the muggiest, stillest days of summer. Lean out over the lip of the viewing platform and you will feel the updraft against your face, cool and unceasing. Ouimet is a sunken garden. The temperature here drops as much as 10 degrees Celsius as the canyon descends, and in the shadowed world at the bottom—off-limits except to those with special permits— an arctic environment has taken hold. You'd have to travel straight north, 1000 kilometres to the shores of Hudson Bay, to come across some of the plants that live in this microclimate, one that is defined by elevation rather than latitude. The same flora you'd find on the tundra of Churchill can be found here.

On the canyon rim, we are standing in the boreal forest. At the bottom lies subarctic tundra, where moss grows thirty centimetres thick in places, on a core of ice that never melts. Arctic wintergreen; the tiny white blossoms of sandwort; Arctic lichens speckling rock in rusty oranges, sudden yellows and earthy browns: they are orphans all, stranded when the glaciers of the last Ice Age retreated 8000 years ago. They are relics of a prehistoric era—the botanical equivalent of dinosaurs.

"Really?" says Alex, hanging over the rails. "Dinosaurs?"

"Well, no—not *really.*"

"Oh."

Beyond the prehistoric cold, the south end of the canyon fans out into the forests and marshlands of the Canadian Shield and, beyond that, the distant haze of Lake Superior.

Sleeping Giant Provincial Park is named for the rocky head-land at the end of Sibley Peninsula. Seen in silhouette, the Sleeping Giant mesas look like the mausoleum rendition of a fallen king lying in silent repose, arms folded over his chest. The name Sleeping Giant suggests both size and strength, a landscape that might awaken at any moment, might rise up and brush us off like sand from a blanket. This is a land of sheer cliffs and abrupt valleys, of deep forests and hidden lakes, a land of secluded inlets and rare orchids.

The slumbering giant is Nanabosho, son of Kebeyun, the West Wind. Ojibwa legends tell of how Nanabosho, having discovered silver, buries the ore on a small islet at the end of a peninsula. He exacts from his people a vow of secrecy, for he knows that if word gets out, white men will come searching for the silver. But one Ojibwa chief, known for his vanity, secretly crafts elaborate weapons from the ore. He is killed in battle against the Sioux, who recover these silver armaments and send an expedition in search of the source. Nanabosho sees the Sioux canoes approaching, with two white men amongst the warriors, and he roars in anger. Stirring the skies like a cauldron, he brings forth a storm that sinks the canoes, killing all on board. In punishment for his deed, Nanabosho is turned to stone, and there he lies. There are as many versions of this story as there are spellings of Nanabosho's name, but all involve a secret cache of silver, Sioux enemies, white intruders. And all point to Silver Islet.

The only community anywhere on Sibley Peninsula, Silver Islet lies in the shadow of the Giant. A crumbling road reaches south to this remote outpost, where the waters of Lake Superior roll in like liquid steel. A mud-splattered SUV bullies its way past us, a canoe on top tied down like a trophy animal. There are only a handful of moose left on the peninsula, but hundreds of deer, and the drive down is rife with them. "Nature's speed bumps," as people say.

Silver Islet is a village of log cabins strung along a lazy loop of road called, somewhat grandly, the Avenue. The village is rich in flower gardens, and the roadside is a froth of saturated colour. Purple flowers hang down like grapes. A mist is settling across the water, but from Sibley Cove we can just make out the small island that gives the town its name. A low outcrop a mile offshore, with a scraggle of trees clinging to it, this was once the site of the richest silver mine in the world.

Below the water, even now, lies an ants' colony of tunnels and mining shafts.

Nanabosho hid his treasure trove well. Seams of pure silver were discovered beneath Lake Superior, but the only access was this tiny island, little more than a shoal, that was constantly swept by hard-rolling waves. Skull Rock, as it was first known, provided the barest of footholds.

The first breakwaters, built on the islet in 1870 to shelter the central mine shaft, were tossed aside by storms. The bigger walls that replaced them were battered down too, smashed by ice, pounded into flotsam. The breakwaters eventually reached 250 by 150 metres, with a coffer-dam of stone and cement—ten times the island's original size. This wasn't a mine, it was a fortress, surrounded by one of the most perilous moats on earth.

Between mining platforms and breakwaters, the island would eventually "grow" to be thirty times its natural size, and a crowded community formed around the shaft and hoists: a pump-house, a blacksmith shop, several boarding homes for the mine workers and a combination library/saloon. (Would that there were more of those around!) Low along the water, the buildings looked like a garrison built on a raft, cut adrift and stranded offshore.

The miners faced cave-ins, violent squalls, flash floods and flammable air. That plus the gnawing knowledge that they were burrowing beneath the largest lake on earth, with the crushing weight of all that water above them. Only the toughest men could hack it. Americans and Canadians usually took one look and left, and in their stead came Cornish and Norwegian miners who blasted their way into the Precambrian underworld. The boarding homes that were squeezed onto the islet were divided along ethnic lines, and the two groups got along about as well as the Montreal men and the *hommes du nord* of yesteryear. The Cornishmen found the Norwegians abrasive and reckless; the Norwegians found the Cornishmen soft and overly pliant—especially when punched in the stomach.

Married men lived on the mainland shore with their families, and a second community grew up there. The miners on shore lived in sturdy log homes, the mine manager in elegance. Churches went up (one Cornish, one Norwegian). A general store was built, as was a dock. A community hall, a post office and a customs house followed (for cross-border lake runs; America is on the other side of an invisible line in the water south of the islet).

By 1883, the miners had tunnelled their way 300 metres below the surface of Lake Superior—as far down as the Giant is tall—and the pumphouse was running all hours to keep the water out. The pumps needed fuel constantly; when a coal ship failed to arrive (caught in an early freeze-up, amid whispers that the captain was drunk at the time), the lake began to seep in. The miners started throwing everything they had into the furnace to keep the pumps running. They began tearing down the walls of buildings, feeding the flames, keeping the lake away. Silver Islet was cannibalizing itself, but to no avail. The waters of Superior eventually flooded in, taking with them any hope of keeping the mine in operation. In its fourteen years, more than $3 million worth of silver ore had been taken from the bottom of Lake Superior, and it made a small number of men very, very rich. Now the islet was abandoned to the elements. Today all that remain are submerged breakwater walls and a mine-shaft entrance just below the water's surface.

The community on shore fared better. The miners' log cabins, cut from stands of virgin white pine, have been converted into summer homes and colonized by artisans and families from the city. It is a handsome, rugged-looking place. The Silver Islet General Store, established in 1871 and built by miners, has been refurbished, complete with tea room and candy counter.

Alex and I walk down to the water's edge along loose shale and jumbled stones. We skip pebbles into Lake Superior, debate the merits of Woody Woodpecker versus Pokémon. So vast a body is Superior that it comes as a surprise when you taste it and discover it isn't salt water but fresh. Superior feels like an ocean—because it is. It is larger in volume than the other Great Lakes *combined*. It is so large it generates its own climate. And yet it's reduced to this: small waves lapping along the shore in cat tongues of water.

Fort, falls, canyon, lake—and next the forest. "We'll be sleeping in the wilderness from today," I tell Alex. "No more hotel waterslides."

"Will there be dangerous creatures?" he asks, ever optimistic.

I chuckle. "No son, the woods are as safe as can be. No need to worry about anything. Why, it's absolutely—" You can see where this is going.

They were baiting the bear trap with doughnuts when we arrived at the campsite. "Doughnuts?"

"Well," the park warden says, "it is a Canadian bear we're trying to catch."

As they joke about waking to find a dozen police officers inside the trap, no one at the campsite seems particularly perturbed about the black bear that has been seen snuffling around the coolers. The night before, a park ranger spotted the bear on top of someone's trailer, and they have now rolled in a heavy culvert-on-wheels that is baited with Tim Hortons honey-dipped specials. "More a nuisance than a danger," I am told. If anything, the staff at the park seem to hold a begrudging admiration for the critter. "He's a smart bear. He's figured out how to open minivans." The swiping action of the typical bruin, it turns out, is perfect for springing a minivan door. And isn't that comforting to know?

Alex and I are not in a minivan, true. But we are deep in the woods, and I remember reassuring Terumi that the camping trip would be harmless fun. "It's not like I'm taking him to Churchill," I said, ha ha. "It's not like we are going to be running into bears, ha ha."

While we're hiking in the woods, I tell Alex that if a bear approaches, he needs to get up on my shoulders right away, so that we look big. Fortunately, Alex is already on my shoulders—with a hi-de-ho and a "Whoa, Nelly!"

This is Alex's first camping expedition, and he has already received several savvy wilderness tips from his ol' man. Namely: to put up a tent properly, you need to have on hand a good supply of profanity. This also applies to campfires and the lighting of. And speaking of fires: to roast marshmallows, also known as "the main course" (with shake-a-pan popcorn for dessert), you will need the following supplies:

- 142 matches
- an entire bag of firewood
- a good half-gallon of lighter fluid
- another entire bag of firewood
- more profanity

Ah, but once that fire goes, she really goes! By the time you're done, the flames should uncurl eleven metres into the air and generate enough blinding heat to be visible from outer space. Then, and only then, are you ready for marshmallows.

"Okay, son. Slooowly lower your marshmallow towards the—" FWOOM! "It's on fire, quick, put it out. No! Don't stomp on it; you do that, you won't be able to eat it. Here, let's try again. Slowly, slowly . . . the trick is to *lightly* brown it as you—" FWOOM!

There is a long pause. We have learned the word "prefer" today. As in "I would prefer you don't yank on my hair any more, son," and "I would *really* prefer you don't yank on my hair any more." Alex looks at the gooey black offering on the end of the stick and says, "I think I prefer marshmallows raw."

That night, I lock our food in the trunk of the car, along with our toothpaste, soap and anything else of fragrant appeal, and unroll the sleeping bags. I show Alex how to wad up his clothes and push them into a stuff-sack to create a lumpy and highly uncomfortable pillow—"Old voyageur trick," I lie. He crawls into bed and is instantly asleep.

It trickles in slowly, like water into an ear: the realization that there is something moving round outside our tent. I drift towards consciousness, like a body gradually surfacing in a lake—and then wake with a jolt. There's a rustle. And another. I can track the sound as it moves through the brush beside our campsite. I check on Alex, see that he is hugging his makeshift pillow. It is leaking mini-marshmallows—delectable, fragrant mini-marshmallows. That's when I get scared.

I have to give Alex credit for his ingenuity. Marshmallows make for mighty soft bedding. But they are also one of a bear's Main Food Groups, right up there with doughnuts and garbage, assorted. I listen, can hear the noise coming closer. I zip open the front of the tent halfway and bang my flashlight angrily against one of the poles, thereby producing a faint *tink* that is sure to frighten off any rampaging carnivores in the vicinity. When I sweep the campsite with my flashlight I see no bears, only deer. They stop, perfectly still, looking at the light. *"G'wan!"* I yell, and they are startled back a few steps. I am about to chase them away for good when it dawns on me that perhaps deer are like canaries in a coal mine. Not that a black bear could ever catch one, but seeing deer in an area probably means it's a safe bet that no bears are prowling about.

I tromp over, open the trunk of the car, dump the bag of mini-marshmallows into the cooler, crawl back into the tent, fall fitfully to sleep and then wake with another panicked jolt when I hear—*nothing*. The deer have gone. Do they know something I don't?

Dawn finally seeps in, and orange light fills the tent. I crick and crack. Crawl out on all fours. Sit at the camp table, try to stir a fire from the ashes, fail, listen instead to the wind searching the trees. Through the open tent flap I can see Alex asleep inside, curled up in a question mark, dreaming. And as much as I would like to believe that I still have an air of the nomad about me, I know that in the running tally of my life, I have long since moved over to the habitant side of the ledger. I try to decide how I feel about this.

The answer lies somewhere inside that tent, sleeping, sleeping.

$$\bullet \quad \bullet \quad \bullet$$

In the north woods of Canada, they speak of a legendary traveller named Atachuu kaii' who "dreamed the canoe into existence." French-Canadian folklore tells of *la chasse-galerie*, a flying canoe that sweeps across the night skies, carrying lonely voyageurs home.

I want to be part of this. But unfortunately, as well as assuring my wife that there will be no bears at Sleeping Giant, I have also promised her, in a vow most sacred, that I won't take our son out in a canoe. Or rather, I promised I wouldn't take our son out in a canoe *on Lake Superior*. Of course not. Superior is an inland sea where freighters go down with all hands, leaving nothing but an oil slick and Gordon Lightfoot lyrics in their wake. I wouldn't dream of taking a four-year-old out on Lake Superior. But note: I said nothing about not taking him out on Marie Louise, which is a lake *inside* Sleeping Giant Provincial Park.

How can I take my son camping and not get into a canoe? If word leaked out, I would be stripped of my citizenship. The CPR may have bound this nation together, but it was the canoe that first called it into being. The birchbark has been replaced, first by canvas and then by aluminum and fibre-glass, but the symbolism remains. Paddling a canoe—why, it's as Canadian as grilled cheese sandwiches.

In his youth, Pierre Trudeau wrote an essay on the aesthetics of Canada's voyageur vessel, concluding: "What sets a canoeing expedition apart is that it purifies you more rapidly and inescapably than any other. Travel a thousand miles by train and you are a brute; pedal five hundred on a bicycle and you remain basically bourgeois; paddle a hundred in a canoe and you are already a child of nature."

A child of nature, mind you. How can we *not* go?

Our guide is Adam Moir, an affable young man with a degree in biology from Lakehead University in Thunder Bay and a wealth of knowledge about the park's flora and fauna. I refer to Adam as a park ranger, but his proper title is— and I quote—"Natural Heritage Education Leader with Visitor Services." Basically, he gets paid to camp out, which is not a bad gig. "I've been coming to Sleeping Giant since I was five years old," he tells me, and it's clear there is nowhere else he would rather be.

Trussed up in our life preservers, the three of us paddle out onto Marie Louise Lake, the Giant rising above us to the west. Though I must admit Adam does most (if not all) of the work. Alex's technique is more "splash and flail" than "cut and chop," and I'm no better, as I try desperately to remember the difference between a J-stroke and, you know, the other one.

"Are there any sharks in this lake?" Alex asks.

Adam laughs. No, there aren't any sharks in Marie Louise Lake. Alex looks out at the water we are crossing. "Any sea creatures?" he asks hopefully.

"I'm afraid not," says Adam. "But we do pull in twenty-five-kilo pike out of here." Northern pike, he explains, are the fish equivalent of sharks.

"How about that over there? Is that a shark?"

"No, that's a piece of wood."

"Oh."

Since visions of ferocious northern pike have failed to capture Alex's imagination, Adam tries another approach, telling him tales of the early voyageurs and the treacherous landscape they had to traverse. "They portaged past waterfalls with heavy packs along narrow trails, and they faced all sorts of dangers along the way."

"Like sharks?" says Alex, optimistic as always.

We glide by an inlet where a great blue heron is poised. "He eats frogs and little fish. He stands perfectly still like that, and then spears them like shish-kebab."

An osprey drifts down on dwindling winds to land atop a gnarled tree. "We have a high concentration of peregrine falcons as well. The body of the Giant is actually a sheer cliff face, ideal for nesting." Peregrine falcons, Adam tells us, are the fastest birds alive. "They dive-bomb at 180 kilometres an hour. You will see them even pick off other birds in mid-flight."

"They're like sharks of the sky," I say, but this only confuses the matter.

"Sharks can fly?" Alex asks.

We pass islands of mossy bog, formed by beaver dams and driftwood jumbles. In the murky shallows we can see submerged logs and drowned trees. The soggy silted lake floor slides by below us. "It's loam," says Adam. "Two or three feet deep." Known colloquially as loon shit, it's pungent too, as we discover when our paddles come up slimy with the stuff.

Adam steers us towards what I think is shore, but the surface is spongy. When we walk on it, it's wobbly. "It's actually a floating mass of sphagnum moss, like a carpet." Adam jumps, and sure enough, the ground ripples. This floating island is home to a colony of pitcher plants, their reddish flowers rising up like TV antennas. "These plants are insectivores. Tiny flies and mosquitoes are drawn in and caught in the plant's sticky hairs, where they are slowly digested," Adam explains. Alex thinks this is exceedingly cool: *a plant that eats bugs*. (Mind you, anything that eats bugs is cool in the eyes of a four-year-old.)

Back in the canoe, Alex and Adam trade knock-knock jokes. Then, when Adam mentions that the voyageurs sang their way across the continent—pacing themselves to the rhythms of their songs—Alex launches into an impromptu tune. *"Somebody once told me, the world is going to roll me."*

"Smash Mouth," says Adam. "Good band."

We paddle all the way to the mouth of Sibley Creek, a cold-water trickle that drains into Lake Superior and was once a key logging route. Once we're ashore, Adam calls us over to a cluster of touch-me-nots.

"The seed pods are spring-loaded. They explode when you touch them." It's how they propagate, he says, and sure enough, when we flick them . . . pow! They erupt like tiny green popcorn.

This is without a doubt the absolute apogee, apex, all-time best highlight of the trip for Alex. He crouches down and bursts dozens of pods, helping the plants to spread—though I suspect it is the spectacle, not the altruism of it, that spurs him on. (Even now, with the week we spent in Thunder Bay several summers in the past, he will sometimes say, with a far-away look in his eyes, "Dad, remember those flowers that exploded when I touched them?")

A hover of dragonflies. A whirligig of beetles skimming patterns across the surface of the water. Lily pads in floating green planes. We are slicing our canoe across the lake, back to camp, with a sun setting in full crimson and a loon calling, its voice like a teakettle run dry, like a whistle in the dark.

In Alex's world, every lake would be filled with sharks, every plant would explode on contact, every marshmallow would be served raw. And every canoe would be paddled by at least one voyageur singing Smash Mouth in a loud, loud voice. *"Well, the years start coming and they don't stop coming . . ."*

By the end of our trip, it feels as though we are shrinking. Or the landscape is expanding; it's hard to say. Thunder Bay, I realize, is all about mass. Sheer unapologetic *mass*. From the cold expanse of Lake Superior to the crowning cliffs of Sleeping Giant to the heavy, almost threatening presence of Mount McKay, the entire region is rendered on a scale larger than we are used to. This becomes clear on our final day, when Alex and I take a boat trip on Lake Superior.

Half of the world's fresh water is trapped inside Canada, and much of that is contained in the Great Lakes. One in three Canadians and one in seven Americans rely on the Great Lakes basin for their fresh water. And plying this nook of it is the *Pioneer II,* a sixteen-metre, twenty-two-ton passenger vessel piloted by Captain Doug Stanton. Stanton looks the role: greying temples, captain's cap, calm air of competence. The boat slips free of the dock and we move past towering grain elevators that line the bay like Saxon castles. A chatter of seagulls reels above. Ocean-going freighters move like minesweepers across the bay.

At the dry docks, freighters have been pulled up on shore like giant canoes. Nanabosho's, perhaps. The *Pioneer II,* impossibly small, slides between the canyon walls of grain terminals, and Captain Stanton points out the graffiti that homesick sailors have scratched onto the waterside surfaces in Greek and Spanish and Chinese. An anchored freighter fills our view like a cliff face, rust-red and mere metres away. We are a long time moving past it.

The grain terminals and pulp mills are inside the protective embrace of a breakwater, itself a massive feat: the Great Wall of Thunder Bay, which holds back the worst of Superior's mood swings. Though they are occasionally imploded (one was taken down on national television), most of the older grain terminals are simply boarded up when their lifespan comes to an end. Cheaper to build a new one on a different site than to dismantle such a weight of concrete, I suppose. In one terminal there have been at least two cases of spontaneous combustion, where the wheat dust suddenly ignited.

Captain Stanton turns the *Pioneer II,* and we enter the delta of the Kaministiquia River. "That's where the original fort used to be," he says, pointing to the CPR rail yards.

We glide past the yards and under the archaic gridwork of Jackknife Bridge. It is a counterweight drawbridge, and the imagery of medieval castles asserts itself more strongly than ever.

We then leave the river delta and run slowly out into the bay, cutting a wide arc past sailboats and an unmanned lighthouse. Evening is settling, and the city has begun to shimmer as we turn back towards the hazy silhouettes of grain terminals.

"Would you like to take the wheel?" Stanton asks Alex. "You can steer us home," he says, plopping his captain's hat on Alex's head.

This will become legend in the preschool playground, how Alex piloted a ship at Thunder Bay. "See the McDonald's sign? You can use that as a guide," the captain advises. "When it gets dark, that acts like a navigational marker."

We look ahead, and there they are on that distant shore, glowing in the dusk, twin arches of gold. A beacon in the wilderness, showing us the way.

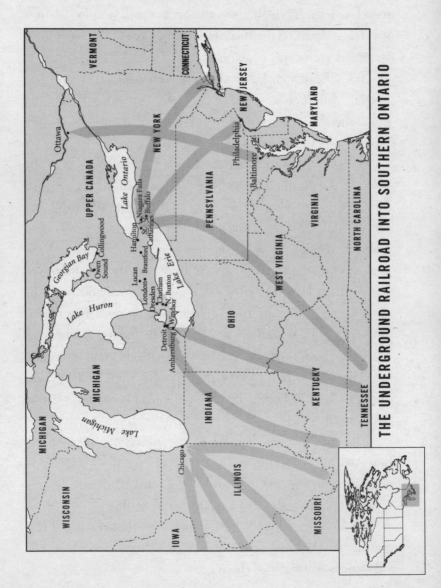

THE UNDERGROUND RAILROAD INTO SOUTHERN ONTARIO

chapter six

THE ROAD TO DAWN

LIKE ANY ROAD TRIP WORTHY OF THE NAME, it was all about freedom. Freedom and escape.

I had been hired to write a cultural study, a "how to" guidebook on being a Canadian, and had immediately brought my brother Ian on board as co-author. Seemed simple enough. All Ian and I had to do was come up with a definitive look at Canadian society. Piece of cake, that. Why, the book would practically write itself!

But as deadline after deadline whooshed by, we realized with a growing sense of unease that perhaps unlocking the secrets of the Canadian soul would be a little more work than we had anticipated. The phone calls and e-mails from our publisher began to pile up, each one more hand-wringingly nervous than the last. "The printing presses are standing by. Still haven't received anything. You weren't planning to write this entire book in a weekend, were you? Were you??"

So here I am. I have flown to Ontario, taken a taxi to my brother's house, have set up camp in the spare room, have said, "Let's get to it, then," in a suitably determined and businesslike tone. Ian nods, equally determined, equally

businesslike. In movies, this is where the montage comes in.
A furrow-browed ensemble sitting around a warehouse table,
planning a heist—with quick cuts of maps being unrolled,
arms being crossed, floors being paced, charts being flipped,
hi-tech gadgets being handled. Alas, in life there are no mon-
tages, and there are no film splices to save us. No matter. Ian
and I have laid out our notepaper and pens on the kitchen
table in a *highly* organized fashion, have brewed up some
coffee and have hunkered down for a brainstorm of *Tempest*-
like proportions. After an intense all-night session, we have
completed an entire chapter: "How the Canadian Government
Works." Unfortunately, this chapter consists of only two
words: "It doesn't."

"You know what we need?" Ian says, stubbing out a cigarette in an ashtray already overflowing. "We need a road trip,
that's what we need. That'll get the old creative energy flowing."

I couldn't agree more. We need to hit the highways and
byways of this great land. So we rent a car and flee the city,
heading west through the small towns and tobacco fields of
southern Ontario. We are searching for Canada.

It was meant to be an afternoon jaunt: out at 4:00 p.m.,
locate Canada by 5:45, back by 7:00. But the road has its own
momentum, and once we slip free of our authorial bonds we
just keep going and going, onward, ever onward, with the sort
of giddy, irresponsible joy that comes from driving a rented
car on corrugated back roads. Ian takes the wheel and
manages to hit every pothole. Intentionally.

"How about St. Thomas?" I say. "I used to live there, it's
south of London, they have a statue of a giant elephant. Want
to go?"

"A giant elephant? You need to ask?" A beat. "Why an elephant?"

"It's a monument to Jumbo, the circus star. Jumbo was hit by a train in St. Thomas. Killed him. They're very proud of this."

"Sounds good. Let's go."

Ian unwraps a fresh pack of cigarettes with one hand, riffles through our box of Timbits with the other and keeps the car on the road with the other hand. (Which involves three hands, now that I think about it. He must have been steering with his knee at this point.) "Bloody paternalistic government," he mutters, looking at the warning label on his package of Export A's. "*Smoking is harmful to children.* Well, fuck'em. Children shouldn't be smoking in the first place."

Ian smokes the way politicians lie: constantly and without reprieve. Window down, we leave a vapour trail that drifts out over the waxy green fields. There are more than 1300 tobacco farms in Canada—and almost every one of them is located here, in Ontario's tobacco belt. Peddling carcinogens, trafficking in addiction. A wholesome tradition, it is.

"Y'know," I say, "those things'll take ten years off your life."

"Screw it," he says. "It's the last ten years." He looks over at me, sizes up my disapproval of someone else's pleasures. "Don't be so Canadian."

The small towns roll by one after another. Harvesters are on the move, working their way slowly along tobacco rows, gathering the leaves and raising a fine dust that colours the air in sepia tones. We weave our way in Etch-a-Sketch diagonals, south a jog, then west, then south, on the endless right angles of concession roads. The village of Thamesville is advertising its annual "threshing festival," which we have just missed.

"Damn," I say. "I would like to have seen that. I'm guessing it's some sort of creepy 'The Lottery'–style event, where the townspeople thresh someone, and I quote, 'to within an inch of their life.'"

"That's 'thrash.'"

"Thrash, thresh—it's the same thing."

This is followed by a lengthy debate about the difference between threshing and thrashing, which resolves nothing and succeeds only in adding to the linguistic confusion on both sides.

Dusk is falling, and a harvest moon, ripe and heavy, swings low along the far side of the sky. We drive into the darkness, and the centreline becomes a staccato of gold, ticking off the distances. On we drive and on, until we reach the ends of the earth (i.e., Chatham). Tired and still unenlightened, we pull off "freedom road," as we have dubbed it.

We miss the city twice—driving past Chatham first from the north and then from the east—but eventually manage to exit onto Bloomfield Road, where we find ourselves in a thicket of motels. When we try them, they are either full or slightly above our Scots-Canadian budget of "sweet bugger all." At the last one, Comfort's End or Journey's Rest or some such, there seems to be a "Twelfth Kid Sleeps Free" promotion underway, and the lobby is swarming with children. "Shouldn't they be in bed?" Ian asks. "Or at least out having a smoke?"

At a Tim Hortons nearby, we stop to consider our options. Coffee, doughnuts and, in Ian's case, a cigarette outside, thus covering all three main nutritional categories—caffeine, sugar and nicotine—in one fair swoop.

"That's *fell* swoop," Ian says.

"Fell, fair—same thing."

"There's lotsa other motels," the coffee-counter girl tells us, when we ask her about less pricey shelter that might be available. "A whole bunch, in fact. What you got to do is go right down Bloomfield here, turn left on Park, then left on Lacroix and then left again on Richmond. Here"—she writes this down on a napkin for us—"easy as pie." We thank her with extravagant grins and a modest tip (we are on a budget, after all) and head out, refuelled and recharged.

Now, those of you keeping track, as Ian and I obviously weren't, may have noticed that she has—mark this—sent us on one right and three lefts, which constitutes a square. We arrive right back at the same Dead Tim's.

"You again," she says, without even the faintest flicker of a smile, when we stomp in.

"Not *left* on Richmond," she scolds. "Right on *Grand.*"

I show her the directions she scribbled down for us not twenty minutes ago. Exhibit A. But she's unruffled by this and is clearly getting fed up with our incompetence. After all, "Why would you go left on Richmond? Richmond is, like, just over there."

Gnashing teeth, we set out again: onto Lacroix, through downtown Chatham at night, past drifting pods of teen-agers; over the river, right on Grand. Sure enough, as we approach the outskirts of the city, we come upon another string of motels. But Ian has a cunning theory. "Never take the first motel you come to," he says, worldly-wise and older-brotherly. "Motels on the edge of town always jack up their prices; they know people are tired and will pull into the first motel they see. You have to go *past* that first cluster of motels. Always."

Except—and again, people keeping track of these things may already have noticed—we are driving *out* of Chatham at this point, which means the first motels we pass are actually the *last*—oh, never mind. I imagine you are as weary of this as we are. Suffice it to say, we choose, with our usual unerring instincts, Chatham's one truly fleabag motel.

We dump our stuff in the room and head for a late-night diner, chosen with these same unerring instincts, where Ian opens his notepad. He writes CANADA across the page in large capital letters, underlines it forcibly and adds a "?"

"There," he says, having done his bit. "Over to you. Canada. What is it?"

I think a minute, but all I can offer is Lower's aphorism about Canada being a canoe route.

"A canoe route, eh?" Ian says. "No, we need something more immediate. Not how Canada began, or what it was— but what it *is*. What drives it forward."

"Doughnuts?"

"Something more subtle."

"Doughnuts with those little sprinkles on top?"

"Sprinkles?"

"You know, multicultural sprinkles, all the colours of the rainbow."

"Too subtle."

We scratch our heads awhile. "A riddle hidden in an enigma, wrapped in a toque?" I offer.

"Too Churchillian."

And so—drawing upon the can-do spirit with which we have been instilled, growing up as we have in the rugged north woods—we decide to give up. "To hell with it, let's call it a night."

Back at Ye Olde Seedy Inn, I sleep lightly but well, lulled into slumber by the sound of trucks passing like breakers rolling in on a distant shore. I wake early and step out, letting Ian sleep. Dawn, and the asphalt is beaded with dew. Autumn wisps of mist uncurl along the highway. Trees are tinged with gold, leaves curling at the edges. I take a long walk and end up in front of "AJ's homecookin'." Yep, one word. Yep, no caps on "home." Yep, an apostrophe on "cookin'." My kind of place. I enter, surprised at the gathering of people inside in these, the earliest hours. And it's not just the sign but the menu, the dialogue—they're all peppered with apostrophes.

"Hello, Paul, how'r'you'n'Dale doin' t'day?"

"Couldn'ta bin better."

"You're just up for Heritage Days, are ya?"

It's a John Deere-hat sort of place, with photos of souped-up race cars on proud display along one wall: hot rods in ribald reds, skanky pink, fluorescent luminescent lime. And I think to myself, *Hot rods are van art come to life. This is an important transitional form, from art on vehicle to vehicle as art.* Not a terrific insight, I admit, but it is still early in the day and I haven't had my morning—

"There y'go," says the waitress, filling my cup with ESP certainty. I peruse the menu, make my selection. And before my coffee cup is empty the platter has arrived, along with another slosh of coffee. Apparently I have ordered the "big ol' bucket o' grease," better known as the Burly Man's Belly Buster Breakfast Special (or words to that effect). It's wonderful. You got yer pork there, in its three natural states—sausage, ham, bacon. You got yer toast slathered with butter. You got yer potatoes fried in the same. And the only vegetable in sight is a frail slice of tomato used as garnish, which I push to one side on principle.

A police officer (a.k.a. "Bill") is speaking with one of the waitresses. He is standing behind the counter, questioning her about an attempted break-and-enter the night before. "They musta come'n'ere," the waitress says. "An' outta there. Didn't take anything, though."

"Jeez, Bill," one of the coffee-counter crowd hollers at the officer. "You'd think you could help out back there, seein' as how you're in the kitchen anyways."

"That's right," one of the waitresses chimes in as she sweeps past, coffee pots in both hands. "You could at least put some toast down'r flip an egg."

At one end of the diner, at a table for six, sits the strangest pair of friends, one round, one thin. They sit not across from each other but side by side, just the two of them, in parallel gaze, looking out as though surveying their realm. The thin one doesn't speak and doesn't move. The round one, however, has a restless leg, which bounces constantly as he talks. And though his thin friend doesn't respond, the round fellow still pauses after each statement, leaving an appropriate gap in the conversation for a reply that never comes.

"I was listenin' to that oldies station, eh?" (pause) "The one with the oldies on it." (pause) "They have songs from the sixties, eh?" (pause) "Some good bands back then." (pause) "And how it works is, you phone in and ask for a song and then they play it." (pause) "So anyways, this guy calls in, right?" (pause) "And the song he requests—it's not an oldie, right?" (pause)

In addition to raising two perplexing questions—namely, what is it with the Ontario habit of pluralizing "anyway"? And surely call-in radio is not a new phenomenon in Chatham?— the interplay of the two men suggests an unusual back-story. As I listen in, I conjure up all sorts of tragic scenarios. A hunting accident in which the thin man saved the life of his friend but was badly injured in the process, losing his voice and his ability to interact with others. His friend has stood by him, refused to give up, even when those high-and-mighty doctors in the city told him his friend would never again be able to— But just as my would-be screenplay soars to new heights, the lanky, silent one suddenly says, apropos of nothing, "Well, enough of this." And he gets up and walks out, leaving the round man with the restless knee to sit sipping his coffee, scanning the room for conversation. I hurriedly avoid eye contact.

Right about then, a pair of post-coital, post-party young'uns slouches in, groggy-eyed and with a full 7:00 a.m. surl on. The boy spots the cop and does a quick U-turn. Outside the window I can see them having a heated debate that ends in hands mutually flung upwards in exasperation, and an exchange of "Fine! Fine!" mouthed with clarity through the glass.

The sun has broken through, and it splinters in, painfully bright. The waitress at the counter is lit with an overexposed radiance as she moves about, pouring coffee and cracking wise. From the haze a familiar figure appears.

"Ian," I say.

He sits down at the counter, heaves a noise somewhere between a sigh and a growl, mutters something under his breath. It's unusual to see him so cranky—cranky, yes, but not *so* cranky.

"You left the light on in the washroom," he says. "Back at the motel, with the door closed and the fan running."

"Did I?"

"I waited," he says. "And I waited. Was wondering what was taking you so long." He turns to the waitress. "Coffee, please."

"So how'd you find me?"

"Well," he says dryly, "there was an Institute of Fine Cooking, an Academy of French Cuisine, and this place." He looks around the diner, nods approvingly. "Process of elimination. You'd be an easy person to assassinate. Predictable."

Reasons you don't want my brother Ian to do you any favours:

"What day is it?"

He tells me.

"*Shit!* I'm supposed to do a phoner with a radio station in Vancouver. I have to call them"—I check the time, do the country-hopping time-zone conversion—"in four minutes. Damn."

"Relax, there's a phone booth out front. It's got a door and everything. Call from there."

I sigh. "I hate this. I know the host, I've been on before, he's one of those guys who has done no research whatsoever and just throws it over to you, expects you to carry the entire show for him. You end up interviewing yourself. I'm telling you, this is the last time I do his show. Period."

"So let me do it," Ian says.

"Tempting, but no."

"Why not? We're brothers. We sound more or less the same over the phone."

I think about his offer. "You'd take the interview for me?"

"What're families for?"

Like an idiot, I not only say yes, I even thank him before-hand.

Here is how the call goes:

Dave! How are you! Great to be on your show again. I've always said that CXJS is the finest radio station in the Pacific Northwest! In fact, I was just telling my brother Ian, who is considered by most to be the best-looking of the Ferguson boys, what an honour and, yes, a privilege, it is to speak with you. Dave, anytime you want me to appear on this fine program of yours—[muffled sounds of me try-ing to wrestle the phone away from Ian]—and that's a promise! And if my brother Ian is out there somewhere lis-tening, I just want to say, "Ian, you have always been a role model for me." Everything I have, everything I've ever done, I owe to—[sound of Ian forcing the phone-booth door closed; muffled cries of *You bastard!* in the back-ground]—why yes, I'm glad you asked, Dave. I agree, brotherhood is important. And I have always looked up to Ian, the good-looking Ferguson, and have admired his quiet dignity and strong moral bearings.

So on and so forth, ad-bloody-nauseam. Ian gives me a big smile and a raised thumb.

"He wants you on his show again next week," he says, after he hangs up.

I simmer awhile in unexpressed rage but decide to let it go. After all, one of us has to take the high road, and it sure as hell isn't going to be Ian.

The two of us kick around town, meander past a Bibles for Missions Thrift Shop and the old Chatham Opera House with its impressive mansard roof, now housing a used furniture store.

"Hey, Ian," I say. "Remember your comic book collection? Remember that copy you had of Captain Canuck #1, limited edition?"

"By Richard Comely."

"The one that would be worth about a million bucks by now, except that Pruney cut out an order form for X-ray glasses in the middle of it? You remember that?"

"How can I forget?"

"Yeah, that wasn't Pruney who did that. That was me." I lick a finger, make a mark in the air. "Point and match."

Antique shops. A few vacant storefronts. Brick warehouses, ivy-clad, converted into shops and studios. And this being southern Ontario, Land of the Loyalists, there is a King Street and a Queen Street. That, and a Tim Hortons on every second corner. The Thames River cuts a grassy green path through the town. The sun is blazing—a hot surge of summer at season's end—and wasps are swarming around garbage bins in a final frenzy. We cross a canal, then wander through the park, past the curling club and the old armoury, a red-brick arrangement of faux-castle turrets.

"Canada," I say, "is like an old armoury. Am I right?"

"You are," says Ian.

"How so?" says I.

He stops. "Nice try."

Chatham is low and made of brick, with few buildings downtown rising higher than two floors, although several oversized church towers do muscle their way into the sky: the twin copper domes of St. Joseph's Roman Catholic Church; the First Presbyterian, with spires that look like smokestacks. And I think to myself, what a pleasantly unhurried place this is.

We wander into the Tasty Lunch Counter Café in the old section of Chatham. It's the narrowest squeeze of a diner. Just one extended counter, really, with swivel stools and wide-backed men hunched over their coffees and grilled cheese sandwiches.

"Have you ever noticed," I say to Ian, as he signals for a refill, "that whenever you and I take a trip together, we always end up spending most of our time in coffee shops?"

"Your point being?"

"We don't really seek out the art galleries or museums, ever notice that?"

"And?"

"I think we have to do this more often."

I unfold the accordion origami of our road map and begin plotting our route home. The entire trip has had the feeling of a shaggy-dog tale, a long loop that ends right back where it started. It's only now, as I ponder the possible paths of re-entry, that I realize how near we are to the town of Dresden. We must have skirted it on our way in last night; it's only a farm field or two away from Thamesville.

"Uncle Tom's Cabin," I say. "It's in Dresden. Want to go?"

"Sure, why not?" says Ian. Anything is better than trying to figure out what makes Canada tick. He finishes his coffee and gets to his feet. Uncle Tom's it is.

He didn't exist. Uncle Tom—the kindly old slave beaten to death in Harriet Beecher Stowe's melodramatic three-hanky tale—was a fictional character. But he was based on a real person: the Reverend Josiah Henson, who was born into slavery on a plantation near Port Tobacco, Maryland, in 1789. Henson's earliest memories, from the age of three or four, were of seeing his father bleeding from the head and back. His father's right ear had been cut off "near his head" and his back had been lashed until it was a bloody pulp, punishment for having struck a white man. Henson's father was sold to a plantation in Alabama soon after, and "Neither my mother nor I ever heard of him again," Henson recalled in his memoirs.

Henson was raised in slave shacks, with dirt floors and thin blankets. "In these hovels were we penned at night, and fed by day; here were the children born, and the sick—neglected."

As a teenager, Henson dragged his owner from a drunken brawl and, in doing so, knocked down a white overseer. Seething, the overseer and three other men later ambushed Henson and beat him with a fencepost. His arm was broken and both shoulder blades were shattered.

"I could feel and hear the pieces of my shoulder blades grate against each other with every breath," he recalled. "No physician or surgeon was ever called to dress my wounds."

The attack left Henson in pain for the rest of his life, and unable to lift his hands to his head. But by then, he had discovered his true calling: forgiveness and the gospel. He worked hard and eventually became an ordained minister, a slave who preached sermons about the children of Israel and their flight from captivity. He was a powerful orator, and through his work was able to save up enough money to buy his freedom—a rare feat. But just when his deliverance seemed at hand, he was betrayed by his owner, who pocketed the money and then attempted to sell Henson to a plantation in the Deep South. In 1830, after forty-one years as a slave, Josiah Henson decided to escape.

In Upper Canada (now Ontario), the importation of slaves had been abolished by Governor John Graves Simcoe in 1793. Though Simcoe's bill didn't set free existing slaves, it did halt any future trade. (Slavery had been a part of Canadian history since the days of New France, and even further back, among First Nations.) Simcoe's bill also made Ontario the first territory anywhere in the British Empire to legislate against slavery—and that includes Britain. By 1803, most blacks in Canada were free. And in 1833, when all forms of slavery were banned throughout British territories, Canada's stature as a northern sanctuary grew. Canada became a mythical place to slaves in the American South. You had only to find the Big Dipper in the night sky and then follow the North Star to freedom.

Estimates of the number of slaves who escaped to Canada range as high as 60,000, though the most likely number seems to be around 30,000. Faced with the sheer brutality of the slave trade, a network of human decency took shape—a secretive relay of safe houses. Started largely by American Quakers and dubbed the Underground Railroad, it helped smuggle runaways to the "cold heaven" of Canada. The journeys were conducted in code. The safe houses were "stations," the fugitive slaves were "passengers," the people who guided them were "conductors." Even the hymns the slaves sang on southern plantations were laced with hidden meanings. "Israel" referred to the blacks, yearning for freedom. "Egypt" referred to the American slave states, and "pharaohs" to the slave owners. "Canaan," the land promised to Abraham, was Canada, and the underground network itself was "a sweet chariot." To "swing low" was to come down south, and "carry me home" meant an escape to freedom. The slaves even had their own saviour, whom they dubbed "the Black Moses": a fearless woman named Harriet Tubman, who established her base of operations in St. Catharines. Having escaped slavery herself along the Underground Railroad, Tubman returned to the Deep South on at least nineteen occasions, often in disguise, carrying forged papers and armed with a pistol, to guide others to freedom. As many as 300 fugitives—men, women, children—were led to Canada by Harriet Tubman. Slave owners in the South put a $40,000 price on her head, but no one ever collected. (During the U.S. Civil War, she would join the Union Army as a nurse, a scout and a spy.)

Although the northern U.S. states had abolished slavery, the threat of bounty hunters was very real. Only Canada offered full protection. And so, on a moonless night in September 1830, Josiah Henson, his wife and their four young children joined this clandestine migration; they caught the chariot and slipped away. Henson and his wife were on a plantation in Kentucky, and they set off northwards, following the star. It took six weeks to reach freedom. They stayed at safe houses and at one point were sheltered and fed by Native Americans on a forest trail. It was a gruelling trek, and the family often went without food for days at a time. But eventually they reached Lake Erie, where a sympathetic riverboat captain smuggled them downriver to Buffalo, New York, and then paid their passage on a ferryboat to Canada, giving them some money as well. When they finally reached Canadian soil, Josiah threw himself on the ground and rolled in the dirt, laughing so loudly that a passerby thought he was having a seizure. "I am free," Henson said. "I am free."

Once the initial elation passed, reality set in. "I was a stranger in a strange land," Henson recalled. "I knew nothing about the country or the people."

Escaped slaves had introduced widespread tobacco cultivation throughout the region. Indeed, they had a virtual monopoly on tobacco, using skills they had acquired in the American South. (The tobacco fields of southern Ontario are, even today, a tangible reminder of the region's role as a terminus of the Underground Railroad.) Henson, however, recognized the weakness in relying on a single cash crop, and from his pulpit he urged the farmers to diversify. He called upon the black community to invest their earnings in land of their own, "where," in his words, "every tree which we felled, and every bushel of corn we raised, would be for ourselves; in other words, where we could secure all the profits of our own labour."

In 1841, with the support of a Quaker benefactor and a Boston abolitionist, and backed by donations from England, Josiah Henson arranged for the purchase of 200 acres of rich farmland and forest along the Sydenham River, near what is now Dresden. Henson secured a further 100 acres soon after, and the Dawn Settlement was founded: a community of free blacks, with a school, a church, a sawmill, a blacksmith shop and a gristmill. The economic engine of the community was timber—the first shipment of the black walnut lumber produced at Dawn was, ironically, exported to the United States—but the cultural centrepiece was the British American Institute, one of Canada's first vocational schools.

Henson made many perilous trips deep into the slave states of the American South to shepherd others to freedom, more than 100 slaves in all. His autobiography, *The Life of Josiah Henson, Formerly a Slave, Now an Inhabitant of Canada*, was published in 1849, and Harriet Beecher Stowe would later name it as one of the key sources she drew upon for her own abolitionist tale, *Uncle Tom's Cabin*. Stowe's novel became a volcanic bestseller that required seventeen printing presses running constantly just to keep up with demand. Translated into thirty-seven languages and considered by many to be the most influential novel of all time, *Uncle Tom's Cabin* ignited an international outcry with its depiction of the cruelty of the slave trade. Abraham Lincoln credited the novel with having helped to spark the American Civil War.

Sleepy Chatham, as it turns out, is swirling in history. It was once both a centre of the anti-slavery movement and a stewpot of racism. At its peak in the 1860s, Chatham's black community made up a full one-third of the city's population. Chatham was also a city riven by tensions and turmoil. It had once been home to Mary Ann Shadd, a publisher of the anti-slavery *Provincial Freeman* and the first black newspaper-woman in North America. (During the Civil War Shadd became a Union Army recruiter, and later, at age sixty-one, a lawyer based in Washington, D.C.) John Brown, the deluded but idealistic anti-slavery crusader whose body "lies a'moldering in the grave," came to Chatham in 1858 to drum up support for an attack on the U.S. arsenal at Harpers Ferry, Virginia. The guerrilla raid, launched the following year, was designed to strike a spark in a tinderbox, to trigger a war of liberation. Two Canadians joined John Brown's small army: a black resident of Chatham, who survived the battle, and another man, white, who did not. The shots fired in the failed attack on Harpers Ferry were, in many ways, the open-ing volleys in the apocalyptic war between the states that ignited eighteen months later. John Brown became a martyr, hanged for treason, "but his truth goes marching on."

Below the city of Chatham is the village of North Buxton, which was the site of the Elgin Settlement, founded in 1849 by the Irish-born, Scottish-educated Reverend William King. A level-headed utopia, the Elgin Settlement (also referred to as Buxton Mission) evolved into a disci-plined, self-supporting community of 2000 citizens, almost all of whom had arrived in Canada via the Underground Railroad. In contrast to the vocational skills that students developed at Dawn, the school at Elgin offered a classical education, and it was soon attracting white students as well,

from Ontario and the United States. There was a waiting
list, and the school proved so popular among parents in the
area that the local public school was eventually shut down.
(A similar situation had occurred in Brantford a few years
earlier; when black children were refused entry to the public school, the town's small black community built their own
school instead. It offered such a high level of instruction
that many whites began petitioning to send their children
there, too.)

The Elgin Settlement, with its well-educated children,
its thriving sawmill and its profitable brickworks, was in its
day the most prosperous black community in North America.
But here, as at Dawn and Chatham, a surprising reverse
migration occurred once the Civil War ended and emancipa-
tion was declared. Blacks in Canada began returning to the
United States. Most of them had left family members and
friends behind. Many felt a responsibility to carry the trades
and skills they had acquired back to the South to help with
the reconstruction.

Many of the original refugees did remain in Canada,
though, and North Buxton is inhabited by the descendents
of these first black settlers. Dawn is no more, but the town
of Dresden, founded by a lumber merchant in 1845, still
has a small black population. And although villages like
North Buxton are the true heirs of the original "flight to
freedom," it is Dresden, home of the fictitious Uncle Tom's
Cabin, that has become the focal point of today's black
pilgrimage route. Convoys of tour buses from the American
South rumble north to the town, following the trail of the
Underground Railroad.

It is into this context that Ian and I have aimlessly wandered.

• • •

Cornfields the colour of tobacco. Tobacco fields the colour of corn. Greens and golds and burnished browns. Old barns, blood red. Houses, pure white. Birds arranged on telephone wires like musical notes.

The road from Chatham is not a long one, and we are in Dresden before we know it. Maple trees, the leaves reddish-orange, line the streets, and we take a slow drive through the village. My dad used to say you could tell a lot about a place by the number of fences you saw. There are very few fences in Dresden.

We park the car near the clock tower of Dresden's town hall, a solid rod-and-brown brick presence in the heart of things, and we stroll the main drag, which takes all of four minutes. Downtown is a single block, basically. The local Stedman's store is offering "Straw brooms. $6: For curling or housekeeping," and the cars honk at each other not in anger but to say hello. Acclimatized to cities, Ian and I keep spinning around, expecting to see a near miss or an impending five-car pileup. No such luck.

A tractor rolls through town. A dog sleeps in the middle of a side street, and a pickup truck gingerly drives around it. We walk down St. George Street, across the bridge and over the Sydenham River. But no matter which direction we take, we soon run out of village. The streets simply end and the cornfields begin.

Turning back, we come upon a gaggle of students, in mixed hues and shades, who are hanging out in front of a convenience store, speaking in that listless teenager way. Lots of "y'knows" and "likes"—entire conversations full, in fact. "It was, like, completely—you know." "I know, it's like—you know." These bons mots are followed by nods of agreement all round. (Was I that inarticulate as a teenager? I seem to remember me and my peers exchanging banter worthy of the Algonquin Round Table.) They are nice enough kids, though. When we ask them for directions to Uncle Tom's Cabin they perk up and talk in competing voices. Some even helpfully point to the large sign we are standing in front of that says *Uncle Tom's Cabin, This Way!*

"Far?" we ask.

"Oh, no," they assure us. "Museum's not far at all."

Museum?

"It's got, like, displays and stuff."

Museum?

"We take field trips there—y'know, like when there isn't enough money to go to a real place. Good museum, though."

Museum?

History, I like. Museums, not so much. History is compelling. Important. But museums? I walk into a museum and within minutes I want to leave. Perhaps it's their dedication to taxidermy, items pinned like butterflies. Perhaps it's the strained attempts at being fun (in the newer ones) or the stifling stillness (of the older ones), but to me they always seem—oh, what's the word I'm looking for—*awful*.

History is not contained in museums; it lies in layers all around us. Consider the "ghost signs" of Dresden: on the side of a building on Centre Street you can still see faint lettering that once read SMOKE SHAMROCK TOBACCO. But with many of the letters having faded out of existence, it has now become *Smoke sham toba*. A picture of an Irish shamrock provides the clue to *sham*. The first word lets you fill in the last one. But take that wall down and put it inside a museum, and it immediately loses its vitality. I have seen the same thing happen to totem poles on the West Coast.

From the 1890s right up until the fifties, Canada's commercial signs were painted directly onto brick walls and barns. Most of these have peeled away into nothingness; some appear only after a rain, emerging like an afterimage on a photographic plate. On others, several layers of lettering blend into each other. There are ghost signs in Moose Jaw and there are ghost signs in Dresden. It is history on the sides of buildings, history as palimpsest.

In Dresden, some of these ghost signs have been repainted, which seems a sacrilege of some sort. One such restored message, on the side of the old Dresden Creamery, reads *Premiums Payed for Milk Fed Chickens*. And below that:

■ Deal Year ●

Get it? Neither did I, not at first. It takes much mulling over before, in a minor eureka moment, it suddenly clicks. I call Ian over. "Five bucks says you can't—"

"A square deal, year round," he says.

"—tell me when that sign was painted. Give up? Ha! No—no, I don't know either, but that's not the point. Buy me dinner and we'll call it even."

And so, as if under the control of a post-hypnotic suggestion, Ian and I once again end up in a booth at a coffee-shop
café, where we settle ourselves in to squander yet another
evening of our rapidly disappearing lives. This café is on St.
George Street, and it's called the Copper Kettle or the Iron
Griddle or the Brass Bucket. A very friendly place. With very
friendly service. Our waitress is cornfed and all smiles, and
she deals us our menus as though they are a pair of oversized
playing cards. Though I don't know why she bothers with
menus, because she has, in her cheerful way, already decided
for us. "Try the hogslop," she says, beaming.

Ian and I exchange glances.

"You're telling us we should try the hogslop."

"Oh yes, it's very good."

Okay. "Two hogslops."

Turns out hogslop is not a communal practical joke played
by Dresdenians on hapless outsiders. Nor is it an actual *slop
à la hogs*. No, hogslop—a Dresden speciality, it seems—is a
churned mix of potatoes, bacon, ham and onions. It has the
texture and aroma of, well, hogslop. But it tastes mighty fine
(potato, bacon, ham, onions: how can you go wrong?), even if
the effect that follows it is not unlike how one might feel after
consuming a half-sack of wet cement.

"Urp," says I.

"Eep," Ian agrees.

"It is, isn't it?" she says, conversant in the language of
stuffed bellies.

The tables fill up, empty, fill up again. Ebb and flow.
Night falls. The waitress tops up our coffee. Again. At the
next table, they are speaking at length about a barn that

went up in flames the week before. Ten acres of tobacco, $60,000 in harvest—gone. "Smoke blew across the roads. Entire area reeked of cigarettes. That was the smell of profits going up."

It's strange to think, but in Dresden, neighborhood cafés like this one were once a battle zone. The simple pleasure of whiling away time at a coffee shop was once a point of racial demarcation.

Dresden is a town with a dark segregationist past. Generations of blacks grew up being barred from restaurants, barbershops, social clubs, the hotel and even some churches. It got so bad and so nasty that in the late 1940s, Dresden's black community organized a formal political campaign aimed at ending racial exclusion in their town. They took as their point of departure the recent United Nations Universal Declaration of Human Rights. Article One: "All human beings are born free and equal in dignity and rights." The key architect of the U.N. declaration was a Canadian, John Humphrey. In Dresden, when a town plebiscite was held calling on restaurant owners "to serve patrons regardless of race, creed or colour," it was voted down, 517 to 108. From there, the battle was carried to the provincial legislature and into the courts. Hard-won anti-discrimination bills were eventually passed in the 1950s and, though hard to enforce, they were evidence that the tide had turned—in Dresden and elsewhere. This small Ontario town, along with the city of Chatham, led the way in the fight for equality, and even though segregated schools in some areas of Canada lasted into the 1960s, that era is almost ancient history. It has faded into memory like sham tobacco on the side of a building. The high-school students in front of the convenience store were a mix of brown and beige and pink. And today, the cafés of Dresden will serve hogslop to anyone brave enough to order it.

We almost don't make it to the cabin.

Dresden, we discover, has a racetrack on the edge of town, where harness racing is the featured event, and Ian and I consider playing the ponies instead. Y'know, raking in a windfall, retiring to the Bahamas, that sort of thing. But it is picking away at us—the end of our shaggy-dog story—and having changed motels in Chatham (a lateral move, as it turns out), we return to Dresden.

Historians have challenged the notion that Stowe's melo-drama was inspired by Josiah Henson's life, and have questioned whether Stowe was even aware of Henson's story when she was working on *Uncle Tom's Cabin*. But the level of evidence they are demanding seems unusually picky to me. Henson and Stowe did become close friends, and Stowe herself drew direct parallels between Uncle Tom and Josiah Henson. Sadder still, the term "Uncle Tom" has since taken on negative, minstrel-show connotations of subservient blacks kowtowing to whites, which is unfortunate, because it undermines the triumph that was Josiah Henson's life. He was no caricature, and his achievements were real.

Uncle Tom's Cabin outside of Dresden is neither Uncle Tom's, nor is it a cabin. It is the Josiah Henson family home, modest but stately. It is not a museum, but a pocket of the past preserved. The Interpretive Centre out front has iron collars and manacles and coiled whips on display, which would be lurid if it weren't that actual events were even worse—almost unimaginably so. If anything, the displays are remarkably understated, all things considered. But the truly evocative space lies beyond the Interpretive Centre, in the small gathering of restored buildings behind: the church, the Henson house, the home of another former slave and a recreated sawmill that spices the air with the scent of cedar and sawdust.

The buildings creak with history. They have been brought together here, on land that was part of the original Dawn Settlement. The cornfields come right to the edge of the yard, making it feel as though we are standing at the bottom of a small lake. The tops of old barns and farmhouses peer from above, like islands in the tidal green.

Inside this clearing in the corn stands a church from the 1850s, with weathered walnut siding the colour of driftwood, and square handmade nails. Inside is the simple tongue-and-groove pulpit from which Josiah Henson preached. Here Henson would have summoned up tales of slavery and freedom, of a Promised Land and a journey through the wilderness. The floor of the church creaks, shifting underfoot, as we walk across it.

The exterior planks of the church's board-and-batten construction are knotted and dry, but the wood is soft to the touch. The grain is like a fingerprint. Beside the church is the Henson home. Weathered frames and old windowpanes, the glass wavy and rippled with age. Musty rooms, faint familiar smells: corn silk and cured tobacco.

The Dawn Settlement and others like it—such as the Wilberforce Settlement, established near present-day Lucan back in 1829—began as havens but eventually outlived their mandates, and as the black community moved into mainstream society, these communal outposts faded away. Dawn in particular was racked by financial woes—lawsuits and countersuits flew back and forth (free men exercising their rights in the eyes of the law), and in the end the community disbanded. The assets were sold and the funds donated to a school in Chatham. Some of Dawn's pioneers returned south after the Civil War ended. Many more moved on to other areas of southern Ontario, Chatham in particular, where their contributions to the business and agricultural communities were second to none.

I talked about this with Brenda Lambkin, a soft-spoken woman who believes her family may have first come to Canada via the Underground Railroad. Records are murky, and understandably so. The baying bloodhounds and midnight crossings weren't conducive to careful record-keeping. But genealogies are slowly being reclaimed, and places like North Buxton, Chatham and Dresden have become key destinations for black Americans tracing their family trees.

Brenda Lambkin estimates the black community in Dresden today at about 150 people in a town of some 2700. "It's very close knit. Everyone knows each other," she says. "There is a lot of intermarriage between blacks and whites. The kids don't much look at colour any more." The segregationist years are behind them, and the problems facing Dresden, like those facing small towns everywhere, are economic. "I have four kids, two boys, two girls," she says. "And they've all moved to the city."

Would *she* ever consider making the trek to the bright lights of, say, Windsor or London? "Oh, no," she says with a laugh. "I'm a farm girl. I live just down the road from here, about five miles down on Twelfth Concession. My husband is a minister with the Baptist Church. He preaches out of Shrewsbury."

She looks across towards the church and the Henson home and the cornfields beyond.

"I like it here," she says. "Peaceful."

Josiah Henson's fame grew, and so closely equated with the character of Uncle Tom did he become that he was sometimes accused of being an imposter simply because he was still alive. "I read that book," readers would say, challenging him. "And Uncle Tom died in the end! So how could you be Uncle Tom?"

In his eighties, Josiah Henson, former slave, was invited to England for an audience with Queen Victoria. "Mr. Henson," the Queen said, "I expected you to be a very old man, but I am delighted to see you are well preserved and good-looking." Henson smiled and said, "My Sovereign, that is what all the ladies say."

From there, Henson travelled to Washington, D.C., to meet President Hayes. After the reception, he continued by carriage to the plantation where he had been born. It was just twenty kilometres away from the White House. The fields were overgrown and the buildings were tumbling into ruin. Hensen's former master had long since died, and the widow was now tending the fading estate on her own. She greeted Henson in a shabby sitting room.

"How do you do, madam?" Henson asked.

"I am poorly—poorly. I don't seem to know you."

Then the flicker of recognition, the startled introduction. "Can it be? Si?" she asked, using his old nickname. "Si Henson?" Looking closer, she said, "Why, look at you. You are a gentleman."

"Ma'am," he replied, "I always was."

Josiah Henson died in 1883 at the age of ninety-three and is buried in the Henson family cemetery, which is now beside the Uncle Tom's Cabin Interpretive Centre. A second burial ground, that of the British American Institute, lies across a gravel road. It contains headstones dating back to 1866, the height of the American Civil War. I walk among the epitaphs and etchings of one graveyard, then the other, past the clouded marble, the doves and lambs and fingers pointing heavenwards. *He's gone, beloved and cherished one, like some bright star he passed away,* reads one headstone. *In silence all lie sleeping here,* reads another.

I find Ian standing beside Josiah Henson's grave. He is reading the inscription and barely notices when I sidle up beside him. "Well," I say, expecting a quip or a wry comment on how far we've driven and how far we still have to go to get home. "What do you think?"

A wind is moving through the corn, swaying the stalks. The air is dusty, the sky an impossible blue. "I don't know what I expected," Ian says. "But I didn't expect this. I didn't expect it to be so moving."

We have inherited an easy life in Canada. A life of calm. It is freedom of a lazy sort, a freedom so pervasive we barely notice it, and one that we claim by virtue of our citizenship. But it is also worth remembering that people—in the words of Bulgarian-born Canadian philanthropist Ignat Kaneff— "crawl across minefields to get here."

When Ian and I started out on our trip, we joked about escape, about freedom. Our choice of words now seems inappropriate. Or maybe not. We also told ourselves that we were searching for Canada. Perhaps we have found it here, or at least caught a glimpse of it. Something elusive, yet always there—faint, but persistent. A whisper. A yearning.

Canada is more than a canoe route after all. Canada is a road trip. And like any road trip worthy of the name, it is ultimately about freedom in its purest form.

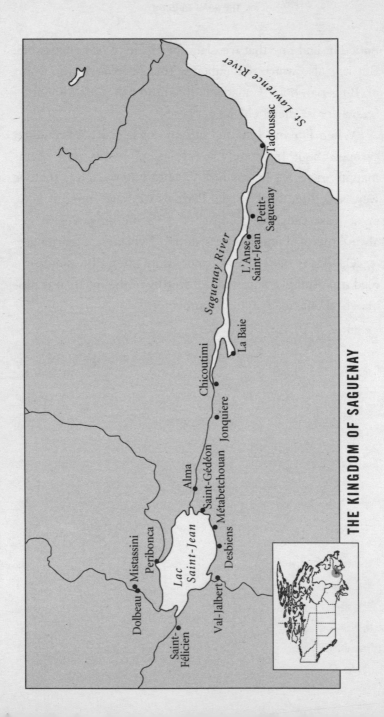

THE KINGDOM OF SAGUENAY

chapter seven

THE LOST KINGDOM

HALFWAY ACROSS THE RIVER, and the landscape simply . . .
disappears. First one shore and then the other, dissolving into
mist, until nothing is left save for a glowing whiteness.

Here at the mouth of the Saguenay River, great currents
collide. The deep-running Saguenay empties into the St.
Lawrence, forcing fresh water up and over the colder briny
depths. Even when surface temperatures reach 20 degrees
Celsius, the lower levels can sit at almost zero. It is a recipe
for fog.

The ferry to Tadoussac acts like a floating piece of highway, a raft that shuttles us across the Saguenay. A cold
wetness hangs in the air; a cumulus cloud has enveloped us.
Passengers slip out of their cars and stand on the deck,
filling their chests with condensation. The boat gropes its
way along, sounding out the far side of the river with blasts
of its horn. Seagulls cry out, unseen. Someone is taking
photographs of the fog. With a flash. "*Regardez, là-bas, une
lumière.*" The air is growing heavier, and my glasses are peb-
bled with water. For a moment it feels as though we are lost
at sea.

There are three of us on this expedition: my older brother Sean, his nine-year-old daughter, Aidan—all arms and knees and laughter—and me. We have come in search of a kingdom.

Sean is the brother who rescued me from a career in minimum wage. He is older than me, younger than Ian. "I couldn't be more middle," he says of his position in the family. I followed Sean through school, and he had an annoying habit of finishing his homework and staying clear of trouble, which was a hard standard for me to meet. When Sean and I were very young, we figured out a way to get onto the roof of our house in Fort Vermilion. We stood there, peering over the edge. Would the lump of dirt below break our fall—or our legs? Sean leaned forward, studying the situation intently, trying to calculate distance, wind speed, rate of trajectory. Was it safe? There was only one way to find out. I pushed him off. *Whump.* There was a pause and then a voice—"Yup, it's okay." We spent the rest of the afternoon clambering up and leaping off. I think this story says a lot about Sean. Sean thinks this story says a lot about me.

Travelling with Sean is very different from travelling with Ian. Sean would never impersonate me for his own amusement. He doesn't smoke. He doesn't try to convince waitresses that I am suffering from a rare form of toxoplasmosis—which I'm not even sure is a real word. Even better, when Sean is driving, he actually glances at the road on occasion, and will usually make an effort to keep at least an index finger on the steering wheel.

Sean, Aidan and I have spent the last two days in a spiffy

new rent-a-car following the St. Lawrence River northeast from Montreal. Aidan has hunkered down in the back like a studious hamster, with a nest of pillows, blankets, books and snack wrappers around her. I am in charge of reading the maps and keeping us on track—not a hard task, I admit. "Just follow the river, Ishmael!" Follow the river.

It is good to be back in *la belle province,* where right turns on red are considered exotic, and the margarine is pale and gelatinous. (In Quebec, spreading margarine on your bread is akin to smearing it with Vaseline, the lack of colouring a result of restrictions argued into existence by Quebec's presumably all-powerful Butter Cabal.)

Quebec is synonymous for me with bewilderment and youth. I lived here first when I was nineteen, and then the following year, when I was not. The places where we shed our teenage years always retain a certain ambivalence in our memory, and so it is with Quebec for me. As a youth corps volunteer, I helped cut a trail through the woods at St-Canut. I worked on a dairy farm near Ste-Scholastique and then—briefly, fired almost upon arrival—at a ski resort in Mont-Tremblant. (Turned out they wanted someone who could (a) ski and (b) speak French—picky bastards.) I ended up in the Latin Quarter of Quebec City and, later, across the St. Lawrence in the town of Lévis. Long story. Buy me a beer and I'll cry into the glass for you. Suffice it to say, Quebec broke my heart like a hoofstrike on a china plate, and I don't think I have ever forgiven her for it.

Just when my Cro-Magnon French was finally coming together, I was accepted into an overseas work program, also volunteer (I am nothing if not astute when it comes to

financial management). I was sent to South America, where
I mashed up the French I had learned with rudimentary
Spanish. Then I went to Japan. By the time I returned to
Quebec, years later, I spoke a bizarre hybrid: *Sumimasen,
una cerveza s'il vous plaît.*

Sean is fluently bilingual, sliding between French and
English with an ease I envy. I do not speak French in front of
Sean. This is for the same reason I do not sing karaoke in public: if I'm going to exert that much effort for so little result, I
would prefer to do it with as few witnesses as possible. Before
Sean and Aidan joined me for the trip to Saguenay, I spent
several days in Montreal and Quebec City, cheerfully mangling
my way through French syntax. I take a Gordian knot approach
when it comes to grammar, and you could see clerks wincing in
pain as I spoke. They all but pleaded with me to stop, tears
welling up in their eyes. You ever want to negotiate a hostage
situation in Quebec, I'm your man. Send me in for a little
parley and the francophone miscreants will flee, hands over
bleeding ears.

Sean has been in Montreal since forever. He moved to the
island city with his wife, Sherry, to pursue a doctorate in music,
and they have stayed on, by turns captivated and beguiled and
maddened by the place. (A common combination, I've been
told.) All three of Sean and Sherry's children were born in
Quebec. This is the family's home now. And though he teaches
at McGill, Sean also works deep within the francophone music
community. He even dresses the part. He has a black leather
jacket, a black sweater, a black scruffy beard and increasingly
expressive hand gestures. He shrugs when I chide him about
this. "It's Montreal," he says. "It's music."

"Hey, I'm living in Calgary now, but you don't see me sauntering about in a Stetson and spurs."

He shrugs—again. A suspiciously *Gallic* shrug, I must say. Next thing you know, he will be smoking in elevators and trying to kiss me on both cheeks. I've been keeping an eye on Sean for some time, attuned to further danger signs, but so far so good. He has not transformed into a wild-eyed separatist citing a litany of humiliations and historical grievances, nor has he become that other dreaded extreme: the Angry Anglo, endlessly carping about minority rights and "oppression," as though he were living under a Stalinist regime.

"You'd almost think there was more to it than that," Sean deadpans. "You'd almost think it wasn't as cut and dried as the extremists on either side make it out to be."

Ah, but Quebec engenders extremes—even extreme neutrality. And politics in Quebec, to a degree greater than anywhere else in Canada (with the possible exception of B.C.), is a Theatre of the Absurd. It's like tumbling through the looking glass, where the Red Queen shrieks and "words mean exactly what we want them to mean." In Quebec, the distinction between *nation* (in the sense of a cultural and linguistic identity) and *state* (as a territorial entity that can include any number of nations) has become hopelessly blurred. The results are often comical and contradictory.

Here's just one example. The Cree and the Inuit in the northern half of the province, making the same arguments for ethnic sovereignty and "distinct status" employed by Quebec nationalists, have been insisting for years that the Québécois cannot force them out of Canada against their will—and certainly not by a simple show of hands. "Go if you want, but you aren't taking us with you" is the message that comes through. This might seem inconsequential save for one interesting fact: the ancestral lands of the Cree and the Inuit encompass the headwaters of Quebec Hydro, that proud nationalist institution. The one that flooded huge swaths of land, swamping ecosystems and drowning more than 10,000 caribou and poisoning the northern wetlands with methyl-mercury. Those guys.

French-speaking Québécois settled in the northern reaches of the province just forty years ago. Compare that to the 4000 years the Cree and the Inuit have been there. During Quebec's last divisive referendum, the Cree and the Inuit each held a referendum of their own, and the results were instructive: more than 95 percent of voters in each group chose to stay in Canada. The irony was sweet. Before it could even attain independence, the would-be glorious Free Republic of Quebec was facing an internal secessionist movement. Separatist leaders in the south sputtered and spewed, declaring Quebec's territorial integrity "sacred." A nation (linguistic and cultural) had magically become a state (territorial, cartographic), even though the borders of the two do not line up. It's a remarkable sleight of hand, that one. A game of three-card monte, a mix of fraud and finesse, played out on a national scale.

But the magic show has grown stale of late, and the carny cries have become fainter and fainter. On the way to Tadoussac, as we drive along the St. Lawrence, through Quebec City and out again, I mention the recent decline of the separatist threat to Sean. "Nice to have that knife taken away from our throats, eh?" I say.

"It's just a lull," he replies. "The separatist movement is never going to die, so we better get used to it."

"Yes, but—"

"We have to come to terms with it; we have to try to understand it."

"Understand it?" I say, scoffing at the suggestion. "How can anyone hope to understand something that's so funda-mentally and resolutely *irrational?* And this notion that 'Canada is divisible but Quebec is not.' What kind of screwy logic is that?"

"Irrational?" says Sean. "Of course it's irrational. *Passion* is irrational. Fear is irrational."

This is why there is no such thing as a rabid federalist. Federalism doesn't ignite the same intensity of emotions. You can't win an argument like this on reason alone. Alas. But I refuse to budge.

"Which is why you will never really understand Quebec," Sean continues. "You know your history, Will, I'll give you that. And you know the political framework behind it—but you don't understand the core of the matter."

I've heard similar alibis, similar claims of inscrutability from the Japanese. ("William-*sensei,* you can never know the True Heart of Japan." That sort of thing.) Sean is my big brother, and he may very well be right, but I'll be damned if I'll concede defeat graciously. "Stooge," I mutter.

"Redneck," he replies, with a grin.

"Are you fighting?" asks Aidan from the back seat.

"Not fighting," I say sweetly. "Just discussing why your father is wrong."

• • •

The Kingdom of Saguenay. *Royaume du Saguenay.* Canada's
own El Dorado, elusive, enticing, false.

The Kingdom of Saguenay started as a tall tale spun by
kidnapped Native guides for a credulous and grasping
Jacques Cartier. The French explorer arrived in the Gulf of
St. Lawrence in 1534, searching for a passage to the Orient,
and made contact with a band of Iroquoians led by Chief
Donnacona. Cartier planted a cross on Donnacona's land,
claimed the region for the King of France and—in the spirit
of friendship and good cheer—kidnapped two of the chief's
sons and spirited them back to Europe. While in captivity, the
young men told Cartier about a great river and a distant land
of unimaginable riches, a realm ripe for plunder. It was an
intoxicating story. Cartier and his men seemed destined to
become northern Conquistadors.

The following year, Donnacona's sons guided Cartier's
ships into the mouth of the St. Lawrence and towards their
village, their *kanata* (spelled "Canada" in Cartier's journals).
Jacques Cartier was the first European to enter the Rivière du
Canada, as the St. Lawrence would become known, and he
and his men pushed on as far as the palisaded Iroquoian city
of Hochelaga (at present-day Montreal), where they were
turned back by the Lachine Rapids. Not to fret. There was,
Cartier had been told, a second route to the kingdom: via the
fjord-like river he had sailed past on his way in, where the seaman had seen porcelain-white whales congregating in the
cold waters. It was the river that today bears the name of
the mythical kingdom of Saguenay.

Cartier and his men wintered near Donnacona's village,
where Quebec City is now located, and the stories their

Native hosts told grew more and more fanciful. Beyond the Kingdom of Saguenay—"where there are immense quantities of gold, rubies, and other rich things," Cartier wrote—there were other lands as well: one where people never ate because they had no anuses, and another where the entire population was one-legged and spent their days hopping about. Cartier dutifully inscribed all of this in his journals and—using decidedly selective judgment—concluded that the Kingdom of Saguenay was real.

Some historians have suggested that the legends of Saguenay may have been referring to the copper deposits inland at Lake Superior, but in the end it didn't matter. Cartier never found his passage to the Far East or his lost kingdom, and the precious ore and diamonds he brought back to France turned out to be fool's gold: iron pyrites, quartz, mica. This gave rise to an expression still used in France today: *Faux comme un diamant du Canada*. (As fake as a Canadian diamond.) Any diamonds in Canada were much farther north than Saguenay.

Cartier had given the name of a Catholic saint, Lawrence of Rome, to a small bay at the mouth of the Rivière du Canada, and this name was later extended to the waterway as a whole. Perhaps it was an omen. After all, Lawrence of Rome had been roasted alive by imperial soldiers for refusing to turn over a rumoured treasure trove.

The Saguenay region *was* rich—very rich. But not in rubies or gold. The river was a natural channel of the northern fur trade, and long before Europeans arrived, Native routes had been established along the waterways, from the St. Lawrence all the way to James Bay. Most of the early contact between Europeans and Natives took place at the mouths of rivers. "Since the Indian canoe could not put out to sea," historian Eric W. Morse writes, "nor the sea-going fishing craft venture far up a stream, river-mouth trading became in this area almost exclusively the rule."

Basque whalers had already staked out the Saguenay by the time Pierre Chauvin, a captain in the merchant marine, arrived from France. Chauvin had been granted a monopoly on the Canadian fur trade in 1599, and he built a small outpost at Tadoussac the following year. The Basques, from the borderlands between Spain and France, had their own distinct culture and language, and they were openly hostile to French colonization schemes. Today, the Basque nation is rife with separatists and prone to acts of political violence. Which is to say, not much has changed. In those early years, the Basques at Tadoussac plotted to assassinate Samuel Champlain, the "Father of New France," after he established a *habitation* at what is now Quebec City. When Champlain discovered the plot to kill him, he had the leading conspirator's head cut off and impaled on a pike outside the garrison walls.

Champlain may have founded New France in 1608, but the colony's roots first took hold here. Tadoussac lays claim to being the oldest European community in North America, which can sometimes irk the good people of Newfoundland and Mexico. (At which point the claim is usually amended to "the first European settlement on the *mainland* of North America *north* of Mexico," which doesn't have quite the same heft, even if it is more accurate.)

The St. Lawrence was a seaway, a highway, the geographic expression of the French colony. In many ways, the St.

Lawrence was New France. The colony followed the contours of the river, and this dictated a pattern of settlement that is even now distinctly Canadien, with narrow ribbon-like farms running back from the water and homes lined up near the water. The northern shore of the St. Lawrence soon came to resemble one long, extended village. And it's a village with one of the moodiest and most wildly changeable climates on earth.

As Taras Grescoe notes in his book *Sacré Blues*, Quebec is "lodged between an icebox and a kettle," and the St. Lawrence forms the dividing line, a thin wedge of water driven between the arctic chill of Hudson Bay and the tropical heat of the Gulf of Mexico. In the St. Lawrence Valley, cold fronts pushing down from one bay meet warm air masses flowing up from the other. The result: humid summers; torrential springs; short glorious autumns—and snow. Lots and lots of snow. The annual amount that falls here is among the highest anywhere, and this extends up the Saguenay and into the Lac-St-Jean basin. If Canada is the Great White North, then the St. Lawrence–Saguenay is its Snow Country.

"It's a heavy snow, as well," Sean assures me. "It's like shovelling wet cement."

No snow to deal with today, only fog. But the air is so thick we could probably shovel that. Our ferry bumps up to the dock, and the cars on board rumble to life and move forward at funeral speed, driving directly into nothingness; the pier has dissolved halfway, like a chalkboard drawing partially erased.

Tadoussac is up and over a hill. We roll slowly into the village, find a small inn, schlep our bags inside. On the roof of our inn is an enclosed widow's walk. In weather like this, the view from there must feel suffocating.

Aidan has been exceptionally well behaved. I think of how
Sean and I and our motley band of siblings acted on long
drives—"Mom! Darla's poking me!" "Mom! The dog threw up
. . . again." "Mom! Billy's looking at me!" "*Ow!* Am not!" "Am
too!" "Am so!" "Am are!!"—and wonder how any of us survived into adulthood. The temptation on our mother's part to
simply release us into the wild must have been almost
overpowering at times. No doubt Aidan's calm demeanour is
partly due to the fact that her little sister, Brynne, is not with
us—Aidan has had the entire back seat to herself, a dream of
non-singular children everywhere—but still. She's nine. It's
remarkable. "Are you feeling okay?" I ask her. "You're not sick
or anything?"

"Nope," she says. "This is fun."

Sean and Aidan settle in for a game of backgammon at a
small café, and I head out into the murky afternoon to explore
historic Tadoussac on foot. At times it feels more as though
I am swimming. This isn't fog, it is rain suspended.

I pass the local youth hostel. I can see the sign, but the
building itself is lost in the swirling grey; it is present only in
the sounds of the inevitable guitar, badly plucked. Spectral
tunes. Disembodied voices. Flashes of hormonally inflamed
laughter. I have long since left my hostel-jumping self behind;
I abandoned him beside a road many years ago, waiting for a
ride. And yet, the nostalgia is always there, and I fool myself
into thinking that I might be able to slip back in, unnoticed—
that I could once again sit in hostels drinking instant coffee
and strumming my youth away note by note.

As I continue down the street, more backpackers appear,
walking in and out of the fog, baggy denim, ratty hair, bodies

lit as though from within. A mother struggles uphill, pushing her toddler son in a stroller. She seems almost grateful for a reason to pause when I ask for directions to the Indian Chapel. (*Note to readers:* Insert horribly mangled French here.) She laughs, brushes back wet strands of hair from her face. Why, the church is just *there*. She points over my shoulder into the ether, past a graveyard. As I focus my gaze, I see the faint outline of a steeple.

I thank her in my *mercy buckets* way and then thread a path through the headstones and crosses, past the outstretched arms of a crucifix. Like something out of Hitchcock or Poe, a raven is sitting on one of the tombstones, shoulders hunched against the damp, calling into the emptiness. Another raven replies, and they caw at each other, back and forth. The red-roofed chapel is milky pink in the mist, and as I approach I hear the *whisk, whisk, whisk* of someone sweeping the front steps. A priestly caretaker in black robes. Wet leaves brushed aside. An easy smile. An open door. "*Merci*." Mercy.

The Indian Chapel is on the site of the original Catholic mission among the First Nations of the Saguenay. The founding Mass celebrated in Tadoussac was held on July 11, 1617, in a makeshift shelter. It is said the early priests used canoes turned upside down for an altar. Legend also has it that Louis Hébert, Canada's first true *habitant* (that is, a settler rather than a woodsman or whaler), took communion here. Today's chapel dates from 1747. It is the oldest surviving wooden church in Canada—possibly North America—and the interior is rough and unvarnished, as befits a religious outpost that was once at the farthest reaches of Christendom. The altar is ornate yet understated. It was carved by a Canadien-born carpenter,

with a motif of vine leaves and grapes, suggesting both wine
and the enduring miracle of transubstantiation. Wine into
blood: the conversion of the everyday into the holy. During the
Quiet Revolution of the 1960s, Quebec jettisoned many of its
religious traditions, but the resonance of Catholic ritual
remains, even if the province's churches now sit half-empty.

I squint up at the chapel's tiny Stations of the Cross,
ink-on-paper depictions just a few inches in size. Farther
along the wall is a painting of the Christ Child, snatched from
the flames of an Acadian church burned to the ground by the
British in 1755. The canvas has the texture of cracked denim
and is painted in the "naive" style, meaning "poorly rendered":
the child's eyes don't quite line up, and his hands seem to be
one finger short of ten. Behind the tabernacle is another
Christ Child, this one a wax figurine with eyes of glass and a
richly embroidered robe. Its gaze isn't lined up properly either.
Is there is a Saint of Corrective Lenses, I wonder. Our Lady of
the Poor Depth Perception? A Church of the Lazy-Eye Jesus,
perhaps? At which point I am struck by lightning. Repeatedly.

As I step back outside, the streetlights are blinking on,
hazy globes in the falling dusk. I follow the boardwalk from
the church past the famous red roof of the Hotel Tadoussac
and down to Pierre Chauvin's reconstructed trading post,
built not far from its original foundations. And thus, in this
short span, I have encompassed three of Tadoussac's historic
lifelines: furs, the church and tourism. Four, if you count the
wooden planks I am walking along.

The "three fs" of early Canadian history—fish, furs, and
forests—were also played out in Tadoussac, in that order.
From fishing cove to lumber town and now tourist village,

Tadoussac has constantly reinvented itself along current market trends.

Hotel guests are promenading along the boardwalk above the St. Lawrence, admiring a view of . . . absolute pale. The great river lies hidden in a heavy cloudbank, but you can *feel* its presence: large currents moving past unseen, the taste of salt water in the air. If every town has its own soundtrack, Tadoussac's is one of foghorns and the low tuba of ferries, always there in the background. It gives the place a certain melancholy mood, just as the plaintive, drawn-out note of a freight train will in a prairie town.

Then the fog lifts, and the harbour appears like a Polaroid developing before my eyes. A curve of beach begins to extend into the distance in a slow arc. A sailboat appears, and then another. A group of Gore-Tex travellers takes shape a few metres below me. They are sitting in a scrum around a small, wistful fire. "There you are!" they say to each other, only half in jest. As the air clears they scramble, gathering up their life jackets, dousing the fire. The game is afoot. Or rather, a-fin.

The white whales that Jacques Cartier first spotted 500 years ago are with us still. They are belugas, a lost tribe, orphans from the arctic seas that took a wrong turn and fol-lowed the Labrador current into a cul-de-sac. Like those at Churchill, the belugas here gather at the mouth of a river that empties into salt tides. Competing currents and temperatures mean the water at the mouth never freezes over, even in the depths of winter. It is rich in plankton and krill—a regular baleen buffet. This attracts whales, which in turn attracts tourists, which in turn attracts souvenir shops. It's the circle of life.

Whaling expeditions still depart from Tadoussac, with Basque harpoons replaced by Zodiacs that skim the waves like police pursuit vehicles. Finbacks, humpbacks, pilot whales, minke, porpoises, seals and even the rare blue whale, largest creature on earth, all gather here. But it is the bone-white belugas, so vocal, so sociable, that are most beloved. They are also, sadly, the single most polluted sea mammals in the world. "Think of the Great Lakes as a giant toilet," a marine biologist once told me, "and the St. Lawrence as the pipe that flushes it out into the ocean."

I've been reading up on the plight of the belugas, and though it appears that things have improved in recent years, the outlook is still sombre. The white whale of the St. Lawrence, with its Mona Lisa smile and alabaster curves, has the highest cancer rate of any wild animal on earth. Fewer than 660 belugas remain in the St. Lawrence, from a population that was once more than 5000. Calves poisoned by their mother's milk, or in the womb, wash up on shore with alarming regularity. The main culprit appears to be not the St. Lawrence but the Saguenay, and the toxic runoff from the many aluminum smelters along its shores. *Suggested tourist motto for Tadoussac:* See the belugas— while you still can. Public awareness can only help, and whale-watchers like those on the beach below may be the belugas' last hope.

"Okay. Do we have everything?" The Gore-Tex brigade hustles towards the dock and the pursuit vehicle that lies waiting, and then . . . as smoothly as it emerged, the harbour again disappears. Slow fade to white. The arc of the bay. The sailboats. The whalers, running. Gone.

Back at the Tadoussac café, Aidan is beating Sean at backgammon, using complicated calculations that render any move my brother attempts to make null and void. Aidan laughs, having won four in a row. "Ha!" she says. Sean absorbs both the defeat and the fluidity of the Rules According to Aidan with admirable patience. He sees me. I am standing near the door, rain jacket open and hair dripping, as I rub my fogged glasses on a damp pull of shirt.

"So," he says, "did you find your kingdom?"

I hold my glasses away from me, squint through them, rub the lenses again. "I think so. I'm not sure."

We wait out the weather in our widow's walk inn. When the skies clear for a few hours one afternoon, we take in some of Tadoussac's finer homes—"cottages," as they are referred to: private residences, many of them tucked out of sight, but well worth skulking about to see.

The present community in Tadoussac dates from the 1830s, when a series of sawmills was built in the region. William Price—industrialist, entrepreneur, capitalist trailblazer—established the first mill, systematically stripping the heights of the great white pine trees that Jacques Cartier had described in his journals. If ever there was a "King of the Saguenay" and a royal family, it was William Price and his sons. When historians speak of the dark days of Anglo rule, a time when the English-speaking minority controlled 80 percent of the wealth and kept the French-speaking Catholics in their place —an era of economic apartheid that Quebec's nationalists have yet to forgive—they are referring to men such as the aptly named Price.

In fairness, the Price family did open up the Saguenay–Lac-St-Jean region, and they contributed heavily to the local economy. Many of Tadoussac's finest buildings date to the days of Price and the lords of lumber. They weren't villains, after all; they were businessmen. (And no, the two terms are *not* interchangeable.) Timber made the town; tourism followed. The magnificent "Great White Fleet" of what would become the Canada Steamship Lines was soon running river cruises to the "Kingdom of Saguenay." A hotel opened to cater to these passengers, touting both freshwater and saltwater therapeutic baths, "of great virtue for curing dyspepsia." The Price family formed their own Tadoussac Hotel and Sea Bathing Company to cater to the newly minted leisure class, and many of Tadoussac's most scenic homes were originally built as summer villas: Fletcher Cottage, the Bailey House, O'Neil, Tudor-Hart, even the wonderfully well-named Ferguson House (though no relation, alas; I checked).

The names attached to these simple yet elegant abodes are revealing, for Tadoussac was the playground for Anglo elites, with more than a whiff of the raj about it. When Lord Dufferin, the Governor General of Canada, chose Tadoussac as the site for his summer residence, the village's status was assured. It became, in the words of author Yves Ouellet, "the focus of the northeastern aristocracy." Even today, *les Anglais* form their own summer sub-culture, a village-within-a-village whose most visible signs are a noted aloofness, a fondness for tennis and a Protestant chapel.

On our final day in Tadoussac, Sean, Aidan and I make the trek out to the sandy plateau and sage-grass dunes of Moulin-Baude, where blond cliffs several stories high slant steeply into the St. Lawrence. In its day, Moulin-Baude was a self-contained village, with a lumber mill and farmhouses and garden meadows. But the mills ate the forests, the soils eroded and the farms were abandoned. That's one version of events. Another is of a more Biblical nature. The village at Moulin-Baude, it is whispered, was once a drunken, rowdy place, filled with wanton dancing and general debauchery. The sacrilegious ways of the people angered the local priest to such an extent that he threatened them with a curse: if they did not cease, he would turn their land into a desert. The townspeople decided, in their danceful manner, to ignore him.

From the top of this wall of sand, the far shore of the St. Lawrence is a quilt-work of burnt orange and russet. A few wisps of yesterday's mist are caught in the forests, like tufts of sheep's wool snagged on a hedgerow. The sun hits the water, and the river shines like a polished tabletop.

The dunes of Moulin-Baude are easy enough to walk down; you simply let gravity tumble you along, rivulets of sand sliding before you with every step. Coming back is harder. Hands on knees pushing against pliant ground, steps half-sinking: it's like trying to run in deep snow. Aidan skips lightly across the surface; Sean and I plod up behind.

Out of breath back at the top, we turn and look out across the St. Lawrence, where a giant freighter is turning as though on a pivot. It is preparing to plunge into the Saguenay, into the Kingdom.

• • •

Travelling through Canada in 1913, shortly before the out-
break of the First World War, the English poet Rupert Brooke
dubbed the St. Lawrence "the most glorious river in the
world." The Saguenay, however, unnerved him. He found it
gloomy and almost sinister, a "Stygian imagination of Dante."
Rock meets water here as cleanly as a knife blade might. No
sandy transitions, no gently sloping shoreline. "There are no
banks," Brooke wrote, " . . . only these walls, rising from the
water to the height of two thousand feet."

At the mouth of the Saguenay, where swirling eddies
and hidden reefs create some of the most turbulent tides
anywhere, Brooke decided to go for a swim. He almost
drowned in the process. "The current was unexpectedly
strong," he wrote. "And it was cold as death. Stray shreds of
the St. Lawrence water were warm and cheerful. But the
current of the Saguenay, on such a day, seemed unnaturally
icy." He pulled himself away, scrambled onshore and ran
through the woods back to his hotel, shivering and grateful
to be alive. Rupert Brooke survived the Saguenay only to die
less than two years later in the Great War—arguably a more
romantic demise than being sucked under by the cold
waters of Canada.

The Saguenay River, one of the deepest in the world, is
better classified as a fjord: a long, steep-sided estuary that
feeds fresh water into salt. It is a cleft in the Precambrian
rock, gouged out by glaciers, and two kilometres wide at
places. Rising above it, in fists of rock, are Cap Trinité and
Cap Éternité—the unknowable and the unimaginable—
which earn their names with sheer drops of 350 metres each.
They are Canada's answer to the Pillars of Hercules. On the

ferry back from Tadoussac, looking straight down the cannon barrel of the Saguenay, we can see the headlands lined up. But we will approach Eternity from a different angle than did England's poet prince. We drive off the ferry and onto the modern equivalent of a river, a highway that rises and falls, over the headlands, into the valleys.

"We are voyageurs!" I say. "Except that we don't have canoes. Or paddles."

"Or furs," Sean says.

"But other than that—we are *exactly* like voyageurs."

The towns of the Saguenay are nestled in—wedged in, in some cases—the coves and gaps between rounded cliffs. It is autumn, and the hills are burning. With each rise in the road, smouldering golds and cold embers of red are layered into the distance. Vibrant pastels, if such a thing is possible. What the Québécois call "the symphony of fire."

These are the forests of the Laurentian mountains, and they remind me of my pencil crayons in grade school. The company that made the pencils was named for these mountains; the package often featured a Quebec valley in autumn. We have fallen into the picture on the pencil-crayon box, and it is so throat-catchingly beautiful that Sean veers to the side of the road so we can get out and just, well, *stare*.

When Margaret Laurence moved from Manitoba to southern Ontario, nothing had prepared her for the sight of blazing hardwood maples. The colours are so different from those of the prairie maples, the birch, the aspen, all predominantly yellow when their leaves change. "These scarlet flames of trees," she wrote, "a shouting of pure colour like some proclamation of glory, have to be seen to be believed. . . .

I could see why the Group of Seven was so obsessed with trying to get it down."

Lakes and ponds are pooled among the trees, their surfaces reflecting the forest in a pointillist rendition. Farmlands, coaxed from the forest. Cattle at pasture, breathing steamy clouds. And the tin-topped farmhouses, roofs sloped hard against the coming snow. Autumn in Canada is always slightly ominous, and nowhere more so than in the snowbelt of the Saguenay. The houses here are garrisoned, bracing for the seasonal siege.

Villages collect along the Saguenay, the homes piled up at the foot of cliffs. Outside one village, we pass through a strange "valley of monuments": crumbling cherubs, lions, griffins, fair maidens—stone sentries standing guard at the manor gates of abandoned estates. The Virgin Mary is here, in Virgin Mary blue, and so is St. John the Baptist, striding out of the wilderness.

As we enter L'Anse-St-Jean, a sign in French reads, "Welcome to Our Kingdom." The village stands alongside a stream that flows towards the Saguenay, and we follow it down to an unexpected covered bridge. Sean reads from the plaque, translating for me: "This bridge was featured on the Canadian $1000 bill since 1954." There is a pause. You'd almost think Sean and I don't see a lot of $1000 bills. "I thought it looked familiar," I say at last, but Sean isn't fooled. We walk through the bridge—wood creaking, air dusty—and ahead of us is a solid canvas of colour. Ochres and auburns, earthy vermilions and the darkness of evergreens, interspersed everywhere with sudden splashes of pure red maple: a thousand Canadian flags fluttering in the foliage. All the more poetic since Saguenay–Lac-St-Jean is the heartland of Quebec's separatist movement.

On our way back to the car, I again deconstruct the flaws in the separatist logic. Sean just as deftly deconstructs my deconstruction.

"Are you fighting again?" Aidan asks from behind us.

"Not fighting," Sean says. "Just explaining why your uncle is wrong."

As we drive in to La Baie, the intestinal tubings and plume-spouting smokestacks of an aluminum smelter and a pulp mill rear into view. It's like finding a sewage treatment plant in the middle of a rose garden. The factory dominates the town, almost *is* the town, and the community curves around it.

The townspeople of La Baie have—without apparent ironic intent—put up a sign near the smelter marking a "scenic lookout." So we dutifully stop to admire the, um, view. It is very scenic if you like (a) smoke, (b) fumes and (c) the aforementioned intestinal tubings. Incredibly, whole families have gathered here, are having picnics and relaxing on lawn chairs. Food stands sell steamed hot dogs and the ubiquitous poutine (cheese curds and gravy on top of French fries, for those of you fortunate enough to have avoided this classic bit of Canadien cuisine). We order some of the goop and dig in, but a chemical smell, like solvent or model glue, has soured the air, and everything tastes tinny. It's like chewing on foil.

With so many people milling about, we start to think maybe we've stumbled upon a festival of some sort—*Festival de la Poutine avec Steamé,* perhaps. But no, it appears that this is simply the place to hang out when you're in La Baie.

A group of boys gawks past, punching and shoving each other amid feigned cries of *"ayoille!"* and *"pissou!"* They are jostling for attention from the girls who sit, imperiously indifferent, on a seawall, kicking their legs in the listless manner of imperiously indifferent young girls the world over. As with any gathering of teenagers in Quebec, the conversations are steeped in religiosity. *"Câlice! Tabarnac! Hostie!"*: an ecclesiastical inventory of chalice, tabernacle and the host of Christ. Though I notice this shifts when the mother of one (suitably mortified) girl comes by with a sweater. *Câlice* becomes the nonsensical but euphemistic *Câline de binnes!* just as *tabarnac* becomes *tabarnouche!* and *hostie* is changed to *hostie toastée!* It's the same way English Canadians employ "friggin'" and "frick" to such a comical extent. (You want real vulgarity? Go to Europe; go to France or England or Ireland, where they don't mince their swear words—they savour them. I had a conversation about this once with an exiled Argentinian writer who was living in Barcelona. He bemoaned how scatological and graphic the Spaniards were, compared to even the most sullen, attitude-riddled members of the Buenos Aires crowd. "It's an Old World/New World divide," he said with a sigh.)

The community of La Baie is located, reasonably enough, on a bay. It's a side spear of the Saguenay known as Baie des Ha! Ha! There is a Lac du Ha! Ha! nearby as well. The "Ha! Ha!" refers to a dead end and, legend has it, to the hearty laugh of voyageurs who followed such passages, thinking they were on a main channel, only to discover *ha! ha!* that they were lost—proof once again that the Québécois have a joie de vivre all their own. Had it been an English-Canadian explorer, the place would no doubt have been named "Shit! Bay" or possibly "Frick! Cove." (Cartographers have of late challenged the "jovial laughter" explanation, pointing out that *haha* is actually an old French term for "unexpected barrier," and one that goes back to the days of Joan of Arc. But that doesn't explain the exclamation marks.)

We have arrived in La Baie in the middle of a crucial social experiment. A billboard announces, in a D-Day–sized headline, that it is now ACCEPTABLE TO TURN ON A RED LIGHT! IT IS AUTHORIZED. The province's ban on right turns on red is coming to an end, and Saguenay–Lac-St-Jean is at the cutting edge of this radical change. Sadly deprived for so long, Sean goes into a whirlwind of right turns at every traffic light we can find, coming at last to the dead end of a pulp mill parking lot. *Ha ha!*

After La Baie the fjord begins to narrow, and by the time we reach Chicoutimi the gap has almost closed, leaving only a fast-running river funnelling through. We come in under a cover of cloud, the slate-grey sky rolling in on itself. Saltwater tides, pushed in from the St. Lawrence, reach as far as Chicoutimi; from this point on, the Saguenay River is fresh. Chicoutimi, located at this strategic point, has always been a major industrial port. Even the factories are historic; a pulp mill built in 1896 is now a protected property, the oldest surviving industrial site in Quebec.

What I know about Chicoutimi is this: it is the hometown of legendary hockey goaltender Georges Vézina, who was renowned for keeping his cool under pressure. Vézina played for the Montreal Canadiens in their barnstorming glory days of the 1920s—which is to say, he *was* the team's defensive line. In one game, Vézina stopped seventy-eight out of seventy-nine shots, a record that still stands. They called him "the Chicoutimi Cucumber."

"Can you imagine?" I say, turning around to talk to Aidan, almost imploring her to be impressed. "Seventy-eight shots! He was a cucumber."

"That's interesting," she says.

"Really?"

"Well, it is a little bit interesting."

The beauty of the fall foliage has exhausted us. Even with the factorial entanglements of La Baie and Chicoutimi, we are so sated on nature it's almost a relief to be in a ragged, dirty-hemmed city for a change. We set up base at Motel Panoramique—*56 chambres, air climatisé, TV couleur avec câble, 3 km du centre-ville!*—and then head out to find a restaurant.

It's ABC, we have decided. Anything but chicken.

So far, we've stopped at every St. Hubert franchise we passed along the way, because I have coupons. St. Hubert is a cultural institution here, named in honour of the Patron Saint of Fried Chicken, I'm assuming. It's Quebec's answer to KFC, and it is famous for the canny marketing hook it uses to draw in customers: "All-you-can-eat coleslaw!" Yes sir. As much raw sliced cabbage as you want. *Menum menum!*

We are now desperate for something else, and we settle on cheese pizza and Pepsi, which we take back to the motel, where we sit around burping and watching equally cheesy Québécois pop videos on "Musique plus." (*Memo to the world*: Disco never died, it just moved to Quebec.)

"Does anybody want to play backgammon?" Aidan asks brightly.

"I would," I say, "but you keep changing the rules."

"Like a true Quebecker," Sean says with a proud smile.

We play. Aidan wins.

When I travel I often have trouble sleeping, and find myself awake in the early hours, before the sun is up, starved for REM. I've seen what 4:00 a.m. looks like in many a city. At the Motel Panoramique, arms behind my head, I lie staring at the ceiling as the first wash of dawn seeps in.

It is a crisp cold Saguenay morning. I step outside and into a view of the bridge to Chicoutimi-Nord. A few bleary-eyed cars are already moving across it. A spattering of water is falling, and the river is pocked with rain. On the far shore: a cross, a row of homes atop a ridge, the single spray of a distant fountain.

Another early riser. A small man, wiry, walking a terrier. He is wearing a short-sleeved shirt—the man, not the terrier—and I find this admirable. I have on a sweater and a windbreaker, and I'm still hugging myself to keep warm. "*C'est bon, eh?*" he says, gesturing to the view.

"*Oui, c'est tres bon*," I reply, instantly revealing my secret identity (i.e., "squarehead").

"*Americain?*" he asks—hopefully.

"*J'suis Canadien*." And even though my cover has been blown, I try to pronounce it *chus* in true Québécois fashion—just as I try to say *wai* instead of "oui"—but succeed only in sounding like an Albertan trying to speak French, or possibly someone with mild brain damage. And no, the two are *not* interchangeable.

In fractured French and halting English we agree that yes, the weather is good, and the river is good and the view is good and the weather—well, yes, the weather is *very* good.

Is it true, I want to know, that this is a separatist heartland? *"Les séparatistes? Beaucoup dans la Saugenay? C'est vrai?"*

Not separatist, he corrects, *sovereignist*. And yes, it is true.

"But everybody has been so . . . so nice."

A smile surfaces, and then a tilt of the head, as if to say, "But of course." And in slow, precise English he says, "We are always happy to have visitors"—and here's the kicker, the line he's been waiting to deliver—"from a foreign country."

I smile magnanimously; pretend I have missed the jab. Lacking the French for a proper comeback, I turn to the view instead and note that it is still good, still very good.

"La Royaume," I say.

"Oui, Le Royaume."

On July 19, 1996, the rain began to fall on Saguenay–Lac-St-Jean, and it didn't stop. Four separate storms had converged, curling up from the Gulf of Mexico, drawing in wetness from as far away as the Caribbean. Turned back by a mass of colder air, the storm stalled, covering the entire eastern half of the continent. Lac-St-Jean was at the epicentre. For three days, torrential downpours pounded the region. More rain fell in the first forty-eight hours than would normally fall in a month. The rivers couldn't drain it, the dams couldn't hold it.

The Saguenay–Lac-St-Jean region has more than 2000 diked dams, an elaborate but disorganized network put into place in a piecemeal fashion over the last century and a half. At Lac du Ha! Ha! a half-forgotten dike collapsed. Water churned out, emptying that lake and a smaller one nearby. A wall of mud and water swept down, tearing up trees by the roots and firing them into houses like battering rams. The city of La Baie, at the head of Ha! Ha!, took the brunt of it. In a way, the Saguenay was simply finding its original riverbed, returning to its true level. The towns, the farms and the cities that lay in its path were on contested land.

Bridges collapsed, roads were washed away. Escarpments fell, houses slid off riverbanks, apartment buildings caved in. The Alcan plant at Jonquière escaped intact more by luck than anything else—a concrete wall diverted the worst of the current. Had the floodwaters hit the molten aluminum inside the smelter, the ensuing explosion would have torn a hole out of the valley.

The city of Chicoutimi found itself caught in a rage of rapids. In a neighbourhood in the middle of town, every home was swept away—every home but one. A single house, perched on the edge of a small cliff, stood fast. It was an image broadcast around the world: that small white house on Gédéon Street, alone against the deluge, as the Saguenay hammered it on both sides. There was an element of the macabre in the way the media covered the story, with cameras trained on the house and reporters standing by waiting for it, too, to topple. It never did.

Damage from the Saguenay floods of 1996 was in the hundreds of millions of dollars. Four thousand people were evacuated. Entire villages were cut off from the outside, and almost 500 homes were destroyed. But not the little white house of Chicoutimi. Today, *la petite maison blanche,* as it is known, is the centrepiece of a city park.

"Does the original family still own it?" Sean asks the young woman at the motel reception, who is showing us the way to *la petite maison blanche* on a town map.

She smiles. "No, no. They sold it to the city. Got a nice little price for it, too" (*bon petit prix*).

"Well," says Sean. "It was the only survivor, right?"

"Oh no, the church beside it survived as well."

"The church?" says Sean.

"Oh yes," she says, and the smile has become a laugh. "It was blessed."

Sure enough, the silver spire of a Catholic church stands on the edge of what is now scoured bedrock. You can see the path the floods took. We park the car and walk up.

From below, the white house stands stark against the sky. It is a modest home with the steep, slightly curved lines of a traditional Québécois dwelling. Perched alone on its exposed foundations, it is at once defiant and vulnerable. It has become a symbol of resistance, courage, resolve.

"You have to understand," Sean says, "that this is how the Québécois see themselves. Alone against the deluge. Holding on. Standing firm."

"It looks like a castle!" says Aidan as she leaps from rock to rock. Sean and I follow her up, and with a start we realize that we are picking our way through the foundations of other homes. Slabs of cement, empty squares, entire basements. They have the feel of unmarked graves.

Cattails and reeds grow in pocketed pools beside the little white house. Water trickles past. It looks like a castle.

• • •

The cloud factories of Chicoutimi. The sweet smell of pulp mills along Technology Street. The cinder-block buildings on Racine, dingy but humming with life. A sign has been posted proclaiming "*Chic*-outimi!" but they're not fooling anyone. We spend the day wandering among the *brasseries* and *dépanneurs*, the tawdry *clubs de nuit* and the dollar stores. A shop on one corner flies a banner announcing the Kingdom of Saguenay, though "flies" isn't quite accurate; in the limp breeze, it droops more than it soars.

The same jangly assortment of youth is here in Chicoutimi as well. "*Parle-m'en pas!*" a girl says breathlessly as she hurries past. "*Ah, c'est la même poutine,*" comes her friend's reply, a phrase I have never heard before.

Back in the car, we drive past Chicoutimi Chrysler—"Le Leader!"—and then follow the smoke-stacks into Jonquière. Overcast skies, overcast streets; the same damp charcoal feel has pervaded both. The industrial cities of Chicoutimi and Jonquière spill into each other, amid the metal maze of the sprawling Alcan aluminum plant—dazzlingly bright at night, as we discover, and a city unto itself. Surprisingly enough, the civic symbol of Jonquière is not an ulcerous beluga whale but an aluminum footbridge, shiny and new, with Hollywood spotlights angled onto it, and triangular support beams that splay taut cables. And I think to myself, *The Saguenay could snap that bridge like a twig.*

We have almost reached the end. We spend the night in another motel and the next day we push on to Lac-St-Jean, at the headwaters of the Saguenay, the source of our Nile.

It is a dramatic moment when we finally break out of the Saguenay Valley and onto flat lands. The fields open up in front of us, and thin grain silos rise in the haze like minarets across the plains. If the Quebec separatist movement has a heart—and some would say it is all heart and very little brain—then we have reached it. The Saguenay is the central circulatory system of the *pure laine,* and Lac-St-Jean is its main pulmonary artery. The lake lies in a shallow glacial pan. It is like a watery continuation of the fields, a mirage.

"A Festival of Blueberries!" proclaims a roadside sign, for we have entered *Le Pays des Bleuets.* "Les Bleuets" is a nickname, as well, used to refer to the residents of Lac-St-Jean in a way that is both affectionate and slightly dismissive. It's not quite an insult. "*Au contraire,*" reads the guide we have been using, "*c'est un honneur!*"

We have arrived at the inner circle. It hardly feels like a kingdom, though like travellers in a fairytale we have fought our way past obstacles—hairpin turns, foul-smelling smelters, dangerously distracting scenery and heart-clogging poutine—just to get here. We drive by clusters of buildings along the lakeshore: St-Gédéon-sur-le-Lac, Métabetchouan, Desbiens. Train tracks loop around Lac-St-Jean like a loosely thrown lariat, and we follow them as one small town skips into the next. Laundry on a clothesline, billowing on a warm wind. Barns and wraparound porches and white picket fences: it's hopelessly picturesque. Piers lead into the lake. Fleur-de-lis flags flutter and snap.

The Lac-St-Jean region is imbued with an illusory nostalgia for many Québécois, for this is a literary landscape as well.

It was in Lac-St-Jean that Louis Hémon chose to set his novel *Maria Chapdelaine.*

Much like Anne of Green Gables in Prince Edward Island or Evangeline among the Acadians, the heroine of Hémon's novel has taken on a larger significance. A fictional character has come to symbolize an entire people. But where Anne is innocent and Evangeline elegiac, Maria Chapdelaine is defiant. Hers is a tale of fidelity. It is a novel of dreams deferred, of dreams subsumed, of individuals who exist only as part of a larger collective identity. Maria chooses traditional French-Canadian values over the riches and slick promises of the Anglo allure, and in case there is any doubt about Hémon's intent, the author lays out his message in clear terms: "Concerning ourselves and our destiny, the duty we face is understood: to stand our ground, to endure. So that centuries from now, the world may look upon us and say, *'Truly, these are a people that know not how to die.'*"

Our journey ends in Val-Jalbert.

Val-Jalbert was a planned community, founded in 1902, very modern in its day, and prosperous. The first sawmill on Lac-St-Jean was at Val-Jalbert, and soon after a pulp-and-paper plant was built to harness the power of a nearby water-fall. By the mid-1920s, more than a thousand people were living here. But it was a company town, and in 1927 the mill closed and Val-Jalbert was shut down.

Sean and Aidan and I have arrived at the end of the day, in the magic hour when the last of the daylight is refracted across the atmosphere, creating a light without shadows. There is no one else around, and the houses—abandoned,

silvery grey—sit as silently as tombstones. Many have begun
to collapse inward with the weight of years. Some list only
slightly; some are as sway-backed as saddles; others have surrendered completely to time and gravity. Second floors have
fallen into first floors, in a jumble of timber and broken
beams. Stairways crawl into mid-air. The windows are dark
and empty.

Val-Jalbert is now a protected site. The lawns out front
have been watered and trimmed, the pathways carefully
raked. "Well-maintained ruins": a contradiction, perhaps, but
an accurate description.

As we walk towards the old mill, the sound of falling
water grows louder. Above us, in a seventy-metre drop, is the
thundering cascade that first breathed life into Val-Jalbert.
We enter the canyon beside it on a pathway wet with the
smell of forest and decay, then climb a long, leg-aching series
of stairs that runs through cedar forests. It takes us alongside
moss-softened foundations and rusting towers, relics of the
village's pulp mill past. So steep is the ascent that our ears
pop by the time we reach the summit. We emerge beside the
waterfall at the very moment of its drop. The river breaks
across water-blackened stones, falling in stages towards the
plains far below. Our faces are misted. Our ears are filled with
white noise.

From these heights we can see Lac-St-Jean laid out in
evening indigo, lights shimmering along the shore. It has been
a good trip, even if the mythical Kingdom of Saguenay has
eluded us. When all is said and done, Lac-St-Jean is still a
cul-de-sac, the ultimate Ha! Ha!, as it were—beautiful, invei-
gling, but without an exit.

Time to go. We start down the stairs, coming out right where we started. Aidan runs on ahead, trailing laughter as she goes.

As we walk, Sean turns to me and says, "If the little white house defying the floodwaters is how the Québécois see themselves, then this"—he gestures to the tidy yards and eerily empty homes of Val-Jalbert—"this is what they fear."

Like a tumbler turning in a lock, it all starts to make sense.

In the early hours of April 17, 2002, an arsonist set fire to the little white house of Chicoutimi.

A dozen firefighters answered the call. They broke the windows and pumped in water, trying to drown the flames. The house survived. In interviews given afterwards, the head of the city's fire department said, with no small amount of amazement, "It withstood the heat—I don't know how. The damage was mainly in the basement, but the rest is okay. I tell you, neither fire nor flood can destroy that home."

The city office agreed. It issued a brief statement to the press, which ended with a simple article of faith and, perhaps, even fact: "The little white house is indestructible."

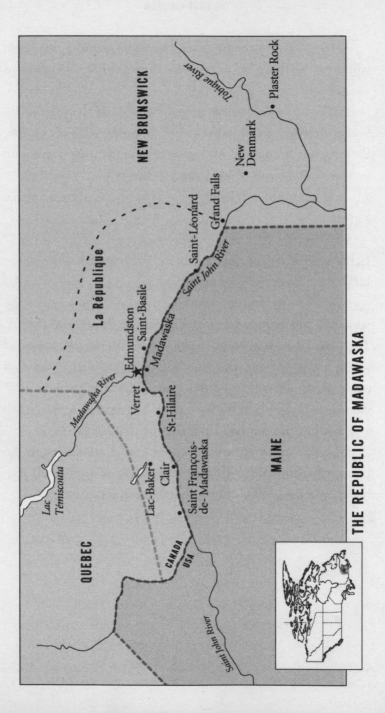

THE REPUBLIC OF MADAWASKA

chapter eight

THE REPUBLIC OF MADAWASKA

I FEEL LIKE JAMES BOND.

It's past midnight, and the rain is bucketing down, washing across the windshield. The wipers slosh back and forth, back and forth. I am hunched over the wheel, keeping an eye out for armed sentries and guard-tower snipers, for we are about to cross over into the renegade republic of Madawaska, deep in the farthest reaches of peace-torn New Brunswick.

I feel like James Bond—though I'm fairly sure Double-O-Seven didn't have a wife. Or a baby booster in the back seat. With a baby in it. Asleep with a cookie in one hand. And I'm fairly sure the cars that Bond drove weren't filled with the faint aroma of poo.

"Alex needs changing," Terumi says, and the theme music playing in my head skids off its tracks like a needle from a vinyl groove. Sigh.

We turn off the highway and drive slowly into the town of Grand Falls, where we find a late-night gas station. We fill up the tank, change the baby and leave a little package—*from Alex, with love*—in the washroom wastebasket. The rain is so heavy it ricochets up from the pavement. The main street, as wide as any parade ground, is awash. Grand Falls, Grand Sault. One town, two official names. The Great Divide.

The Maliseet called it Chik-un-it-pe, "the destructive giant." It is one of the largest waterfalls east of Niagara, and in the early years it blocked all but the most determined settlers from pushing past. To this day it forms an inland rift, a fault line. In this corner of New Brunswick, a geographical barrier has become a linguistic divide: above Grand Falls is French; below it, English.

The water thunders through a bottleneck gorge, dropping more than twenty metres as it goes. They say the spirit of a young Maliseet maiden permeates the mist. Her name was Malabeam, and she was captured by Mohawk warriors who tried to make her lead an invasion force against her own village. She guided the armada of war canoes over Grand Falls instead, sacrificing her life to save her people. *They say you can hear her voice crying out from the watery embrace of the Destructive Giant even now. . . .*

Terrific legend, that. Shame it isn't true. After all, how could anyone possibly know what really happened? Everybody died, so who was left to tell the tale? Ah, but the story has since been revised. In an effort to address such inconsistencies, Version Two has the Indian princess slipping free of her canoe just before it goes over the edge and then swimming to shore. I've seen Grand Falls. Good luck trying to make it to shore. You'd be dragged over by the current— unless you slipped free so far upstream that the element of surprise was completely lost. This version also assumes that the marauding band of warriors was either congenitally hard of hearing or profoundly gullible. "What's that echoing roar we hear?" "Just a secondary river," Malabeam coos.

Anyway, I have heard the same story told of northern Ontario's Kakebeka Falls (Ojibwa princess; Sioux villains), and a similar one about Niagara, where it is Lelawalo, "the maid of the mist," who is sacrificed. I doubt whether any of these tales is of authentic Native lineage; they smack of Victorian melodrama. Though why, when confronted with the power and beauty of an untamed waterfall, our instinctive response is to put an Indian maiden in a canoe and push her over the edge, is a mystery perhaps best left to psychologists.

We have arrived at the French-English divide of Grand Falls in the most unlikely of ways: via Denmark. Our trip began in the Loyalist town of St. Andrews, on the Bay of Fundy, in fine form and clear weather, and we have followed the map north, leaving wrapped packages at regular intervals as we go. Alex has pooped his way across New Brunswick, something I am sure will become a point of pride for him later in life. So far, we have seen the Unusually Large Stuffed Frog of Fredericton, the Giant Axe at Nackawic and the World's Longest Covered Bridge in Hartland.

We have always travelled this way. When my wife and I moved to the Maritimes after living in Japan, one of our very first trips was to the Acadian community of Shediac, self-anointed "Lobster Capital of the World," to see the Giant Lobster. And a very realistic-looking crustacean it was, weighing in at fifty tons, with the figure of an unsuspecting fisherman about to be caught in its claw. Terumi was duly impressed.

"Canadians are . . . interesting," she said.

Shediac is on the east coast, though, on the Gulf of St. Lawrence. This trip has taken us north, into forests so thick they seem cross-hatched. Under brooding clouds, we drove into the town of Plaster Rock, gateway to the interior highlands. We are using a guidebook from 1966 that I found at a yard sale for a dollar. Actual quote: *Plaster Rock has sidewalks and lawns and many other sophistications.* . . . Unfortunately, being a tad out of date, the book doesn't mention the Enormous Chainsaw Sculpture of Fiddleheads that is now the all-star attraction and main tourist draw of Plaster Rock (sidewalks and lawns excepted, of course). Among Canada's many and varied Large Objects by the Side of Road, these are, I believe, the only ones erected in honour of an edible fern. Considered a delicacy in New Brunswick, fiddleheads are the sprouts of ostrich ferns. Their tightly curled tops give them their name. At least fiddleheads are edible, unlike that other great New Brunswick dish, dulse. For those of you not familiar with it, dulse is the stuff that's left behind after the tide pulls back—the slimy, sour-smelling seaweed that makes you go *"Eew!"* when you step in it by accident. In New Brunswick this is considered food.

Alex tottered around at Plaster Rock, legs moving almost independently from the rest of him, arms out, astonished look on his face—there's a reason they call them toddlers—as I stepped back, arms crossed, to admire the majesty of the Giant Fiddleheads.

"Fiddleheads, but no dulse?" said Terumi.

"Not to worry," said I. "I'm sure that someone, somewhere, is working on it as we speak." (*Memo to Maritimers:* The title of World's Largest Dulse is still up for grabs.)

From Plaster Rock, we cut across a plateau where the forest suddenly opened up. Farmlands appeared, like a meadow in the woods. It was pure storybook: tidy white houses and neatly lined-up fields met the road at right angles, bordered by windbreaks of trees that looked almost like hedgerows. These were not the riverfront ribbons of land found in New France. Nor were they the large, quilted squares of Loyalist farms. This was Scandinavia transposed— for we had entered a Danish outpost.

We were in New Denmark, the largest colony of Danes in North America, though that suggests a scale that isn't apparent to a visitor. It's more secluded than one would expect, and smaller. Halfway between Plaster Rock and Grand Falls, New Denmark was once the terminus of a Danish exodus. The people who came were pulled, not pushed. Agressively courted by Canadian officials—to act, it was rumoured, as a buffer between French-speaking Acadians and English-speaking Loyalists—the first families arrived from Copenhagen in 1872. They had been spun sugar-cone tales of abundant free farmland, and that part was true. There was farmland—somewhere underneath all those trees. The "settlement" they had been promised, though, consisted of a single dormitory-style immigration hall in a mucky, stump-filled clearing. As one history described it, the newcomers were like children "abandoned in the woods."

The Danish settlers barely survived their first year in New Brunswick, forced to eat stewed weeds and seed potatoes. Canadian history is littered with failed experiments, doomed colonies, lost causes—but New Denmark was not among them. The settlers persevered. The forests gave way to fields. A Scandinavian church, St. Ansgar's, went up in the wilderness, and slowly a community took root along Klokkedahl Hill—and there the town remains, even today, an island onto itself.

"Isn't your grandmother from Denmark?" Terumi asks.

"*Norway*," I say. "She's from Norway, not Denmark."

"There's a difference?"

"A world of difference. The Norwegians were brave, seafaring folk. The Norwegians were Vikings. The Danish were named for a breakfast pastry."

Terumi thinks a moment, does the math. "So Alex is 12.5 percent Viking."

"He certainly eats like one. Have you seen what he does with mushed peas?"

We stop in New Denmark for a hearty (*read*: heavy) meal at the Valhalla, a sprawling restaurant beside the train tracks, where Terumi indulges her strange affection for pickled herring and Alex chows down on—what else?—pancakes. As we work our way through the food, the restaurant fills up with ambly old men and loud, rambunctious families. The Valhalla is as much a community drop-in centre as it is an eatery, and I am pleasantly astonished to hear Danish being spoken at the other tables, interlaced with English and even a dollop of French. The cultural continuity of New Denmark is a remarkable achievement, even if it does involve pickling that which should not be pickled.

Alex looks up from his pancakes, a deep, philosophical expression on his face. We know what that means. Terumi hands me the diaper bag. "Your turn," she says.

It is late when we leave New Denmark, and a wild wind is shaking the trees. As we follow the road out of town—past potato sheds like bunkers half-buried in fields, and mailboxes painted with Danish crosses—the sky rumbles. When the storm comes, it is so severe, so sudden, that we are forced off the road. We sit on the soft shoulder, illuminated by Frankenstein-flashes of lightning, as the car rocks on its suspension. The rain sounds like hail rolling across the roof.

After creeping through Grand Falls, wipers flailing, we enter the New Brunswick panhandle, a thin strip of land between the province of Quebec and the state of Maine. It is a cartographic heel-spur, a territorial anomaly, an extra piece of puzzle that didn't seem to belong anywhere else.

Our luck holds, and we manage to slip through, unnoticed, into *La République*. The fact that there are no roadblocks to run, no customs or military checkpoints to pass through and no armed guards to outwile doesn't hurt. Truth is, the only thing to indicate we have crossed an international border is a small sign caught fleetingly in the sweep of our headlights: *You are now entering Madawaska County.*

The name "Madawaska" is derived from the Maliseet words for "porcupine" (*madawes*) and "land" (*kak*), making it the Land of the Porcupines. And what is a porcupine if not simply a beaver with better weaponry?

The Republic of Madawaska may not have an army or a currency or a seat at the U.N., but it is, I assure you, quite real. The republic is older than Canada itself. It has its own coat of arms, a national capital, a president. And in defiance of Canadian constitutional law, it has separated unilaterally. There were no referendums, no October crises, no kidnappings, no assassinations. Although a renegade republic, Madawaska is also a peaceable kingdom.

Tadoussac may have been France's first permanent base in the New World, but it was a seasonal one, abandoned in winter and claimed again in the spring. The first true European community to take root in Canada was not along the St. Lawrence but on the Bay of Fundy: Acadia, founded in 1604.

Acadians did not exist in France; they were formed here, in the marshlands and meadows of that tidal bay. The society that developed in Acadia was more egalitarian and more tolerant of religious differences than that of New France and later Quebec; their numbers included Protestant Huguenots. The Acadians spoke their own dialect, followed their own customs and were far more open to Native culture than were their St. Lawrence cousins. Indeed, as historian Naomi Griffiths and others have shown, the rapport between the Acadians and the Mi'kmaq and Maliseet was arguably the best ever to develop between European colonists and First Nations. There was no equivalent to Quebec's Iroquois wars in Acadia. The early Acadians and the Mi'kmaq became so mutually dependent and intermeshed that they were on the verge of merging, of becoming a prototypical Metis nation.

But that never happened. Acadia was a richly abundant region, caught in the crossfire of competing imperial designs. These dual claims were reflected in its name; as early as 1621, the Fundy region was being referred to on maps as "Acadie or

Nova Scotia." The settlements were looted and burned constantly, and Acadia changed hands no fewer than fourteen times between its founding and its final capture by the English in 1710.

Under nominal British rule, the Acadians prospered in relative peace for the next forty years, obstinately independent and loyal to neither Britain nor France. In 1755, they paid for this obstinacy. The governor of Nova Scotia, fed up with their neutrality, ordered the population expelled. Entire villages were rounded up at gunpoint and deported. British troops torched their homes, leaving the crops to rot and the livestock to starve. The Acadians became a lost tribe, cast out of the garden, scattered amongst hostile English colonies from Boston to the Falkland Islands. As Anglo-Acadian author Clive Doucet has noted, their expulsion was a sinister act, and one ripe with foreboding: "The Acadian exile marks the beginning of geopolitics—politics based on the attempt to enforce a planetary agenda. . . . It was an eighteenth-century precursor to ethnic cleansing."

When the American colonies took up arms against British rule, another diaspora began, this time moving in the opposite direction. Families who remained loyal to Great Britain fled north. One population had been removed and another now poured in. So many Loyalist refugees arrived that a new colony had to be carved out of Nova Scotia to accommodate them. It was named New Brunswick, and the motto was *Spem Reduxit*—"Hope restored."

In the years that followed the *Grand Dérangement,* or "great upheaval," the Acadians also began to return, by boat, on foot, in carts. But when they arrived, they found that their farms and land had been claimed by others. Crowded out from all sides, one group of Acadian families petitioned the British governor to be allowed to settle beyond the formidable barrier of Grand Falls, in the northern reaches of New Brunswick. Permission was granted, and in 1785 they pushed past the falls and into a verdant valley, half-hidden from the outside world, where the Madawaska River flowed into the St. John. It seemed, in the words of historian Charlotte Lenentine, "like a promised land." The Acadians settled near a Maliseet camp. They drew maple syrup from the trees and crops from the fields. Some traded in furs. Others cut lumber. Villages grew along the rivers, and for thirty years no one bothered with them.

Others drifted into Madawaska. French-speaking settlers arrived from Quebec (or Lower Canada, and later Canada East). They were joined by a small band of Irish, English and Scottish settlers in the mid-1800s, and then by Americans moving west from New England. The region acquired a certain Yankee flavour, but for the most part it remained strongly, defiantly French. A new identity was born, one neither Acadian nor Québécois nor American, but a mélange of all three: les Brayons. Though sometimes denigrated as merely "backwoods Acadian," the Brayon identity is more subtle and more confused than that. "On the forms," the people there joke today, "we are classified as 'all of the above.'"

The word "Brayon" may be derived from braie, or "flax breaker," an agricultural instrument used to prepare material for weaving. The Brayons are renowned for the skill of their weavers, and their traditional "homespun blue" is still treasured. Another possible explanation is that the word refers to a type of trousers, called *brayères,* that were popular with the men in the region. But to my mind, the most likely explanation has to do with geography. A good number of the first settlers traced their ancestry back to the Bray region of France, and the term for such people is "Brayon."

The Acadians crossing Grand Falls had sought sanctuary in isolation, and they might have found it, but for one unfortunate fact: they had settled in a political no man's land. The Treaty of 1783, which ended the American Revolution, set the boundary between the newly formed United States and Britain's remaining colonies, but the descriptions of the border were notoriously vague. The line between New Brunswick and the U. S. ran through these forests, but no one knew exactly where.

Events unfolding on the far side of the world rippled across the ocean and up the St. John River, into the remote communities of the region now known as Madawaska. Napoleon had signed a treaty with Russia that effectively closed the Baltic timber trade to Great Britain, and with it access to the tall pines needed for masts and ships. A mad timber rush began across Britain's North American colonies and, as it happened, the Madawaska and the Aroostook River regions along the U.S.–New Brunswick border were rich in virgin pine. Lumberjacks from both sides met headlong in the disputed territory.

The rain has chased us all the way to Edmundston. We arrive in the early hours to streets that shimmer, wet beneath the streetlamps. Edmundston is the largest francophone city in Canada outside of Quebec, pinned between *la belle province* and the Pine Tree State, with the United States of America just across the river. Border towns are always slightly surreal, but they aren't unusual. After all, Canada itself—historically, demographically, psychologically—is one extended border town. Terumi shakes her head in wonderment. "The United States. Just there." Those trees, that shore. She finds it fascinating, this idea that you can walk over a bridge or drive across a street and be in another country—and not any country but *America*, that sprawling carnival to the south, that empire of empires. This is a new concept for her. Japan borders no one. It is an archipelago nation, a collection of islands.

But then, so too is Canada.

The would-be founder of the Republic of Madawaska was a hot-headed Yankee by the name of John Baker. Baker was either a selfless liberator or a lowdown agitator, depending on where you stood. He was also a late convert to the cause. For all his later bluster, Baker had been on his way to Fredericton in 1825 to apply for British naturalization when he met a pair of land agents from Maine. The men were in the region illegally, presenting deeds to American settlers as part of a pre-emptive claim on the region. No one knows exactly what transpired but, in a conversion worthy of Saul on the road to Damascus, Baker turned around and headed back to Madawaska, determined to lead the fight.

On July 4, 1827, John Baker hoisted a homemade flag—an eagle beneath a semicircle of red stars—and declared Madawaska an independent American republic. (Before the Civil War, American states were considered semi-autonomous entities within the union.) When ordered by a British magistrate to lower his banner, Baker refused. "Nothing but a superior force to ourselves shall take it down," he said. "Great Britain has no jurisdiction here." The governor sent in an armed posse to arrest the Yankee firebrand.

Rather than deny the charges against him, Baker simply refused to accept the authority of the court. He was an American citizen, and Madawaska was an independent American republic. How could Great Britain presume to have jurisdiction? Baker was fined and sentenced to time already served. Steamin' mad, he returned to Madawaska to continue his campaign. The struggle for the region now became the Clash of the Census Takers, the Battle of the Surveyors, as each side tried to lay claim to the timber-rich borderlands.

When an arbitration ruling on the disputed territory failed to win approval on either side, Baker and his supporters began holding town meetings. In a bid to curry favour among the French-Canadian majority, the Americans attempted to draft Pierre Lizotte, a local Brayon leader, as their representative to the state legislature. Lizotte refused but they elected him anyway. When word got out, the governor of New Brunswick marched his men back in and arrested the ringleaders.

Tensions rose, tempers flared, spittle flew. The conflict reached the boiling point in 1839, in what has become known, rather grandiosely, as the Aroostook War. The governor of Maine sent in 200 armed men as part of a state-sanctioned vigilante squad. The British promptly arrested the leader, and the Americans replied in kind, taking a New Brunswick land warden into custody. Tit-for-tat it went. Armed fortresses

were thrown up along both sides of the frontier, at times
almost within sight of each other.

"Maine and her soil, or BLOOD!" the American press
cried. "Let the sword be drawn and the scabbard thrown
away!" Ten thousand Maine militiamen prepared for combat,
practising their musket skills on effigies of Queen Victoria.
Newspapers sent "war correspondents" to the front lines.
Other states threw their weight behind Maine, and the U.S.
Congress approved $10 million for the war effort. American
troops marched into the woods of New Brunswick singing a
fine bit of doggerel known as the "Maine Battle Song."

> Britannia shall not rule the Maine,
> Nor shall she rule the water;
> They've sung that song full long enough,
> Much longer than they oughter.

It wasn't really a war. No shots were fired and no one
died, at least not in combat. A farmer who wandered into an
American firing range paid the price, and a soldier keeled over
from a case of acute measles, but that was it. The worst clash
of the entire Aroostook War was a drunken fistfight outside a
local tavern.

Local lore also tells of a cook from a New Brunswick lumber camp named Paddy McGarrigle and his large girlfriend,
who went for a stroll one day over to the American side, with
her in her new red dress, only to find both the town and the
fort deserted. The American soldiers had apparently run away
when they caught sight of Paddy and his girl, convinced the
entire redcoat army was heading in. Finding himself in

possession of the American base, Paddy claimed the town for Britain. A dubious tale, to be sure, and one not helped by the fact that Paddy McGarrigle's enormous girlfriend figures largely—if you'll excuse the pun—in other tales as well. One version of John Baker's 1827 rebellion even has him hoisting not a flag but a pair of her gigantic bloomers.

In retrospect, the Aroostook War has taken on the aspects of a comic opera. But the situation was deadly serious. A last-minute truce defused things, but it wasn't long before tensions again escalated. Troops from New Brunswick marched back in. Maine again prepared Articles of War.

In a final attempt at preventing an all-out conflagration, the U.S. Secretary of State, Daniel Webster, met with Lord Ashburton, an emissary from Great Britain. The two men knew each other, were friends, in fact, and together they threaded their way through the myriad claims and counter-claims. Swords were slid back into their scabbards, war correspondents were sent home, and Maine's battle anthem was replaced by "The Great Song Written to Mark the Occasion of the Webster-Ashburton Treaty of 1842," which began:

> O'er the Lion and Eagle now hovers the Dove;
> To-day there's a banquet of national love.

Poetry: so often the first casualty of war.

The Webster-Ashburton Treaty split the Madawaska region along the St. John River. Britain maintained its overland link between Quebec and the Maritimes. Maine received title to the timber-rich lands of the Aroostook. Opposition members in London may have denounced the deal, calling it "Lord Ashburton's capitulation," but the border held and the threat of war ended.

There was just one problem. It wasn't an empty valley they were carving up. Brayon communities lined both sides of the river. Marriages, church congregations and businesses straddled the line, and with a stroke of a pen Great Britain had abandoned more than a thousand Brayon families. They had petitioned the government, asking to stay in British territory, but to no avail. (British rule was the lesser of two evils. French rights were safer under the British Crown than under the Americans, and it's no coincidence that today the French in Maine have been almost entirely assimilated, while New Brunswick is an officially bilingual province.) Ironically, when the border was finally drawn, John Baker found himself on the wrong side of the line. The once fiery patriot quietly lived out the rest of his life under British rule.

You'd think they would have a statue of John Baker somewhere in Edmundston, or one showing two men in top hats furiously negotiating a treaty—"Webster and Ashburton heroically hammer out details of the 1842 boundary between New Brunswick and Maine," that sort of thing. Or even one to Paddy McGarrigle's girlfriend and her gigantic bloomers. But we find no such monuments. What we do find are flags. Flags a'fluttering.

"I counted six from our hotel window," Terumi says. The Canadian maple leaf, the fleur-de-lis, the stars-and-stripes, the New Brunswick boat carrying Loyalists away, the State of Maine's pine tree and moose, and finally, rounding it out, a modern version of Baker's pouncing eagle: it reminds me of the overlapping circles of a Venn diagram. Madawaska is where multiple flags make counterclaims.

The squabbling didn't end in 1842. As soon as the American threat was removed, Quebec and New Brunswick began bickering over the territory that remained. Quebec reasserted an earlier claim on Madawaska, insisting that the region was simply an extension of Rimouski County. New Brunswick had a stronger case: the St. John River was the natural water route; it was New Brunswick that had transported and supplied the settlers; and it was New Brunswick that had defended the region during the Aroostook cold war. This new dispute between competing British colonies would drag on for another fifteen years before finally being settled. In the end, the land was divided yet again, with Quebec awarded the northern half. What was once a "promised land" is now divided by three borders into two countries, one state, and two provinces.

The legend of La République du Madawaska was born during this time. Pulled in three different directions at once, *les Brayons* declared themselves independent. A pox on all your houses! New Brunswick author Stuart Trueman claimed that the use of "republic" to describe the region actually began as an insult. "Madawaska," Trueman wrote, "was first called a 'republic' in derision long years ago when its carefree inhabitants became notorious for ignoring provincial regulations about such minor things as Sunday bars, movies, and sports." The people of the region, according to Trueman, accepted the criticism "as a compliment."

Well, not quite.

The legend of the republic goes back much further than that. A story—apocryphal, perhaps, but based on historical events—is told of a beleaguered Brayon farmer, a government nose-counter and a defiant answer to a volatile question.

A census taker making the rounds in the days before the Aroostook War demanded to know the loyalties of a local farmer. Was the man American? Canadian? A Quebecker? A New Brunswicker? Where did he belong: to which province or state? The farmer, inspired no doubt by Baker's earlier sedition, drew himself up to his full height and proclaimed, with the pride of an ancient Roman, *"Je suis citoyen de la République du Madawaska!"*

The existence of this republic was revealed to the outside world only in the 1920s, when Dr. Lorne Violette, provincial representative for the area, began referring to his riding as "the Republic." The legends grew, Dr. Violette's stories became more and more outlandish and on April 5, 1949, a coat of arms for the "Republic of Madawaska" was registered in Ottawa. The design shows two hands shaking over a fleur-de-lis in what can only be described as Summer Camp Gothic.

John Baker has been embraced as the spiritual founder, and the flag chosen for the Republic of Madawaska is none other than an adaptation of the eagle-and-stars banner first raised by Baker back in 1827. The new flag was commissioned in the 1960s by Edmundston mayor Fernand Nadeau. Nadeau liked to sign official documents with the title "President of the Republic of Madawaska," and he ran a thriving trade in barter with the Americans across the river: medallions, plaques and other republican regalia in exchange for cases of maple syrup. He was later convicted on tax evasion charges.

Ten knights sit on the High Executive Order of the Republic. The capital is Edmundston and, post-Nadeau, the mayor of that city is acclaimed president when he or she takes office. The republic even has its own Betsy Ross, the Reverend Sister Marthe de Jesus, a nun with the Order of Immaculate Conception who hand-painted on silk the first official banner, still on display in the Edmundston city hall.

The symbolism behind the Madawaska flag was concocted after the fact. Mayor Nadeau came up with an official explanation more or less on the spot, when a visitor persisted in asking him, "But what does the flag *mean?*"

Nadeau held his breath for a moment, thought about it and then, with a deep exhalation, replied, "The eagle is for this powerful neighbour of ours, the United States of America, to whom in 1842 Daniel Webster and Lord Ashburton refused the privilege of having the Madawaska region in its realm. A great loss for Uncle Sam! The white background is for the openness of the Madawaska landscape and its people: a purified crossbreed of Acadians, French-Canadians, Aboriginals and Anglo-Saxons."

Nadeau was only warming up. Pointing to the flag's six stars, he continued, "These represent the first settlers. The people whose toil, sweat and blood helped build Madawaska: the Natives, the Acadians, the Quebeckers, the English, the Scots and the Irish. Six stars. Six founding peoples."

Today, the "six stars of Madawaska" are represented in everything from signposts to water fountains. Chainsaw sculptures of the founders—Indians, Irishmen, Scots and the rest—are lined up beside the Edmundston city hall, and adorn the entrances of restaurants and inns.

The irony is that Madawaska is now one of the most culturally homogenous regions in Canada, with current estimates putting the population at 94 percent francophone. But language alone is a deceptive standard, and the notion of "one people out of many" is given extra credence in the unifying myth of the Brayon nation. This first became evident during the rise of the Quebec separatist movement in the 1970s, when the Brayons—and the Acadians to the south—were once again caught between competing loyalties. A survey taken in Madawaska during those tumultuous years revealed the extent to which the phenomenon of multiple identities had entered the consciousness. In response to the question "How do you define yourself?" the results were instructive:

Acadian: 41.8%
Brayon: 62.7%
Citizens of the Republic of Madawaska: 65.1%
French-Canadian: 89.8%
Canadian: 91.2%

The population of *les Brayons,* in Maine, New Brunswick and Quebec, is estimated at around 65,000 people. It is a culture that defies borders. The nearest hospital may well be in another country; babies are born on either side of the river, and dual citizenship is common—triple citizenship even, if you count the republic.

When I asked Gilbert Lavoie, director of the Madawaska Museum, how he defines himself, he says, "Well, my mother was Acadian. My father was a Quebecker. I live in Madawaska, so I guess that makes me Brayon."

We are in Edmundston for the annual Foire Brayonne, a five-day cacophony of music, sports and rowdy public dancing, and we wade into the celebrations.

I remember my sister-in-law Sherry talking about moving from Alberta to Montreal. One of the first things she noticed was how much the Québécois adore children. "They would dash through traffic to see our baby," she said. It was one of the things that won her and Sean over to Quebec.

The Brayons and Acadians of the Maritimes are just as smitten by children. They too are a traffic-dodging, baby-viewing breed. If ever you want to convince French New Brunswickers to run with the bulls at Pamplona, you have only to tell them there is a wee cute baby at the other end, and off they'll go. Terumi and I are taken aback. It is like a family reunion every time we step outside. Wherever we go, people gather around to beam at Alex and exclaim with joy at seeing him trussed up in his little stroller. We are celebrities. Getting through the crowd becomes a slow process, and when we stop at a restaurant the people at the next table more or less move over, into our booth, dangling keys and chattering in French at Alex.

"Jeez," I whisper to Terumi, as we push our way back into the street. "You'd think we have the world's cutest child."

She gives me a withering look. "Oh, right," I say. "We do. I forgot."

The mascot of the Brayon Festival is a six-foot-high porcupine named Typique, who wears a plaid shirt (*Brayonne*

plaid, we are told) and jaunty suspenders. Alex is terrified of
him. "C'mon," I say. "Scoot in for a picture. It's just a six-foot-
high porcupine."

The food of choice at the festival—a standard Brayon
dish, as we discover—is pancakes. Yup. Pancakes. I suspect
some sort of Danish-Brayon conspiracy is involved. *Ployés*, as
the thin buckwheat pancakes are called, are served with cre-
tons (a pork pâté) and the ever-present Brayon baked beans.
Everywhere we go, they throw a ladle or two of baked beans
into the bargain. "Postcards? Sure, over there, and here"—
sloop—"have some baked beans with that."

Where the Danes below the falls eat *vælling*, a soup made
from buttermilk and thickened with oatmeal, and gosh
doesn't that sound appetizing, and *grønkaalssuppe*, made from
pork hocks and chopped kale, the Brayons above the falls eat
headcheese and tourtière and spiced *boudin* sausages. Yet
both agree on one inexplicable requirement: pancakes with
your main course.

"They come out West for a visit," I tell Terumi, "and I'm
serving them corn flakes for supper. I'll tell them it's part of
our culture."

Among the traffic-dodging, bull-running, baby-grinning
Brayons who fall all over Alex is a group of university students from the Edmundston campus of the Université de
Moncton. They speak with bubbling energy and varying
degrees of bilingual proficiency. The students swap words in
French with Terumi for words in Japanese, like visitors
exchanging gifts at a public event. Alex sits very still
throughout this conversation, a deep, philosophical look on
his face.

One student, a girl named Valerie, says something that has stayed with me ever since. I've been telling her how fascinated I am by their republic. "The United States is just over there." I point towards the steel bridge that spans the St. John. "Quebec is somewhere over there. English New Brunswick is back that way. Don't you ever feel sandwiched in?"

"No, no," she says. "We are in the middle of everything. We live *between* the borders. It's fun."

And perhaps it is the elated summer air or the festive music or the free-flowing sense of good cheer, but at that moment it seems that perhaps *les Brayons* represent the best of Canada, what the rest of us might aspire to be: an eccentric, eclectic, fluid nation, one of layers and multiple meanings. A nation that lives between borders.

"You know Bonhomme Carnaval?" I ask the students. "The snowman mascot—the one in the Quebec Winter Carnival?"

"Yes, of course."

"And Typique, the giant porcupine here at La Foire Brayonne?"

"Sure."

"Well, if Bonhomme Carnaval and Typique ever got in a fight, who would win?"

Valerie laughs out loud. "*Mais, non!* They are friends, I am sure!"

"True, Bonhomme Carnaval is usually invited to the Brayon Festival, and yes, he walks beside Typique during the parade, but let's say they had a falling-out. Say they were drinking and one thing led to another and someone threw a punch. Who would win?"

Valerie's friend François mulls this over. "Hmmm. A fight between a snowman and a porcupine, eh? I think who is victorious would depend on the season. In winter, Bonhomme will always win—made of snow, right? But here, in summertime, Typique—always Typique."

Ah, the smell of pulp mills in the morning. The sad truth is, Edmundston, even with the rivers curving through, even with the bicycle paths and the footbridges and the gardens, is not a handsome city. It tumbles down one side of the valley and up the other, a blue-collar town, a Chicoutimi of the backwoods, where the mills spew smoke into the sky and pipelines channel steam and factory waste through the city centre. The engine that runs Edmundston is the Fraser Pulp Mill, which straddles the international border. Pulp from Edmundston is turned into paper across the line in Edmundston's mirror community of Madawaska, Maine. The blue-and-green tubing carrying pulp and waste runs along the valley. As we walk beside the river, Terumi says, "Look! Water slides!" and I don't have the heart to tell her. Edmundston is a city with its circuitry laid bare, its arteries and veins revealed. A city of church steeples and smokestacks, where the Cathedral of Immaculate Conception is still the tallest, most imposing presence in town.

In fairness to the rest of the republic, it should also be noted that Edmundston, although designated the capital, is not necessarily the cultural heartland. The true spirit of *les Brayons* lies in the smaller towns and villages along the St. John River: in the wooded hamlet of Verret, home of the Festival de la Ployé, the only festival in the world dedicated to

buckwheat pancakes and pâté; in the Irish-Acadian community of Clair; in sleepy little St-Hilaire, once a Prohibition
boom town, from which bootleggers smuggled truckloads of
whisky into the U.S. and where a local moonshine known as
bagosse was openly available for years; and—above all—in the
attractive and somewhat haughty town of St-Basile, site of
the earliest Acadian settlement and the first religious parish
in the area. It is a town that considers itself the true *Berceau
du Madawaska*, or "Cradle of Madawaska." (Mind you,
St-Basile was also the home of pop star crooner Roch
Voisine—the Brayon answer to Céline Dion—so the place is
not entirely without fault.)

Clearly, the Republic of Madawaska is larger than the
sum of its parts. Back in Edmundston, I leave Terumi and
Alex surrounded by paparazzi and adoring fans, and head off
to confront the one man who has all the answers: the
President himself.

Jacques P. Martin was mayor of St-Basile for several
years, and he now heads the city of Edmundston. From the
cradle of the republic to *la capitale:* Monsieur Martin stands
at the pinnacle of power in Madawaska, and a newspaper in
Ottawa has asked me to speak with him about serious issues
of national unity. I'm not exactly sure what those issues are,
but the paper is picking up the tab for our hotel, so I figure
I should make an effort. Mr. Martin is a hard man to corner,
and having postponed my interview twice already, he now
decides to cancel it outright. "Urgent business," says his secretary. "A trip to Fredericton," says his assistant.

The President of the Republic hasn't counted on my
dogged determination as a newspaperman, and I do what

any hardened foreign correspondent faced with having to pay for his own accommodation would do: I decide to accost Mr. Martin directly, braving bodyguards and certain imprisonment. True, ambushing the mayor of a community of 18,000 people isn't *that* difficult. There's no scrum to fight my way through, no roped-off areas, no bodyguards at all, in fact. Just a very pleasant secretary and a twenty-minute wait in the lobby.

I spot the president as soon as he walks in the door.

"Mr. President! Mr. President!" I yell. "Answer my questions! The people need to know!" We are standing only a few feet apart, but you never know when an executive helicopter might land and pluck him away to some high-level international meeting.

Mr. Martin looks at me. "Sure, step inside. Just stop shouting."

The Office of the President of the Republic. I have entered the inner echelons of power. The lights are dim and the office is plush and comfortable, with dark wood panelling and soft leather chairs. All we need are cigars to smoke and a puppet regime to topple and the moment will be complete.

"Tell me about the republic," I begin.

"It's the *legendary* republic," he replies. "Being the president is an honorary title."

"So you're sort of a figurehead. You don't have any real authority."

"Exactly."

"You can't order executions or anything."

He blinks several times, not sure if he has heard me correctly. "Executions?"

"Political opponents who conveniently 'disappear.' *Off with their heads!* That sort of thing." I lower my voice. "I understand if you'd prefer not to discuss it. Wink-wink."

"Yes. Well. Personally," he says, "I believe that this role of president should be shared among all the mayors in the area."

"Are they jealous, the other mayors? You know, because you're the president. Do you kind of rub it in their faces?"

"No, no."

"How should we address you, then? Your Worship? Your Highness? El Presidente?"

He starts to laugh, but it trails off. You can tell he's having his doubts about me. "No, no, no. It's the legendary republic. It's a selling tool."

"As citizens of an independent republic—"

"A *legendary* independent republic."

"—do the people of Madawaska support the separatist movement in Quebec?"

"Not at all," he says. "For myself, I will always respect the decision of the people in Quebec. But my wish is that they never separate from the rest of Canada."

Mr. Martin mentions the Saguenay floods, when people from across Canada sent supplies and support to the ravaged area, which is, remember, a separatist heartland. He was active in the Edmundston effort, helping to organize shipments of blankets and food. Four large transport trucks left from Edmundston alone.

"The solidarity expressed for the people of Saguenay in that difficult time—I think it brought people in Quebec to realize how important it is to have neighbouring provinces that care. Not to be alone. The francophone community in New Brunswick mobilized; so did the anglophone community. English and French people got together to help out. It sent a message. Canada is one country, the best country in the world. I believe that. I really do."

The president feels this is why there has been a sudden increase in tourists from Quebec visiting Atlantic Canada. It's not just the poor exchange rate abroad. No, he insists there is more to it than that. A shift in thinking has occurred. "They are curious," he says. "They want to find out more about this country they live in. This country called Canada."

It's apt, I speculate, that the citizens of the republic made such a concentrated effort to aid those of a kingdom.

Jacques Martin laughs. "That's right, the Kingdom of Saguenay. They even elected a king a little while ago."

"A king? And they *elected* him?"

"It's a legendary kingdom," he adds quickly, cutting off that route.

"So, are you the king too, in a sense? The King of Madawaska?"

"No, no, no," he says. "I'm not the king. I'm not so pretentious as that."

"Whatever you say, Your Highness." And since we are comparing kingdoms and countries, regional republics and larger allegiances. . . .

"Mr. President," I say, "one final question. I would like your honest opinion. If Bonhomme Carnaval and Typique were in a fight, who would win?"

The question doesn't faze him, not in the least. By this point, he has gotten used to fending off my maddening non sequiturs. (I use the Kangaroo Technique of interviewing, involving sudden unexpected leaps of logic.)

"Bonhomme Carnaval and Typique?" Jacques P. Martin, President of the Republic, straightens his shoulders and says, with all the pride of an ancient Roman, "You better believe Typique would win. He's a porcupine. You mess with a porcupine, you get hurt."

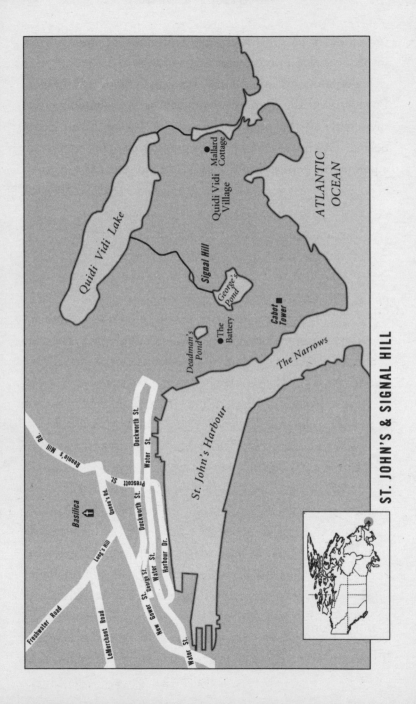

ST. JOHN'S & SIGNAL HILL

chapter nine

"ST. JOHN'S IS GNAWING ON MY BONES"

ALL I REALLY KNOW ABOUT NEWFOUNDLAND is that it's always raining, they eat fried food every day of their lives, and they drive on the left-hand side of the road. Or maybe I'm thinking of Ireland.

An understandable confusion: both places are located in the same general vicinity—somewhere out there in the cold North Atlantic, right? But this was not Ireland we were talking about, this was Newfoundland, and the response above came in reply to a message I had sent to a friend inviting him to join me on a road rally across the southern part of the island.

I e-mailed him back. "Does that mean the answer is no?"

"Are you kidding? Count me in!"

I had thought that I could bring passengers along, that it would be like any road trip, only faster. But as it turned out, no. Only one spot was available in the rally, and it was reserved for a journalist—or, in my case, a reasonable facsimile thereof. My friend, neither a writer nor a race-car driver, was disqualified.

I had been approached by Porsche to sit in as a passenger/ observer in one of the rally's cars. My duties were simple enough. I would be with a professional driver inside a Porsche Targa as the designated navigator. "Navigator?" I thought. "How hard can that be? Once you get outside of St. John's there's, like, one road in Newfoundland."

I was set to go. *Hoo-ha*. Then I got a call from Rick Bye, the driver of the car that I would, *snork,* be "navigating." That's when the trouble began. Rick was a great guy, terrific, with an upbeat—albeit untested—confidence in my abilities. "It's a timed race," he said, "with staggered starts. They'll close off sections of the road along the coast, and you'll be given a detailed map of the route. As we approach each turn, you'll count down using the odometer, first in kilometres and then by units of a hundred metres. You have to tell me what type of corner we're approaching as well, so I can adjust— gearing up or down—to take every bend as smoothly and effi- ciently as possible. So, it would be 'T-intersection, hard right, in five, four, three, two, *one*—,' that sort of thing."

There was a dead silence on my end.

"Hello?" said Rick. "Are you still there?"

"Ah, just curious," I said. "But what happens if I screw up?" The use of "if" was, of course, unduly optimistic. I wanted to know what would happen *when* I screwed up.

"Don't worry, we'll teach you the turns and the terminol- ogy and how to read the map. No one's perfect. We all make mistakes. Last year my mechanic acted as navigator, and even he had trouble once or twice."

This did not reassure me. In fact, it did the opposite; it *un*assured me. If a race-car mechanic, someone who lives and breathes automotives, can't pull this off without a glitch. . . .

An image appeared before my eyes, strikingly clear, of a Porsche being launched into the sky through a guardrail, floating in mid-air for just a moment, almost in slow-motion, before slamming down hard into the Atlantic. I tend towards absent-mindedness while driving. I'm not as attentive as I could be to such trifles as traffic lights, lane changes, elderly pedestrians, BRIDGE OUT signs, the frantic waving of work crews, international borders or oncoming freight trains. I do have a knack for admiring the scenery as it drifts by, though this is perhaps not a trait one looks for in the co-pilot/navigator of a Porsche doing 200 kilometres an hour along hairpin turns. Even worse, I was familiar with the stretch of coastline Rick was talking about. I'd driven it. It's not a road, it's a series of corners linked together. And there it was again, that oddly compelling image of a Porsche airborne over the North Atlantic. Did I mention that the racecourse would be winding through small towns along the way, and that the streets of these towns would be *lined with spectators*? Can you say, "carnage ensues"?

And so I declined. I felt bad about bailing on them like that, and I tried my best to arrange a replacement. But any writers I knew who were crazy enough to try something like this weren't available, and those who *were* available weren't crazy enough. Crazy, yes. Crazy enough, no.

Like a dog pursuing its own tail, I even went back to my friend—the one who thought they drove on the wrong side of the road in Newfoundland. But when I explained what was involved, he balked as well. "I don't mind impersonating a travel writer," he said. "I mean, it's not like what you do is difficult. But no way am I going to guide a speeding car through Newfoundland fishing villages. I'll kill somebody, I know it."

"Relax," I said. "Newfoundlanders are surprisingly quick on their feet. Chances are, most of them will dodge out of the way in time." But he was having none of that.

It broke my heart, having to say no. As it was, I did travel in Newfoundland that summer, but it wasn't in a Porsche, it was in a dinky little Neon rent-a-car with all the pickup-and-go of a hamster inside a plastic ball. "Vroom," I said to myself sadly as I steered my hamster ball along the coastlines of the Avalon Peninsula. "*Vroom.*"

And thus ends today's shaggy dog. By now, you're probably wondering why I've spent so much time telling you what I *didn't* do. "Hey, Will, you didn't go hang-gliding, either! You going to write about that as well?" When an author has written himself into a corner like this, the temptation is to simply put a break in the text, add a space on the page, and then start fresh with a new paragraph. But that is not the sort of device to which I would ever stoop.

When I wrote a travel column for *Maclean's,* I got into the habit of carrying a small notebook with me wherever I went, to jot things down in: bits of advice, street directions, pithy insights, snippets of conversation, the phone numbers of the many beautiful and, so far, purely theoretical women who throw themselves at travel writers. That sort of thing. It sometimes requires a concentrated effort later on to decipher what I have scribbled down, but I can usually tease out a meaning. Not this time. Not after a night on the town in St. John's, when I discover a note to myself that reads: *St. John's is gnawing on my bones.* Waking with a God Almighty hangover, and still not sure how I made it back to my B&B, I'm baffled by this cryptic sentence. I don't remember writing it, and it doesn't even look like my handwriting, though that may have something to do with the amount of screech I swallowed the night before. Screech being the rum which Newfoundlanders are so fond of forcing down the throats of unsuspecting Mainlanders. (*Please note*: One does not "drink" screech, one swallows it, hard, the way one might ingest cough medicine or lighter fluid.)

And so it is with St. John's, as well. You can't take it in with small sips; you have to choke it back, swig it down. You have to wheeze about and stagger.

This is Canada's "Far East." Our oldest city and Atlantic bookend, St. John's stands in stark contrast to Victoria at the other end. Where Vancouver Island is draped in moss and towering with Douglas firs, Newfoundland is a wind-blasted, raw-knuckled rock—an island of stunted, tenacious trees and fierce wet winters.

The four standard-issue Interesting Facts about Newfoundland and Its Capital City, listed below, give a sense of St. John's' position in Canada, geographic and otherwise. (The correct name of the province is, of course, "Newfoundland and Labrador." I apologize to Labradorians out there for using the informal, shortened version.)

Factoid #1: Newfoundland lies in its own distinct time zone, unique in the world.

Factoid #2: St. John's is where the Trans-Canada ends—or begins, depending on which way you are going.

Factoid #3: St. John's is closer to London than it is to Winnipeg, closer to Dublin than to Calgary. And not just in terms of distance.

Factoid #4: St. John's is where the British Empire began.

These are well-known tidbits of information; flip through any travel article or guidebook and you'll come upon them, often under a heading that reads: *Hey! Did you know . . . ?* But trivial pursuits aside, what these items tell us, collectively, is that Newfoundland is both the beginning and the end, the alpha and the omega, the gateway to and the outer barracks of a country, a continent, a New World.

Newfoundland exists in a pocket of time all its own, thirty minutes behind the rest of eastern Canada. Or is it thirty minutes *ahead*, because the sun rises first here and, well, never mind. I never could figure that out. No matter how you define it, this oddball time zone puts the province a half-step out of sync. Broadcasters are constantly adjusting to fit Newfoundland into the greater scheme. *The world will end at midnight, twelve-thirty in Newfoundland,* as the old joke goes. The sun rises on Newfoundland, sets on British Columbia, island to island. Chilly Atlantic mornings and warm Pacific sunsets. An arc that traces a path from the dawn of an empire to its twilight.

The Trans-Canada Highway connects Victoria to St. John's, like a wire stretched between two tin cans, the messages shouted down the line becoming muted and muffled along the way. Both cities claim to be the starting point of our national highway, which is why—in a classic Canadian compromise—we have two separate (*but equal!*) Mile Zeros. I've been to both ends of the Trans-Canada, and once again the differences are striking. In Victoria, Mile Zero begins on the edge of a lush green field, with the Olympic Mountains of the United States as a backdrop. In Newfoundland, Mile Zero is officially tagged at the St. John's city hall—a soulless slab of architecture if ever there was one—but everyone knows the road really begins at Cape Spear, a short drive south of the city at the easternmost point of North America. At Cape Spear, the windy heights look out onto the bruised blue of the North Atlantic, towards Britain, that other island, just beyond the curve of the sea. Canada: we are bracketed by empires.

Newfoundland is England's oldest colony, Canada's youngest province. It may have joined Confederation in 1949, but its roots as a European outpost go back to the dawn of First Contact and the days of Christopher Columbus. An Italian seaman, Giovanni Caboto, better known as John Cabot, came upon this New Founde Lande in 1497 while sailing under commission from an English king. The Portuguese followed Cabot in and were soon joined by large fishing fleets from Bristol, France, Spain and the Basque region. By the time the Elizabethan adventurer Humphrey Gilbert arrived in the summer of 1583 to reassert England's claim, St. John's was already a thriving seasonal community—a freewheeling International gathering place of ships from many nations, where a rough and wild transitory population had taken hold. St. John's was an open port, beyond the reach of European duties and taxes. Behind the wharfs and the fish racks, between the merchant stores and the shanties, were a pair of cart tracks called the Lower Path and the Upper, now Water Street and Duckworth and still the commercial heart of the Old Town. Humphrey Gilbert had walked these tracks, dreamed of a "colonial utopia" in the New World, but it was never to be. He went down with his ship in a North Atlantic squall, his final words overheard by those on an accompanying vessel: *We are as near to Heaven by sea as by land!* Which only proves, a friend of mine from St. John's likes to point out, what a poor navigator Gilbert was. "After all, Newfoundland is *nowhere near* Heaven."

St. John's has been described as "the world's largest fishing village." In the words of Newfoundland author Harold Horwood, the island capital is simply "the biggest outport of them all." The usual clunky array of office towers—unimaginative, uninspired, unloved—lines the waterfront, but for the most part the character of St. John's has survived the infliction of modern architecture with remarkable grace. Aplomb, even. The clapboard homes, the gingerbread trim, the narrow lanes and the stone stairways cutting between streets: from Hill O'Chips to the cliff-clinging buildings of the Battery to the parade of colour on Jellybean Row, St. John's is a patchwork of neighbourhoods. The city began as a series of small towns—Cookstown, Monkstown, Dogtown, Turbid's Town, Maggoty Cove and so on—that have long since been subsumed into a larger civic identity, but this sense of St. John's as a gathering of small towns continues. Lanes wander about like someone looking for an address only half-remembered. The houses tumble *uphill,* if such a thing is possible, and the entire place seems to have been laid out without the aid of a ruler.

I once won a bet with a Newfoundland colleague who insisted that St. John's is, empirical evidence to the contrary, an orderly sort of place and easy enough to get around in. So I threw down a challenge: "Show me one intersection anywhere downtown where two streets actually meet at right angles." Off we went, this way and that, but every single intersection had some strange kink to it, some arbitrary bend or jog. It's a city filled with angles that don't quite add up. (This is a fun pastime, by the way, the search for right angles in downtown St. John's. My friend Mike Dinn has told me that the next time I come through his fair city he will take me to Prescott and Water, which he says do meet at a clean 90 degrees. We'll see.)

If Victoria is our nation's veranda, sun-dappled and drowsy, then St. John's is the attic, stacked with shelves and boxes and old sea-chests, dank and dusty, the air heavy with the smell of mildew and old books, the nooks crammed full of sepia-faded photographs and rumours of lost treasure. It's a city of cluttered foregrounds, of bric-a-brac and ad hoc add-ons, jury-rigged and well worn. In Calgary, the streets are laid out with a checkerboard certainty: wide, empty, clean. In Calgary, there are alleyways that you can look down and almost see tomorrow. Not here. In St. John's, the past always blocks the view—*is* the view.

That said, the streets are not unreasonably narrow. These aren't the single-car squeezes or rabbit-warren lanes you'd find in Japan or Ireland. Neither claustrophobically thin nor wide enough to preclude easy jaywalking, the streets of St. John's are just the right size. As a pedestrian you can pinball lazily from side to side, back and forth—until you suddenly snap awake and realize you are stranded in the middle of one of the city's yawning, inexplicable crossings. The map I picked up at the St. John's city office lists the following pieces of advice, presented here verbatim:

INTERSECTION	ADVICE
Queen's Rd./Gower St. & Church Hill Area:	*Just pray & hope you are going the right way.*

Cavendish Square/ Hotel Newfoundland:	*Pass thru unscathed and* *you've passed the Nfld.* *driver's test.*
Rawlin's Cross:	*Site of the city's first traffic* *light and no doubt traffic* *accident.*

This from a map they hand out to visitors, mind you.

Actual exchange witnessed at one of St. John's more ambiva-
lent intersections: A car jerks to a halt, a pedestrian jumps
back, a window rolls down. I'm expecting a few choice words,
invective flung, threats hurled, perhaps even a bit of the ol'
fisticuffs. This is what I get instead:

The woman in the car: "Pardon me, dear, didn't see the
crosswalk."

The gentleman who has had to leap backwards into the
air: "Well, it's very faint—etched in the imagination."

A laugh on both sides, a wave and a nod and off they go,
weaving their respective ways through the city. Now, I'm sure
there's road rage in St. John's as there is anywhere, but I
suspect that there is markedly less of it, and that even when
tempers do flare, those involved will still find time for an
artfully delivered quip prior to the actual fight.

Another helpful tip: while visiting St. John's, carry cigarettes, even if you don't smoke. Perhaps it's just me. Perhaps
I look like a diehard nicotine addict or, more probably, like an
easy mark, but everywhere I go, people keep asking me if they
can bum a smoke. Some offer me a quarter or even a loonie—
this is apparently a common transaction in St. John's—and I get

approached so often I eventually duck into a corner store and buy a pack, to see if I can turn a profit. (I know, I know— a Calgarian at heart.) I don't make any money, but I do have a string of eccentric conversations in a language that at times almost resembles English. *Some fine figgin' wit a guppy for da bluff, eh b'y?* I mention this without any negative nuance whatsoever. I think it's wonderful, especially the use of "b'y." When I was growing up in northern Alberta, people regularly called each other "partner," something that gave even the most fleeting of exchanges a Western flavour. *Hey, partner, you got the time?* I never hear that any more, which is why I am glad to see "b'y" still used in Newfoundland, not in a self-conscious or a folklorey way, but peppered in amid everyday speech, as ubiquitous and invisible as the Canadian "eh?" *Can I borrow a smoke from you, b'y?* comes the query, and I happily comply. (Though how one "borrows" a cigarette is something best left for another day.)

Small one-act plays constantly unfold. It's as though Newfoundlanders hate to see a silence pass between them; they need to fill it. As someone who's Irish on my mother's side (Scots-Norwegian on my father's), I think I know where this tic comes from. The Scandinavian strain of our extended family is exactly that, *strained.* Taciturn. Economical with their words. But the Irish side, by jeez, give us a cuppa and we'll blather away for hours on a topic of your choosing. There was a definite love of banter in our house, of back-and-forth, of conversations that were not so much carried onward as kept aloft, like a shuttlecock at a family picnic. So too in St. John's.

Two women on adjoining door stoops, and it could be a scene right out of Dublin or Derry:

"Where's your Kelly then?"

"Away. Went to Boston."

"Boston?"

"That's what he told me. My guess, he's been down at the pub all week."

"Away to Boston? Must be quite the thrill."

"For him or for me?"

She laughs. "It's same with my Jimmy. I been tellin' him for years now, 'How can I miss you if you won't go away?'"

In the patterns of speech and the fondness for tea, in their fierce, almost aggressive pride in their own friendliness, in the serrated edge of their humour—homespun and good-natured on the surface, but like a shiv between the ribs below—Newfoundlanders have always struck me as being the Irish that the Irish aspire to be.

This is not my first sojourn in St. John's, so the city is no longer completely confusing, but neither is it comfortably familiar. I have a nodding acquaintance with shortcuts. I know where I am more often than I don't. I recognize shops and streets and individual houses—and even cats—but the place never completely jells. It feels as though I am suffering from a mild form of amnesia: every morning I walk out into a city that is vaguely reminiscent of something but still slightly skewed. I experienced the same thing when I was staying in Enniskillen, Northern Ireland, a city of bridges that *almost makes sense,* but not quite.

Many times in Newfoundland, it feels as though I have fallen through the surface, not into Ireland but into a richly reimagined version of Ireland. Not a parody, not in any sense; this is most certainly *not* Victoria. There is no aura of cargo cult here, no genuflecting homage to Ye Olde Country.

It's deeper than that. Before arriving in St. John's, I spent a week following the coastline of the Avalon Peninsula, from cove to cove and town to town—and I often forgot that I was still in Canada. I kept expecting to see castles crumbling on the hillsides. I kept expecting to receive foreign coins as change in the shops. I was surprised at times that they *didn't* drive on the left, and I was taken aback when I saw a maple leaf flag—it's a shade of red not normally seen in Newfoundland, where the greens and blues of the sea dominate. This wasn't Ireland. It was Ireland lost. And Ireland found. It was Ireland cast adrift and washed up on a cold island. It was Ireland reconstructed, like a portrait assembled by someone working from memory, getting the mood right if not the details.

I've been reading *The Irish in Newfoundland*, by Mike McCarthy, which gives a blow-by-blow account of this history—in every sense. The following is from a July 6, 1752, dispute between a pair of Irish workers named Quinn and Murphy, who were in the employ of a man by the name of Haggerty. The incident occurred while the two men were laying fish out to dry on wooden racks, called "flakes."

Quinn found fault with the way Murphy was washing the fish, and when Murphy made an uncomplimentary comment about Quinn's ancestry, Quinn slapped him across the face with a wet fish. Murphy retaliated by slapping Quinn across the face with the fish he was washing. Quinn beat Murphy over the head with a mop handle and then went to find Haggerty to complain about Murphy. While he was gone, Murphy pulled up a flake lunger and when

Quinn came back he beat him about the head and
crammed the lunger down his throat. Quinn died in the
attack and Murphy was charged with murder.

Which pretty much sums up the last 400 years of Irish
history, now that I think about it. It's also worth noting that
when Murphy was put on trial for killing Quinn, an inter-
preter had to be brought in, because the man spoke no
English, only Gaelic.

Newfoundland was founded by Irish boys, English merchants and a motley assortment of pirates and privateers—
though the three categories often overlapped. The pirate
admiral Henry Mainwaring loved Newfoundland; it was the
easiest place on earth to recruit. (*Note:* The difference
between pirates and privateers is mainly a matter of paper-
work. Privateers were licensed. Pirates were independent
operators. Both pillaged, robbed, torched and terrorized, but
privateers had official sanction from their governments.)

Fishing is a hard life. Piracy paid much better. The young
men brought over to work the fisheries, Irish "youngsters" as
they were known, came to the island as seasonal workers. It
was bondage in all but name. When their usefulness ended,
they were often abandoned like so much ballast on the
beaches and in the fishing coves. Caught in a web of debt,
many of them took years to pay their way back to Ireland.
Others stayed on and married the daughters of English
planters, planters who themselves were usually the victims of
some ill-planned colonization scheme. *We'll churn butter and
plant gardens and harvest bounties of wheat from the rich
Newfoundland soil. It'll be swell!*

Newfoundland's history is a series of mass immigrations, usually from Ireland and usually after yet another political upheaval back home, starting with the turmoils of the 1690s. The Irish in Newfoundland, soldiers and servants alike, had a disconcerting habit of abandoning their posts and joining the French whenever the French swept through on one of their periodic bouts of mayhem and ruin. Indeed, some of the Irish took a certain joy in turning on their English masters, and understandably so. Most stayed loyal, though, or at minimum neutral, and they were duly captured by the French army and later swapped for French prisoners. (The prices varied: whereas the English would happily trade one Frenchman for one Englishman, they required *three* Irish prisoners for every French captive they released.)

By the 1750s, the Irish population in Newfoundland had outstripped the English. With this perceived threat to British authority came religious persecution. The Catholic church was proscribed, Mass was outlawed, and any building where communion had been taken was burned to the ground. Irish Catholics were excluded from owning property or holding public office, but even with restrictions on Irish immigration, the influx continued. Newfoundland became an arena of second chances. Following the failed Ireland uprisings of 1798, the United Irish Movement regrouped, gaining clandestine support among soldiers in the Newfoundland Regiment. A dark tea was brewing. One of the governing officers warned of a possible insurgency, noting—ominously, in his mind—that "nearly nine-tenths of the inhabitants of this island are either natives of Ireland or immediate descendants from them and . . . the whole of these are of Roman Catholic persuasion."

His numbers were off—it was closer to two-thirds—but his fears were well founded. By 1800, Newfoundland soldiers had formed a mutinous cabal and were planning an attack on a Protestant church in St. John's. It was a cunning plan, all right. By capturing the church they would capture the city, and by capturing the city they would capture Newfoundland, and by capturing Newfoundland they would be able to create a free Irish state. It was to be a "theocratic republic" ruled over by Bishop O'Donel of St. John's, who would be crowned both President of the Republic of Newfoundland and, presumably, high priest—which came as news to the bishop. Honestly, they should have checked with him first, because when word reached him of their scheme he hightailed it over to the British, and the plot was broken up before it could even be launched. Five of the ringleaders were hanged in St. John's, and the rest were transported to Halifax, where several more were hurled into infinity on the end of a noose. Like similar schemes of this nature (*see*: Fenian Brotherhood, invasions of), it ended not in glory but with bodies twisting in the wind.

The Irish of Newfoundland fought amongst themselves as much as they did with the English, and the internecine nature of these squabbles was notorious. Factions and feuds from the Old Country, often running along specific county lines, were carried over into the New. Newfoundland's itinerant priests helped stir the pot as well. They were a fiery lot even by Irish standards: they drank, brawled, tore down Protestant fish racks, were excommunicated and criticized—and were fiercely loyal to their parishioners.

With Britain's repressive Act of Union in 1801, a new wave of Irish emigrants arrived. More than 7000 landed in St. John's in 1814 alone. The city doubled in size in the span of a few years, and the Irish Catholics now outnumbered their Protestant counterparts 7500 to 2500. Still, the British authorities kept them under heel. It was only in 1829 that Catholics were fully emancipated in Newfoundland, and with this came an upsurge in Irish militancy. Catholic priests became enmeshed in the island's politics to such a startling degree that the local bishop was formally censured by Rome not once but twice.

In the 1880s, the sectarian violence finally came to an end with a grudging recognition that, given their numbers, Irish Catholics should be granted equal representation in their governance. A key point in all of this is that neither the Irish nor the English could lay claim to Newfoundland as a true "home-land." Moving beyond a stalemate, the two sides began to share a sense of commonality, even kinship. Newfoundlanders, whether Irish or English, Catholic or Protestant, had more in common with each other than with the home countries they had left behind.

The Irish made their mark on Newfoundland. The twin spires of St. John's Basilica define the skyline of the city even now: a monumental pastiche of Dublin granite, Galway limestone and local stone cut from Kelly's Island. But more important, Newfoundland left its mark on the Irish.

In his history of the island, Patrick O'Flaherty writes of the Irish "habits of mind," and how the "fear and paranoia, and the shame that sprung from centuries of ignominy and failure, were transported to Newfoundland and put to use." Newfoundland seemed to offer the Irish a shot at redemption. "Here, after all," O'Flaherty writes, "was another Ireland, with the 'people' in bondage as in the homeland. This time the Irish and their leaders would not wait to be given their rightful place in society. They would take it, and quickly. They would rule, as they should rule back home. . . . " But as O'Flaherty points out, "Newfoundland was not another Ireland. It was a British North American fishing colony," and to try to turn it into "a surrogate Irish state, to make it into something it could never be, a compensation for failure back home, was to wrench it out of shape."

Newfoundland would not become another Ulster. And St. John's would not become another Belfast. Newfoundland was where the English and the Irish—and the *Irish* and the Irish—finally made peace with one another.

In Newfoundland, the past is played out daily in the shops and homes and on the street corners; it is evident in the pitch and roll of the language and in the turns of phrase. History here is laced into the conversation, and Newfoundland's varied dialects are steeped in ancient Irish and old Devonshire from England's West Country, with the earth still clinging to the roots.

When Newfoundland workers travel to Ireland—or are recruited, as is increasingly common—they regularly stump their Irish hosts with their accents. "We can pass ourselves off as Irish with ease," I was told more than once. "We speak what seems to be a regional dialect, but they can't quite place it." Their hosts will throw out names of remote Irish villages and islands until eventually, having exhausted the choices, they will say, "Where then?" It's not only a matter of distance but of time as well. Stranded on the other side of the ocean, Newfoundland is a linguistic time capsule. Phrases and words long vanished in Ireland or England have been preserved here in brine and isolation. Irish-born author Kildare Dobbs has explored the way Devon dialects and Irish Gaelic came together in Newfoundland. "West-Country English is also a distinctive burr," he writes. "Blended together, the two idioms became a new version of English, with more music and poetry in it than any other North American speech."

I concur. I spent two months in Ireland prior to this visit to Newfoundland, and if anything, I find the patterns of speech here even more rhythmic, more melodious, more richly layered. Ireland seems almost restrained in comparison to the sheer gallop and grin of Newfoundland. It's a fun accent.

Want to blend in? Want to pass yourself off as a Newfoundlander? Who wouldn't? Here is a quick course, a selection of Newfoundlandisms presented in no particular order. Not every Newfoundlander in every town will use these, but all are culled from actual encounters I had.

"Wit" (humour, dry; also: together with, as accompanied by). "Odder" (an alternative choice: as in, "he went wit da odder one"). "A narber" (a sheltered inlet of water used for docking vessels). "Shore" (yes; why not?; certainly). "Shore ting" (without a doubt; that which will certainly transpire; a bet one cannot lose). "Toime" (time). "Witchya" (accompanying: as in, "Lemme know da toime and I'll go witchya"). "Hog" (farm animal; also: friendly embrace; as in, "Give us a hog!") "Buddy dere" (yonder fellow, the person to whom we are referring) "is askin' for it" (will soon be given a pummelling). "Mainlander" (not of Newfoundland; of slightly inferior stock; an object of pity). "Hi! I'm from the Mainland, and I just love to use the term *Newfie*. In fact, I have several"—air quotes—"'Newfie jokes' with which to entertain you. Would you like to hear one?" (invitation to a pummelling). "Nointy tree cens" (a price, under one dollar). "Soin dat" (please attach your signature to the following credit card slip). "Jaysus Murphy" (exclamation of disbelief; the little-known surname of a Nazerene carpenter, not commonly thought of as being of Irish descent). "Me son" (used in reference to friends, strangers, people one has accosted, people one likes, people one dislikes, people to whom one is about to give pointed advice—as in, "Listen, me son"—in short, anyone and everyone except one's actual son. He is referred to by his name.) "Lord" (the fat rendered from animals; as in, "Fried in lord, it was."). "Lard" (Our Saviour; Christ the Redeemer; Our Father in Heaven; as in, "Lard love us!")

I hear these two final terms wielded with admirable dexterity at the B&B I'm staying in, after I happen to mention the name of a certain fish-and-chips shop where I stopped to eat earlier. The lady of the B&B is beside herself, almost literally: her sister is sitting next to her, both have cups of tea and immaculately arranged hairstyles, and both have the same expression on their faces—namely, one of apologetic disbelief. That some poor, uninformed Mainlander should wander into such an awful site!

"They ought to close that place down," she says to her sister. "They fry their fish in lord."

"Lard love us, in lord?"

Then to me, with a sympathetic hand on my arm, "That's no canola oil, my dear. Next time, it's best you go to—" (Insert name of much better fish-and-chippery, owned by—and shore ting, it's just a coincidence—her brother-in-law).

"And they . . . they do use canola?" I'm expecting a triumphant nod.

"No, they use lord."

"But a better lord," her sister cuts in.

"Oh, wait, there's Annie—" and the conversation is put on hold as they lean forward to peer conspiratorially out their window. "Now where's she goin' wit da bons this hour of day?"

"Da bons?" I repeat.

"Da bons," they say gravely.

"Da bons?" I'm still not clear on what they are—

"Have some tea, dear."

I never do figure out what *da bons* means, and there are times, especially when I leave St. John's and poke around the smaller villages, when I swear my comprehension is less than it was in French-speaking Quebec. Out in Alberta, we have these little phrase books listing Western Canadian expressions—"Cold as a Bay Street banker's heart," that sort of thing. In Newfoundland, they have an entire friggin' *dictionary*. And even then, it doesn't list "da bons" or any known derivatives of such. I checked.

Here's something else that surprises me: although fishing has long been the core of the community, it isn't fish that Newfoundlanders are obsessed with; it's berries. Right here—in the city, in a B&B in the heart of town—the conversation, if left untethered, will drift towards the subject of berries: preferred seasons, the picking of, secret spots in which to find, areas overpicked and best avoided. In Newfoundland, Tim Hortons carries partridgeberry muffins. You've never heard of partridgeberries before. Right? Exactly.

"Now my sister, she's a berry-holic." This is the owner of the B&B speaking—confiding in me the shortcomings of her sister the moment said sister has stepped out the door. "A berry-holic, it's true, it's true. Anytime, night or day, if you want to be goin' berry-picking, she's ready. Call her up on a full moon and she'll meet you in five in her housecoat and wit a pail in one hand. It's a kind of sickness. She'll pick and pick the berries, and she don't even eat them herself."

"She doesn't?" I say.

"Oh, she has no life. Take it as a rule: anyone who considers berry-picking an excitement—they have no life. She especially loads up on partridge, and those are some ugly berries. Tart? Oh, dear. When we were children, our punishment was going berry-picking. How I hated the flies" (*da floies* in original). "I had a tendency to eat the blueberries as I was picking them, and that didn't help. Now, my sister, that's when she got addicted to it—the berries that is."

And on it goes. Accents aside, I feel right at home.

The B&B I am staying at is on a hill so steep I entertain the neighbours daily by stepping out and immediately stumbling to one side, like an amateur act yanked stage left by a pole. In St. John's all streets eventually lead to the sea; you have only to follow the natural slope of the city, past the homes leaning hard against the angle of the hills, and eventually, like a trickle in a drain, you will reach water. Walking downhill is easy in St. John's; you just take that first step and let momentum do the rest. (Try to stop before you stork-walk into the harbour, though.) Walking uphill, however, is not as much fun. Which is why I spend most of my time in the lower town. Everything slides towards the harbour, anyway. Should a massive earthquake ever hit the city, most of St. John's would end up in the bay—and I find that uplifting, in a strange sort of way.

From the water's edge in the early evening, the harbour looks like a landlocked lake, its narrow entrance sealed off by distance and the angle of view. In among the derricks and the hoists, the ropes and the rigging, great ships lie slumbering. The *Volstad Viking* out of Norway is tied to the dock. A towering wall of sea-going metal, bleeding rust from its portholes and rivets, it rises and falls on slow exhalations of water. Other ships are moving in, and a cold wind comes with them, like air off an iceberg.

Don't speak to me about isolation; the whole world comes to St. John's. This is a port city, a merchants' town, and it always has been. For more than 500 years, different crews from different lands have jostled for position here. If there is an inferiority complex at work—as some have claimed—I have seen no evidence. As Horwood notes, "St. Johnsmen sincerely believe that they are several cuts above just about everyone else, and that they can lick the world single-handed."

From the harbour, I make my way to Water Street. It is summertime, and the city has taken on a giddy air of excitement. The gloom of grey winters is gone, and the days are long. You can feel the tempo building. People are hurrying down the streets, disappearing in and out of doorways, appearing and reappearing like characters in a bedroom farce. I end up at the Westminster Pub, where the menu offers "Fine English Fare." I'm assuming this is meant to be taken ironically—the words "English" and "fine fare" being mutually exclusive—and so it proves.

"You have grilled cheese sandwiches?" I ask. I'm in the mood for ethnic, and it's been a while since I've had some proper Canadian cuisine.

The waitress says she'll check but never comes back with an answer, and I settle instead for English food involving peas and (possibly, but it's hard to tell) kidneys. It's the only cuisine in the world that makes Canadian fare look good.

St. John's is a city of pubs. My favourite story is one told of the old Traveller's Joy, a tavern that was built on the west end of the city, on the road out of town. A sign hanging out front read: *Before the Traveller's Joy you pass, Step in and have a parting glass.* And on its opposite side, the one facing people coming into St. John's, it read: *Now that your journey's almost over, Step in, your spirits to recover.* They get you coming and going in this city, and whether it's to mark a departure or celebrate an arrival, there is always cause enough for cheer. It's also worth noting that they rhymed "over" with "recover."

In 1807, a Newfoundland governor noted that among the good folk of St. John's "rum was no luxury, but a necessity." Still is, even if lager has surpassed rum as the quaff of choice. I follow the crowds to George Street and what the tourist board calls a "continuous carnival in the heart of Old St. John's." This is because "rowdy piss-alley full of bars soaked in beer" doesn't sound quite as appealing. When I'm here, I always end up on George Street, which I admit gives me a somewhat warped perspective on the city. No doubt there are fine art galleries in St. John's, and overpriced bistros and wine shoppes catering to upper-middle class aspirations, but so far I have managed to avoid them.

I prefer George. It's a single street squeezed into the Old City, and I'm told it has more bars per square foot than anywhere else in Canada. I have heard that same claim made about streets in Moncton, Halifax and elsewhere—the title of Most Bars being a highly coveted one, especially in the Atlantic provinces—but George Street may well be the true champion. This street isn't simply lined with pubs, it is packed with them. It's "pub stuffed," "pub engorged," and it is fast approaching some sort of critical mass. There are manic sports bars and smoky caves, there's Trapper John's Museum & Pub (pure St. John's, that), there are patios crammed full and spilling onto the street, there are side-alley entrances and even a few, ahem, "gentlemen's clubs." Though, from the looks of the clientele entering, no one is checking peerage at the door.

It's a boozy, brawling, caterwauling place. Crowds clot the doorways and huddle on sidewalks as they map out the night's strategy. "Right. We'll start with Pub X, and then it's off to Bar Y before Band Z ends their second set." A voice in the back: "So, we'll catch the last of the fiddle, then?"

Tonight is more frantic than usual. It's a holiday weekend coming up, and the bands are pouring in. Buddy Wasisname and the Other Fellers are warming up, as are the Irish Descendants, and Celtic Connection, and Arthur O'Brien & the Navigators (not to be confused with Dan O'Brien & the Wanderers, who are also slated to appear). There is a band called Shanneyganock and another called New Ireland. It's Celtic Night in Old St. John's. Although, really, every night is Celtic night in Old St. John's, no?

Shades of Moose Jaw: tunnels! Tunnels running below

George, *aye!* Burrowed by bootleggers, they were. A tall tale, clearly. The city is built on bedrock, and even then, rum-running was hardly a covert operation in Newfoundland; there was no need to go underground. When a barkeep at one pub tries to convince me otherwise—"Oh, there are tunnels all right, it's true. I'd swear on an open Bible"—I tell him about the jack-alopes that roam the Alberta plains (i.e., rabbits with elk horns, a favourite of taxidermists) and of the fish that are covered in fur farther north. And the iceworms up in the Yukon. "Why, there're probably some jackalopes running around in your tunnels," I say. "Pursued by Elvis."

He laughs and comes clean. "No tunnels, true. But we have fun with it, with the new staff. We'll send them out to look for the keys to the tunnels, to the bar next door, where they'll say, 'Oh, the keys? We passed those on to So-and-so,' and we'll send him door to door all the way down George and back again. Just yesterday, a young fellow comes in, new at the job and in a panic, saying he's supposed to fetch the keys to the tunnels but can't find a set anywhere. So I tell him, 'You go tell your manager, I'll lend him my set of keys if he'll let me use his bacon-stretcher.' Off the lad goes, comes back not ten minutes later, red in the face and out of breath, and he tells me his boss has upped the ante, will trade his bacon-stretcher for my fish-polisher. I would'a kept it going—maybe send him back for a toothpick sharpener or some waterproof tea bags—but the girls took pity on him and made me stop. The women, they don't understand the beauty of a perfectly executed practical joke." He smiles at the memory of it. "Oh, it was an absolute riot."

The greatest practical jokes are, of course, reserved for use on Mainlanders. Which is why I take pride in the fact that, in all my travels to St. John's, I have successfully avoided being "screeched in." This is a ritual—a completely bogus ritual— staged mainly to amuse the locals, wherein gullible tourists are forced to recite some fishlore gibberish and drink a kick of rum (the infamous screech) and then kiss a cod, all in the mistaken belief that they are ingratiating themselves with their hosts. They aren't. I suspect being screeched in began as idle talk over a kitchen table. "Why, these Mainlanders are so thick, I bet we could make them kiss a smelly old codfish. I bet we could make them kiss its arse—long as we tell them it's part of our heritage."

As it turns out, I *will be* screeched in. Inadvertently, but nonetheless. (Though from a distance it must have looked more like a kidnapping than an initiation.) Having hopped my way through a couple of pubs, I am captured by a fishing crew from Portugal Cove.

"Alberta? How about dat? I've got a cousin in Fort McMurray." Everybody in Newfoundland has a cousin in Fort McMurray. "Maybe you know him? Small guy, looks like me."

The legendary highwayman John Flood gained his fame by holding up the stagecoach to Portugal Cove—before he was nabbed and dangled, that is—but the crew I am with are not highwaymen. They fish for snow crabs, or at least I think that's what they have said. Maybe it's "there's no crabs, no crabs." Hard to say; it's all a blur. They torment me with screech and second-hand smoke, and tell me about how their families were so poor "back when" that they were reduced to eating lobsters. Lobster, mind! This is not the first time I have heard this. Apparently, half the population of Newfoundland has subsisted entirely on lobster at some point or another. *Memo to Newfoundlanders*: We have all heard the story about

how your mom/dad/uncle/aunt/grandpa and/or in-laws used
to be embarrassed to have to eat lobsters. It's a good story, but
we've heard it. Please find another.

Eventually, I stumble free of my captors and back into the
goodwill and lawlessness of George Street. I have an unfailing
instinct when it comes to these things: I've been captured by
truck drivers in Japan and *campesinos* in Ecuador, yet I never
learn. My eyes are raw and red, and the pavement keeps buck-
ing beneath my feet, trying to throw me off as it sends me
staggering into progressively larger men. "I'm sorry," I gasp.
"I'm from the Mainland, you see." Spared a pummelling, I
somehow make it back to the B&B and flop into bed.

Morning claws its way up the sky—too soon, too soon—and
I wake with a hangover of medieval proportions. And there it
is, that note to myself, scratched in a notebook: *St. John's is
gnawing on my bones.* There's a phone number as well, along
with assurances from myself that I am supposed to call this
person right away (*Right! Away!!* in the original). I dial and
the phone rings and rings, until a groggy voice appears on the
other end to mumble something in my ear and hang up.

I blame it on the screech. I am sweating the stuff at this
point. Screech, for those as yet unsoiled by it, is a low-grade
dark rum imported from Jamaica, bottled in St. John's and used
to strip paint and start briquette-fire barbecues, as well as, on
occasion, to drink. Mainly, though, it's used to torment the
tourists. When Newfoundlanders drink rum, it is usually
Lamb's or Captain Morgan, not screech. Even so, I've been told
that today's screech is not *real* screech. What I glutched back
on George is a watered-down, government-approved version.

Real screech is much stronger. "One fella, he went to blow out a match, hiccuped, inhaled and set his throat on fire. Burned right into his belly. True story, I swear." If nothing else, screech has inspired the sommelier in me: *How to describe the national drink of Newfoundland? Horrible, and yet at the same time revolting. Appalling, yet dreadful. Vile, but wretched.*

One could make similar pronouncements about seal flipper pie, though I imagine you would have to throw some "really, very, truly's" into the mix. Lorraine McGrath and Leslie Thomas, two lovely women from the Avalon Visitors' Centre, have heard I am in town and have decided to treat me to an early lunch of seal flipper pie at Chucky's Restaurant.

Chucky's is a St. John's institution, though, as I discover, it is also the subject of divisive sectarian opinions. Forget the old "Be ye a Protestant? Or a Catholic?" bone of contention. In St. John's the question that reveals your true character is whether you go to Chucky's or the "odder place." It reminds me of the overblown importance that Montrealers assign to smoked meat sandwiches. "Be ye a Schwartz's man? Or are ye of The Main?" If you want to have some fun in Montreal, tell them you prefer Ben's—and then step back and watch the sputtering begin. "Ben's? Ben's is for *tourists!*" Claiming an allegiance to Ben's over Schwartz's or The Main has been known to cause spontaneous cardiac arrest in certain Montrealers. So it is with St. John's. Next time the topic of fish and chips comes up, pipe in with "Personally, I prefer the new fishburger at McDonald's. I think it's called the McHaddock. *Mmm-mmm,*" and watch the room freeze in stunned silence, the way a saloon will when someone orders a sarsaparilla.

One of the ladies I am with—I won't say which one—

leans in while the other is wrestling out of her coat and confesses, "Personally, I prefer the odder place." She won't even say the name out loud, lest she be immediately hoisted from the gunwales. (I'm not sure what gunwales are, but this was definitely a hoisting offence.)

There really is a Chucky. He has his own boat and everything, and much of what he dredges up in his net ends up on the menu. As a fisherman's restaurant, Chucky's is a suitably sprawling, undisciplined place—both larger and smaller than it seems—and we have to squirm our way to a table through an early crowd. Eleven a.m. and the place is packed. Chucky's is known for its seal flipper pie, though I'm told in a hushed voice (speaker's identity again concealed) that what's served here is not *true* flipper pie. It's real flipper, sure, but it's prepared in a non-conventional fashion. For one thing, it's almost edible, whereas real flipper pie—*authentic* flipper pie—should be so godawfully bad that the mere whiff of it can be used for crowd control. "Jayzuz George, dey're bringin' out da flipper pie—run for it!" I have heard many things about flipper pie, none of them good, and I am bracing for the worst. Moose stew and caribou meat also appear on the menu at Chucky's. "But not bottled moose," Lorraine says, with a twinge of disappointment.

"Bottled moose?"

"Pickled." A pause. "Not the whole moose, you understand, dear. Just some of the bits."

Now, as noted, I'm sure there are some perfectly fine French restaurants in St. John's, but why would I bother? If I'm going to travel to the outer edge of Canada, to this Atlantic island that is closer to Ireland than to Winnipeg—closer historically, geographically and in popular sentiment—if I am going to go to all that trouble, why on earth would I dine on something I can get just as easily anywhere else? No, I am here and, God help me, I am going to eat seal meat. Egged on by Leslie and Lorraine, I place my order—though I notice, with mild consternation, that they stick with the fish and chips. "You go ahead," they urge. "Seal flipper pie. It's a Newfoundland tradition."

I am very wary of things fobbed off as "tradition"—after all, *piracy* was a Newfoundland tradition—but having taken the plunge, I am pleased to see a solid block of what looks like shepherd's pie arrive a few minutes later.

"Doesn't seem so bad," I say, poking at it with my fork. Perhaps the stories have been exaggerated.

"Seal's *under* that," Lorraine says.

Oh. Turns out I was looking only at the dumpling-like top layer, covered in sauce and scattered with carrots. Beneath this is a slab of seal meat. Oily, dark and pungent. Very pungent.

"Dig in," they urge. "Dig in."

Flipper pie is the sort of food that's eaten almost exclusively on a dare, like prairie oysters or 7-Eleven hot dogs. Not the sort of thing you want to face while under the influence of a lingering rum-induced hangover. I manage a few mouthfuls and then discreetly push my plate to one side. "Has anyone ever finished an entire serving?" I ask. Not sarcastically, you understand; I'm genuinely curious.

"I've never seen it done," whispers one of my hosts.

Round Two: *cod tongues*. The seal flipper is cleared, and out comes a plate of small medallions of fish. These, I like. They are tender and tasty and have a delicate, slightly gelatinous texture to them. "And which part of the codfish are these taken from?" I ask.

Lorraine looks at me. "You're talking about the cod tongues?" she says.

"That's right."

"You're asking me which part of the cod the cod tongues come from?"

"Yes."

"They come from the tongues," she says.

Oh. Of course. "I, um, thought it was a metaphor or something." I'm feeling a wee bit foolish. I didn't even know codfish *had* tongues. (When I later read Charles Gordon's book *The Canada Trip*, I am relieved to see that he made the same gaffe. Asking which part of the cod the cod tongues come from is apparently high on the list of Stupid Things Mainlanders Ask.)

Nor is this the first time I have felt foolish when it comes to fish. I remember in my first visit to St. John's mulling over the selections at a neighbourhood chip shop. I was trying to figure out whether the various platters used different types of fish. Were some platters haddock, some cod, some flounder? But that's not how my question came out:

"Um, yeah. Listen, can you tell me," I said, flustered, as a line formed behind me at the counter, "what's the difference between a *large* fish and chips and a *small* fish and chips?"

There was a lull in the lunch-counter chatter. The owner looked at the other customers and then back at me, with a crooked smile on his face, and he said slowly, the way one might address a particularly dim-witted child, "Well, generally speakin,' da large fish'n'chips is *slightly bigger* dan da small fish'n'chips."

It was the "generally speaking" that really twisted the

blade. I can hear the laughter ringing in my ears even now. And as I later discovered, in Newfoundland "fish" means cod, plain and simple. The two words are interchangeable.

Back at Chucky's, my head is throbbing worse than ever, in an either pre- or post-Apocalyptic manner, it's hard to say which. After the flipper pie and the tongues of cod, followed by a chaser of aspirin and vows of temperance from that moment onward—vows made to the gods themselves—I climb in with Lorraine and Leslie for the drive up Signal Hill.

This is the city's crowning height of rock, as striking a promontory as the headlands of Quebec City, but more exposed, more dramatic. It's a windy day, but clear, and the road curls up the hill. We pass Deadman's Pond, looking dark and cold in its crevice of bedrock.

"They say it's bottomless." This is Leslie from the back seat, her voice sunny and sweet. "Men who drowned in it—their bodies never surfaced."

"Really?" A tall tale, perhaps. And perhaps not. At times the city itself feels like one large bottomless pond. I can imagine it perfectly: plunging into St. John's headfirst, disappearing into the narrow alleys, never resurfacing.

"And prisoners, too," says Lorraine. "After they hanged them, they would dump their bodies in the pond. That's what I heard."

Leslie and Lorraine are warming to the topic, and I am regaled, in that peculiar Newfoundland way, with lurid tales of gallows and hooded hangmen and an entire roster of unsolved murders. "Now, I heard," says Leslie, making it sound like a juicy bit of gossip recently gleaned, "that they would hang them up on top, and then put them in barrels and roll them down the hill, so they wouldn't have to lug the bodies."

"Dead weight, I suppose," says Lorraine, and they both chuckle. "I guess it would depend who was on duty that day, whether they felt like carrying them or not. Just imagine if those barrels got smashed apart on the way down." More chuckles. "That would stop 'em in their tracks—dead in their tracks, I imagine."

The noonday gun does nothing to ease my headache, nor does the Signal Hill Tattoo, with its infernal drumming and incessant firing of muskets. We arrive in time for the *ten-hup* and *about FACE!!* of military formations. The Royal Newfoundlanders march and wheel to the roll of the Regimental Fife and (very loud) Drum Band. "It's wonderful," I say to my hosts, wincing from splinters of pain with every volley of musket fire. It ends with a barrage of cannons, at which point my temples begin to bead with blood.

Ah, but the Atlantic air works wonders, and we continue to the top, soaking it up. I can feel the knots in my forehead slowly loosen; I can feel my vows of abstinence start to dissolve. Signal Hill takes the brunt of what the Atlantic Ocean can dish up—sentries have frozen to death, hikers have been blown off to their deaths—but today the weather is glorious and the buffeting wind is uplifting in a spiritual sense only.

This is where the youth of St. John's used to go to neck—before the tour buses started showing up. "Oh, it was a popular place to go and park," Lorraine confides, though adding quickly, with a laugh, "I'm not speaking first-hand, now, you understand."

"I hear they'd go up for the view even in the fog," says Leslie. Signal Hill is where the last battle was fought in North

America between Britain and France. After the Fall of Quebec, the French needed a bargaining chip in the coming post-war negotiations, and in 1762 they launched a surprise attack that captured St. John's. The British counterattacked, taking Signal Hill and turning their guns on the French base below (on what is now the site of the Hotel Newfoundland). A single night's bombardment was all it took. If St. John's is where the British Empire began, Signal Hill is where the dreams of New France came to an end.

At the top of Signal Hill sits the lonely landmark of Cabot Tower: a solid, squat, Gothic-revival structure. It looks as though it has been cut out of the stone it sits upon, and in a way it has; most of the tower's blocks were originally cut from Signal Hill. Cabot Tower, completed in 1900, resembles a military outpost—part lookout, part bastion—more than it does a tower. Where I'm from, you aren't allowed to call something a tower unless it has a revolving restaurant and coin-operated binoculars on top. This looks more like a castle, that missing piece of the Newfoundland landscape I have been looking for in vain.

It was near Cabot Tower, in an old hospital now gone, that the young Italian scientist Guglielmo Marconi received the first transatlantic wireless message, on December 12, 1901: the *click-click-click* of the Morse code for the letter S, repeated, sent around the curvature of the earth from a base in England. In Marconi's own words, "Distance had been overcome."

Marconi described the heights of Signal Hill as "a lofty eminence overlooking the port and forming a natural bulwark which protects it from the fury of the Atlantic winds." A Gibraltar of the New World, in effect. At Signal Hill the cliffs dive directly into the sea, and only a narrow gap allows access to the protected waters of the inner harbour. Ships approaching the Narrows are confronted with a wall of solid rock until, at almost the last minute, an entrance appears: just 275 metres wide at its mouth, it soon narrows to a mere 125 metres. And even then, ships threading their way in have to watch for submerged rocks and hidden shoals. Some vessels have been driven back by storms just short of sanctuary. In one case, a ship had actually entered the Narrows—one of the passengers could reportedly see his house—when a gale forced the vessel back out to sea and eventually pushed the ship to the coast of Ireland. Think about that—blown off course across an entire ocean.

It requires almost preternatural skill to navigate these shores. Caught in a "foul wind with thick fog," one sea captain ordered his men to fire the ship's guns repeatedly. He then steered his way along the cliffs by the sound of the echoes and slipped in unscathed. A nineteenth-century traveller compared entering the Narrows to sailing through a mountain pass and coming into an open coliseum.

Fishing fleets have caused nautical traffic jams as they squeeze out of the harbour at the start of the season, and the Narrows have been the site of so many shipwrecks and drownings and mid-channel collisions that I almost expect to find the water floating with flotsam and corpses. Steamers have collided with schooners. Schooners have rammed into sailboats. And tugboats have driven over dories. After a young woman died during a summer outing in 1884, when the sailboat she was on capsized, an advisory warned, "[In the Narrows] the wind doesn't blow with that steadiness characteristic of places where the land around is level, but comes down from the high hills in fitful gusts." *Fitful gusts* is right. I have been above the Narrows when the winds suddenly pick up. It's exhilarating—and frightening.

Sharks have been snagged in the Narrows, ice floes have blocked it, fogs have swamped it; pirates have prowled its waters and German submarines have fired torpedoes through its entrance. There's even a resident mermaid, although, this being St. John's, 'tis no delicate lass who lurks here, but a roaring girl with seaweed-like hair who attempts to climb aboard fishing boats and has to be beaten back with oars.

I return to Cabot Tower from a ridge walk along the edge, and climb the stairs for the full 360. On the open platform, a father and son are looking across the Atlantic. They are Newfoundlanders, in from Bonavista Bay, and it is important that they get their bearings straight. "Ireland and England are just *there*," the father says, pointing not east but a few degrees off, on what I suspect is an exact compass reading. "And Boston—Boston is over there." He again lines up his sights.

"And Canada?" his son asks.

"Canada?" the father says. "Canada's that way." He gives a slight wave of his hand, indicating a vague, undefined place somewhere out there past St. John's.

In the early hours of morning, the sun spills through the Narrows, fanning out into the harbour, warming the city. At the day's end, the sun falls back the other way, and the heights glow like copper.

At the top of Signal Hill, a hiking trail leads along the heights to Quidi Vidi, a self-contained seventeenth-century fishing village tucked within the city limits. I have been to

Quidi Vidi by car, have been whisked up to the reconstructed battery that sits above it and whisked back down, but on my last day in St. John's I make the trip on foot.

Quidi Vidi (pronounced "Kiddy Viddy") is the city's historic back door. It's one of the prettiest coves in Canada. It is St. John's in miniature, with a one-boat narrows, a scale-model village, a small chapel, a pond-sized harbour. It even has a brewery—a *micro*-brewery. The gap in the rock that leads to Quidi Vidi from the sea is only four metres across at its gut, and at low tide the water is just one metre deep. The Quidi Vidi inlet is deceptively small, for it too is a bottleneck. Men have drowned here, fishing boats have tipped, storms have smashed ships to splinters. In bad weather, fishermen have to count the waves, timing their entrance to roll in with a surge. It is the equivalent of threading a needle in the dark.

Set against the gold foil of the water, fishing dories are silhouetted along the dock. Quidi Vidi is a ship in a bottle: a village and a harbour in the most improbable of containers. It is also home to Mallard Cottage, the oldest surviving home in Newfoundland. The cottage was built by the Mallard brothers, who arrived in Quidi Vidi in the 1750s, and is patterned on the thatch-roof cottages of Ireland, with a central chimney, a low-hipped roof and a simple symmetric design. It was used as a dwelling by the Mallard family right up until 1985, when the last of the family line died off and the cottage was put up for sale. At the time, Mallard Cottage had no electricity, no running water, no indoor toilet and twenty-seven layers of wallpaper. The basic amenities have been added and the archaeological levels of wallpaper pulled back, but that aside, Mallard Cottage has scarcely changed, with the original windows and doors still in place.

The home has been turned into a curio shop and craft store, and I nudge around its cluttered collection of knick-knacks. It feels like a garage sale held in a closet. Old books, nautical brassware, vintage postcards, coins, crockery, tobacco tins, Oriental vases and Newfoundland rugs: every available shelf and nook is filled. There is barely enough room for two people to pass in the aisle without becoming intimate. A well-dressed couple are ensconced in one corner, looking at something small and porcelain, and they are whispering excitedly, "Do you know what this is? *Do you know what this is?*"

In Mallard Cottage the ceilings are low and the floor creaks. The sunlight seeps in through old panes feathered with dust. The cottage smells of mildew and memories, like a grandmother's shawl or a grandfather's workshed. If I were asked to choose the one building that embodies the city of Victoria, it would be the Empress Hotel: solid, certain, central. In St. John's, it would be a small ancient cottage in Quidi Vidi, filled with rickety reminders and half-forgotten heirlooms.

I leave Quidi Vidi, following the long path back across Signal Hill, and the vista opens up. The sudden cliffs and headlands, the plunge and gap of the Narrows, the inner harbour and the city beyond. Can you miss a place before you leave it? Can you feel homesick for a city that isn't your home? That is how I feel. I miss St. John's, and I have not yet gone. I'm homesick, and this is not my home.

St. John's. It's a good city, this outport on the eastern edge of North America. It gnaws on you.

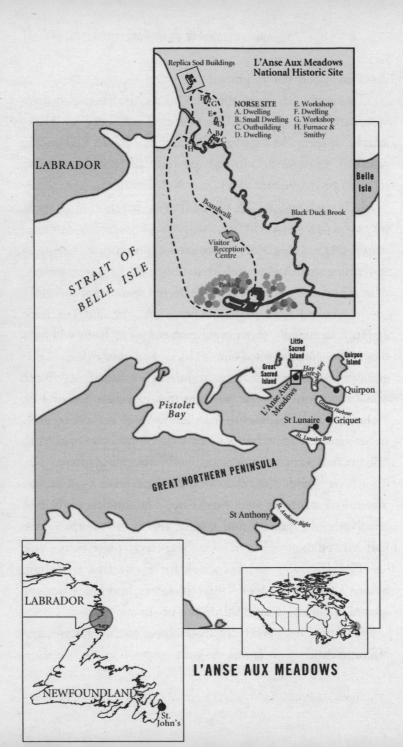

L'ANSE AUX MEADOWS

chapter ten

AT L'ANSE AUX MEADOWS

I STAGGER AWAKE IN THE DARKNESS and crawl into my clothes. It is an hour before sunrise, in a small guest home in Hay Cove, on the upper reaches of Newfoundland's Great Northern Peninsula.

My plan is to hike down to the land's end and watch the sun break across the Atlantic on this, the first day of July. I tiptoe out, into pale moonlight, closing the door quietly behind me. Clapboard homes line the road. Clusters of wildflowers form perfect bouquets, and everything seems to glow a low blue. A wind is coming off the sea. I can hear the lap and roll of waves on the shore. There are tales of a whale in the inlet. "He's been scoopin' up the krill," I was told when I arrived last night.

The road from Hay Cove slopes up and onto asphalt, where a lone highway unrolls along boggy barrens. A congregation of shadows has gathered beside the road. Moose. Four, maybe five. They come out from the scrub on knob-kneed legs and move towards me, clip-clopping across the blacktop, so close I can hear their puffs of breath. Large. Imposingly so, when set against the stunted vegetation and shrub-like trees

up here. Like moose everywhere, they carry with them a
certain dignified ugliness. They are the inbred Habsburg mon-
archs of the animal kingdom, combining regal deportment
with huge, misshapen noses. *Prehensile* noses. They clop
nearer, loom larger. I think a moment. When was the last time
I saw a moose up this close? Well, never. And the rutting season for moose, when exactly does that begin? I try to look
uninterested in the females. I try to look big. I try to look calm.
I try to look like someone who is Not Afraid, even as the moose
begin to outflank me on either side. "G'wan. Go away," I say,
my voice disconcertingly high.

It's no use. I am about to be mugged by a gang of moose,
and the only comfort I draw from this is the knowledge that,
if nothing else, this is certainly the single most *Canadian* way
you could possibly die. I can see the headlines already:
BELOVED AUTHOR TRAMPLED TO DEATH BY MOOSE. A NATION
MOURNS. But then, on some unspoken cue, they lurch to one
side and lope away.

Pulse pounding, chest tight, I walk back to Hay Cove at a
brisk pace—so brisk it's more of a sprint than a walk, really.
"Think I'll drive," I gasp aloud. And as I ease the car out of
Hay Cove and onto the highway, I can't help but wonder if my
CAA insurance plan would consider moose an Act of God.

I have come to L'Anse aux Meadows for Canada Day (1st
July), because this is where Canada—the *idea* of Canada—
was first forged. In many ways, Newfoundland's northern
peninsula represents our nation's vanishing point, where parallel lines converge. A geometric impossibility, perhaps, but
not when it comes to the history of who we are.

The shift from *kanata* to Canada begins here at L'Anse aux Meadows. It starts with a ship lost in the fog, a Viking vessel blown off course en route to Eirik the Red's colony in Greenland. The Norsemen on board caught sight of a distant, unknown shore, and the existence of this new land, poised at the end of the world, fired the imagination of Leif Eiriksson, son of Eirik. On or around the year A.D. 1000, Leif set sail with a small crew.

The end of the world was not that far away, after all. Leif and his men soon arrived at a barren coast, which they named Helluland (Flat Stone Land, most likely Baffin Island), and then, turning south, came upon the wooded shores of Labrador, which they dubbed Markland (Forest Land). Continuing south for two more days, they discovered a shallow bay surrounded by sloping grassy fields. A stream trickled down, teeming with fish, and the hills were ripe with wine-berries. They named it Vinland (Wine Land).

Loading his ship with timber, as good as gold in treeless Greenland, Leif Eiriksson sailed for home the following spring, and with that single voyage he made both his fortune and his name. He would be known as "Leif the Lucky": the first European to set foot in North America, legends of Irish monks and ancient Phoenicians aside. And though Leif himself never went back to Vinland, others soon followed.

His younger brother, Thorvald, led an expedition down the same coast, and in one bay came upon a band of hunters asleep beneath skin boats. The Norse referred to them as *skrælings*, a term of contempt meaning "wretches" or "barbarians," but from the description of the boats and the men beneath them, it would appear they were Inuit or possibly

Innu. This encounter between Norse explorers and Native hunters was a pivotal moment in world history. Spilling out of Africa, the human race had pushed north into Europe and east into Asia, through Mongolia and either across the sea or over the Bering Strait to the Americas. And now, on this windswept coast, the two sides had once again met. Humanity had come full circle. It was as much a reunion as it was "first contact."

Alas, as with many a family reunion, things were a little strained. The Vikings—being Vikings—immediately attacked, killing all of the hunters but one. He managed to escape, which was bad news for the Vikings, because he returned with a whole armada of kayaks. A pitched battle ensued, during which Thorvald was hit by an arrow. He made a farewell speech and then promptly died.

That first meeting set the tone for much of what would follow. A later expedition ended in a full-scale war between the Norse colonists and the *skrælings*. During one melee, Leif's half-sister Freydis grabbed up the sword of a fallen Norseman and, ripping open her shirt, slapped the blade against her breast. She stood her ground, ready to fight, but the Inuit attackers stopped, speechless at the sight of this. Freydis was pregnant at the time, as well, and one of the cardinal rules of combat is "Never piss off a pregnant woman when she's holding a sword." The Inuit scattered, and Freydis, bare-breasted and defiant, became a Viking legend. Never mind that another account of her voyage to Vinland paints a very different picture, with a bloody feud breaking out between competing Norse camps that ended with Freydis butchering her rivals. (When her own henchmen refused, Freydis killed the female prisoners herself. With an axe.)

Relentless *skræling* attacks, isolation and loneliness and the creeping cold of a "little ice age" helped doom the Norse settlements. Vinland the Good was abandoned, fading into the myth and memory of Norse sagas. Clues about the lost colony were woven into these narratives, and in 1914, Newfoundland historian W. A. Munn was able to trace the location of Vinland to Pistolet Bay, at the northern end of the peninsula. "They went ashore at Lancey Meadows," he wrote.

Munn was only slightly off. They hadn't simply landed at "Lancey Meadows," they had built their base camp there. A Finnish geographer followed the path of the sagas to northern Newfoundland, as did a Danish archaeologist, who explored the area around L'Anse aux Meadows in 1960 and just missed the site. The very next year, Norwegian explorer Helge Ingstad arrived at the northern strait between Labrador and Newfoundland, and he too came ashore at L'Anse aux Meadows. (The name seems descriptive—there are meadows here, indeed—but in fact it is probably derived from *l'anse aux méduses*, the French for "bay of jellyfish.") When he looked out at the sloping shore and curved bay, the open views and low height of land, Ingstad was struck by a sense of déjà-vu. He recognized this place. He had seen it before: in Norway, in Greenland, in other ancient Norse locations. *They would have felt at home here*, he thought. He knew, before he had turned a single sod of bog-iron peat, that he had found Vinland.

The Norwegian explorer also had the good fortune to strike up a friendship with a local fisherman, a gregarious, bewhiskered, brogue-speaking, pipe-smoking old-timer by the name of George Decker. Decker took Ingstad to a series of grassy humps that Decker referred to as "the old Indian camp." The hillocks and hollows were not "Indian," however; they were Viking.

Ingstad's wife, archaeologist Anne Stine Ingstad, paced out an excavation site the following year and, with a team of volunteers, began peeling back the peat. A village slowly emerged. A smelter, a bathhouse, a boat shed, firepits and living quarters. With this came a wealth of artifacts: iron nails, ship rivets, a stone anvil, a bronze cloak-pin and a spindle whorl. More than 2000 items have been recovered, but it's the last one—the spindle whorl—that was the single most momentous. A small piece of rounded soapstone used to spin wool into yarn, it is considered one of the great archaeological finds in North America. The reason? Spinning and weaving were an exclusively female occupation in Norse culture, and this stone spindle provided irrefutable evidence that the settlement at L'Anse aux Meadows was not a temporary camp. It was an attempt at establishing a permanent community. *They brought their families with them.* It calls to mind heartwarming images of Viking longboats ringing with cries of "Are we there yet?" "Mom, Olaf is kicking me!" "Am not!" "Am too!" "By the Blood of Thor, if you kids don't settle down, I'm turning this boat around right now!" True, no direct evidence of children has turned up at L'Anse aux Meadows, but the Norse sagas do tell of at least one child born in Vinland, a boy with the sleepy name of Snorri.

L'Anse aux Meadows was a Norse settlement. But was it Vinland? This is a question that continues to vex historians and archaeologists, with much of the mystery turning on the meaning of *vin*. Wild grapes are not found this far north.

Perhaps the Norsemen were referring to the plump berries that grow in such abundance here, the currants, the squash-berries, the bakeapples and partridgeberries. Journals from English explorers refer to "wild grapes" and "grapevines" in Newfoundland well into the 1740s, so it was an easy enough mistake to make. Helge Ingstad has suggested that the refer-ences to wine and grapes were added later, in error, and he points out that in Old Norse, *vin* (with a short "i" sound) refers to meadows rather than grapes, making it not "Wine Land" but "Land of Meadows."

Personally, I think we can end the entire debate about Vinland by using basic common sense. The settlement uncov-ered at L'Anse aux Meadows is the only authenticated Viking site in North America. And how was it discovered? Through a careful reading of the ancient Norse sagas, and the sailing times and geographical descriptions they provide. What are the odds, in following these clues, that archaeologists and his-torians would, by sheer coincidence, have stumbled upon a *completely different,* heretofore unknown Viking village? Pretty damn slim, I imagine.

Is this where Lief Eiriksson first landed? Of course it is.

Today, the pale blue of a U.N. flag flies above L'Anse aux Meadows, marking it as a World Heritage Site. I wander through the Interpretive Centre, peer at the spindle whorl, now on display behind glass, then follow the trail down. The archaeological excavations have been covered again with sod to protect them from the elements, leaving impressions in the grass that are somehow more evocative than the gaping, gravedigger squares of a scientific worksite. Reconstructed Norse dwellings stand to one side, sod-built and peaty, filled with the smell of woodsmoke and wet grass. A brook trickles into the bay, the curve of low beach leads towards islands anchored offshore: the Great Sacred, the Little Sacred. And behind them the coast of Labrador, forming a dark curtain along the water.

Hello! Meet Egil, the Chieftain, who is a bit flamboyant, single and in love with Halbera. Thorgerd, the town gossip, is married to Kvelduf. If you enjoy the spoken word, say hello to Lambi the *skald*, who spends his time carving as he recites passages from the Havamal, the Viking book of sayings.

Not far from the L'Anse aux Meadows historic site is the tourist village of Norstead, a full-scale replica of a Viking settlement, complete with Great Hall, sod-covered dwellings, some soggy-looking sheep, and people walking around dressed up like Vikings and speaking with Newfoundland accents. "Valhalla, and all dat," one of the Vikings is telling a group of visitors when I arrive. "Now dis yere, dis would be da mighty Viking sword, b'y." It is not incongruous in the least. Newfoundlanders make excellent Vikings. Both are of the sea, and both—I imagine—would be equally good in a fight. The tourist brochures "cast of the characters"—quoted above—could, I'm sure, be as easily applied to any neighbourhood or outport in Newfoundland. *Now where's Kvelduf da Mighty goin' wit da bons dis hour of day?*

In the town of St. Anthony, I pass the Vinland Motel and the Viking Mall, and in the former fishing cove of St. Lunaire a local family now takes passengers on excursions out of Noddy Bay on board the *Viking Saga*. This is a hand-built replica of a *knarr,* the type of vessel that Leif the Lucky sailed in—except that this one has a motor hidden in it. And snacks. And very little hand-to-hand combat. I board the *Viking Saga* for an iceberg tour, the square sail flapping furiously for dramatic effect as we putter out of port. The captain angles us towards a floating mountain just as a slice of ice falls away, dropping into the water with a crash. "We'll hang back on this one," he says prudently.

Icebergs are not white. They are blue on blue and veined with green. Translucent marble, Matterhorns on the move, they roll under the waves, grind along the bottom of bays, lurch to a dead stop, melt themselves free.

The captain reverses the engine, bringing us to an abrupt stop, and we bob on the waves as he grabs a long snare-net and darts to one side of the ship. He is scooping up 10,000-year-old ice cubes: the crumbling debris of icebergs, to be used by restaurants to chill the drinks of tourists. He rinses the salt water off a fist of smooth ice and tosses it over to me. "There you go," he says. "Purest water you'll ever taste." I press it against my tongue. It numbs my mouth and makes my teeth ache with its clear, clean cold.

Against a backdrop of icebergs, a whale breaks the surface, spouting a plume of fishy breath. It's a humpback, and it arcs into the water, tail sliding up and in like a hand waving goodbye. Silence. And then suddenly it reappears on the other side, having crossed below us. That something so large could disappear with such ease. . . . I think of villages that lie in stillness for a thousand years, of currents that run in a northern sea, of all those things that lie just below the surface of who we are, nine-tenths unseen.

My grandmother was of Viking stock. My grandfather, from Scotland. "And Scotsmen," my grandma liked to say, "are just shipwrecked Norwegians." How did I get here? I ascended. I ascended from Cape Breton coal mines and the Barnardo orphanage of Belfast, from nomadic Czech migrations and Australian penal colonies. These tales converge in me, and this is not unusual. From the first Vikings to the shattered displacement of the First Nations, from resistance to revival, from New France to the New West, from dreams of utopia to dreams of prosperity, from Loyalist boat people to modern-day refugees, Canada is more than just a country: it is a sum of its stories. We are all orphans, are all survivors of shipwrecks, and we carry these stories of exile and renewal within us, whether we are aware of it or not.

As the captain turns the ship back towards the grassy shores, with a harvest of ice in the hold, a stanza of poetry surfaces. It's a fragment of verse from "The Canadian Boat Song," something I once had to memorize for school. It's a song about a nineteenth-century Scottish emigrant, but it is more than that.

> Mountains divide us, and the waste of the seas—
> Yet still the blood is strong, the heart is Highland,
> And we in dreams behold the Hebrides:
> Fair these broad meads—these hoary woods are grand;
> But we are exiles from our fathers' land.

The broad meads, the grassy mounds. Vinland lost and Vinland found. *"We look / like a geography but / just scratch us / and we bleed / history."* This last line is from Miriam Waddington's poem "Canadians." Scratch us and we bleed history.

ACKNOWLEDGMENTS

Michael Schellenberg was the acquiring editor and driving force behind *Beauty Tips*. It was four-and-a-half years ago that Michael first approached me about writing a Canadian travel memoir, and he has seen this project through with enthusiasm, a steadfast confidence and no small amount of finesse.

Barbara Pulling edited the final manuscript, and her clarity and insight have been invaluable. Barbara is, without a doubt, one of the finest editors in publishing today. Deep thanks as well to copyeditor Gena Gorrell for her meticulous work. Between Michael, Barbara and Gena, I had an amazing band of editors. Any eccentricities of style or flaws in the writing should be ascribed to author intransigence and not to a lack of editorial input.

I am very fortunate to have a great group of people behind me at Knopf Canada. Books don't fall fully formed from the sky (alas!); it takes an entire team of people in editorial, distribution, publicity, design and marketing to make them work. I would like to express my appreciation to everyone at Knopf, especially Louise Dennys, Brad Martin, Frances Bedford, Duncan Shields, Matthew Sibiga, Constance MacKenzie, Deirdre Molina, Angelika Glover and designer Kelly Hill.

My literary agent, Carolyn Swayze, has been with me from the start, and I thank her once again for her unflagging support and astute advice. An overdue thank you to Barry Jones for his continued good cheer, and to Douglas Coupland for taking an author photo that actually resembles me—only better. (Thanks, Doug. The *mochi* is on me!)

Some sections of this book first appeared in much abbreviated form in *Maclean's* as part of a series entitled "Will Ferguson's Canada," and in the *Ottawa Citizen* ("Republic of Madawaska") and in *Flare* ("The Moose Jaw Spa"). I would like to thank Tony Wilson-Smith, who invited me to write for *Maclean's*; Berton Woodward, who edited my columns the first year; and Michael Benedict, who took over after Berton and who was the editor on "Polar Bear Haven," which went on to win the Northern Lights Award for Travel Writing. I would also like to thank Sue Allan, formerly of the *Ottawa Citizen*, and Kim Izzo, Features Editor at *Flare* and a dear friend.

Travel writers must always rely on the kindness of others, and I have been aided and abetted by a great number of people along the way. I hope I haven't missed anyone.

In Victoria, I would like to thank May Brown, Ross Crockford and Brian Dodsworth. In Port Alberni, I would like to thank Aili Jowsey, who took the time to speak with me about Tom Sukanen. And in Vancouver, my sister Lorna Robson for all her help arranging travel schedules and tickets.

In Moose Jaw, I would like to thank Donna Fritzke, who was with Temple Gardens Mineral Spa when I went through, and the staff at the Oasis Beauty Spa, in particular, Brad Moffatt, Jackie Hill and Damara Brown. Thanks also to Bruce Fairman, Jocelyn Okoktok, Tim and Kathy Smith at the Oak & Rose Book

Shoppe, Poet Laureate Gary Hyland, and Irene Grobowsky, Lori
Dean and Karen Basky at the Saskatchewan Festival of Words.

Warm thanks to my aunt and uncle, Priscilla and Steve
Lazaruk of Regina, Saskatchewan; and to my honorary aunt,
Kay Parley of Saskatoon; to Helen Kaeser in Regina, and my
sister Gena Ferguson in Gilbert Plains, Manitoba—though
she'll always be Margaret to me—and Randy Peters, who
packed up the White Lady and made sure she got to me safe
and sound.

For my trip to Churchill, I am indebted to Cathy Senecal
and Colette Fontaine with Travel Manitoba; Stacey Jack and
Jackie Schollie at Parks Canada; Tony Bembridge and pilot
Scott de Windt at Hudson Bay Helicopters; Merv and Lynda
Gunter at Frontiers North; buggy guide Hayley Shephard and
driver Chris Hendrickson; and, of course, Dennis the Bear
Man at www.polarbearcam.com. Thanks also to photographer
Kevin Spreekmeester and his son, Ben, for sneaking me back
in for another encounter with Dancer. And, last but not least,
a toast to the gang in Tundra Buggy #13: Polly Chevalier, Jane
and Peter Evans, their daughter Liz Evans, Rob Woodland,
Kerrick James, Larry MacGregor, Michael Park, Candyce
Stapen and Jorge Zepeda. *Salut!*

In Thunder Bay, I would like to thank Marilyn McIntosh
with the Travel Bureau; Captain Doug Stanton and family
with *Pioneer II;* Marty Mascarin at Old Fort William; and
Lynda Harmon at Kakabeka Falls. Many thanks, too, to the
great bunch at Sleeping Giant Provincial Park: Cam Snell,
Ryan Lehr and our intrepid guide, Adam Moir.

I would like to express my thanks to Brenda Lambkin in
Dresden, Ontario, and to my brother Ian Ferguson for sharing

the road with me. Raucous thanks as well to the Fergusons of Montreal: my brother Sean, my sister-in-law Sherry and their children, Aidan, Brynne and Liam—with a special thanks to Aidan for being such a great traveller.

In the Republic of Madawaska, I would like to thank Roger Gervais and Gilbert Lavoie, as well as Valerie Lebrun, François Thériault and Charles Louis Pelletier for debating the finer points of a Bonhomme vs. Typique match. I would also like to thank Jacques P. Martin, Mayor of Edmundston and President of the Republic, for being such a good sport.

In Newfoundland, a hale and hearty thank you to Lorraine McGrath and Leslie Thomas of the Avalon Visitors Centre; Bernadette Walsh at Tourism St. John's; Peg Magnone and Stephanie Page at Mallard Cottage in Quidi Vidi; Beverly and Eric Roberts in St. Anthony; Paul Compton with the Viking Boat Tours in St. Lunaire; Marilyn Pittman at Hay Cove, L'Anse aux Meadows; and my friends Marcia Porter and Mike Dinn in St. John's.

Travel can take its toll on a family, and above all I would like to thank my wife, Terumi, for being so supportive and understanding. I also thank my mother, Lorna Bell, and our friends in Calgary who watched out for Terumi and the boys while I was on the road: Heather Abdel-Keriem, Kirsten Olson, Trish and John Clark, and Yvette and Kenji Nakamoto. *Arigatō ne!*

SOURCES

GENERAL

Francis, R. Douglas, Richard Jones and Donald B. Smith. *Origins: Canadian History to Confederation*. 5th ed. Nelson: 2004.
———. *Destinies: Canadian History Since Confederation*. 5th ed. Nelson: 2004.

CHAPTER ONE: VICTORIA

Barefoot, Kevin, et al. *Victoria: Secrets of the City*. Arsenal Pulp Press: 2000.

Green, Valerie. *Upstarts & Outcasts: Victoria's Not-So-Proper Past*. TouchWood Editions: 2000.

Holloway, Godfrey. *The Empress of Victoria*. Revised ed. Empress Publications: 1980.

Jenson, Philip. "The Architect and the Lady." In *The Beaver: Canada's History Magazine*. June/July 1999.

Lee, Barrie. *Victoria on Foot*. Terrapin Publishing: 1989.

Lillard, Charles. *Seven Shillings a Year: The History of Vancouver Island*. Horsdal & Schubart: 1986.

Reksten, Terry. *The Illustrated History of British Columbia*. Douglas & McIntyre: 2001.
———. *"More English than the English": A Very Social History of Victoria*. Orca Book Publishers: 1986.

Taggart, Jim. *Circular Self-Guided Walking Tours of the Architecture of Downtown Victoria*. Blue Steps: 2000.

CHAPTER TWO: FORT VERMILION, SASKATOON & DAUPHIN

Bell, Lorna, and Florence Letts Sutherland. *No Need for Drums*. Lilybell Books: 1990.

Bicentennial Association. *Fort Vermilion People 1788–1988*. Fort Vermilion and District Bicentennial Association: 1992.

Ferguson, Ian. *Village of the Small Houses*. Douglas & McIntyre: 2003.

Francis, R. Douglas. *Images of the West: Changing Perceptions of the Prairies, 1690–1960*. Western Producer Prairie Books: 1989.

Fryer, Harold. *Ghost Towns of Alberta*. Stagecoach: 1976.

McCourt, Edward. *Saskatchewan*. Macmillan: 1968.

Senecal, Catherine. *Pelicans to Polar Bears: Watching Wildlife in Manitoba*. Revised ed. Heartland: 2003.

Note from Will: *Village of the Small Houses,* by my brother Ian, is "a memoir of sorts," and though it combines fact and fiction, it does capture the feeling of what it was like to grow up in Fort Vermilion.

CHAPTER THREE: MOOSE JAW

Bruce, Jean. *The Last Best West*. Fitzhenry & Whiteside: 1976.

Dederick, Paul, and Bill Waiser. *Looking Back: True Tales from Saskatchewan's Past*. Fifth House: 2003.

Fairman, Bruce. *Moose Jaw: The Early Years*. HomeTown Press: 1999.

Grey, James H. *Booze: When Whisky Ruled the West*. 2nd ed. Fifth House: 1995.

———. *Red Lights on the Prairies*. Fifth House: 1995.

Jensen, Philip. "Urban Legend: The Tunnels of Moose Jaw." In *The Beaver: Canada's History Magazine*. June/July 2001.

Larsen, John, and Maurice Richard Libby. *Moose Jaw: People, Places, History*. Coteau Books: 2001.

Mullin, L.J. "Moon," Dick Meacher and Eldon Owens. *"Together at Last": Tom Sukanen and His Ship*. Sukanen Ship Pioneer Village and Museum: 1976.

Rees, Ronald. *New and Naked Land: Making the Prairies Home*. Western Producer Prairie Books: 1988.

Russell, E.T. *What's in a Name: The Story Behind Saskatchewan Place Names*. 3rd ed. Western Producer Prairie Books: 1980.

Schroeder, Andreas. "Mad Prairie Mariner of Macrorie." In *Sailing Canada Magazine*. Vol. 4, No. 2: 1982.

Wheaton, Elaine. *But It's a Dry Cold! Weathering the Canadian Prairies*. Fifth House: 1998.

CHAPTER FOUR: CHURCHILL

Coutts, Robert. *On the Edge of a Frozen Sea: Prince of Wales' Fort, York Factory and the Fur Trade of Western Hudson Bay*. Parks Canada: 1997.

Fast, Dennis, and Rebecca L. Grambo. *Wapusk: White Bear of the North*. Heartland: 2003.

Fleming, Mark. *Churchill: Polar Bear Capital of the World*. Hyperion: 1988.

Hansen, Thorkild. *The Way to Hudson Bay: The Life and Times of Jens Munk*, trans. by James McFarlane and John Lynch Harcourt. Brace & World: 1970.

MacIver, Angus, and Bernice MacIver. *Churchill on Hudson Bay*. MacIver: 1982.

McGoogan, Ken. *Ancient Mariner: The Amazing Adventures of Samuel Hearne, The Sailor Who Walked to the Arctic Ocean*. HarperCollins: 2003.

Schuster, Carl. "Into the Great Bay: Henry Hudson's Mysterious Final Voyage." In *The Beaver: Canada's History Magazine*. August/September 1999.

Shipley, Nan. *Churchill: Canada's Northern Gateway*. Burns & MacEachern: 1974.

Wrigley, Robert E., ed. *Polar Bear Encounters at Churchill*. Hyperion: 2001.

CHAPTER FIVE: THUNDER BAY & AREA

Bisaillon, Cindy, and Andrea Gutsche. *Mysterious Islands: Forgotten Tales of the Great Lakes*. Lynx: 1999.

Black, Arthur. *Old Fort William*. Old Fort William Volunteer Association: 1985.

Brown, Jennifer S.H. "A Parcel of Upstart Scotchmen." In *The Beaver: Canada's History Magazine*. February/March 1988.

Dyke, Gertrude. *Historic Silver Islet*. Drake Printing: 1979.

Francis, Daniel. *Battle for the West: Fur Traders and the Birth of Western Canada*. Hurtig: 1982.

McWilliam, Scott. *The Island Mines: The Story of the Silver Islet Mines, 1864–1884*. The Silver Islet General Store: 1999.

Morrison, Jean. *Superior Rendezvous-Place: Fort William in the Canadian Fur Trade*. Natural Heritage: 2001.

Morse, Eric W. *Fur Trade Routes of Canada: Then and Now*. 2nd ed. Macmillan: 1979.

Poling, Jim. *The Canoe: An Illustrated History*. Prospero: 2002.

Raffan, James. *Bark, Skin and Cedar: Exploring the Canoe in Canadian Experience*. HarperCollins: 1999.

Tanner, Ogden. *The Canadians*. Time-Life Books: 1977.

CHAPTER SIX: DRESDEN & THE UNDERGROUND RAILROAD

Blockson, Charles L. "Escape from Slavery: The Underground Railroad." In *National Geographic*. Vol. 166, No. 1: July 1984.

Cavanah, Frances. *The Truth About the Man Behind the Book that Sparked the War Between States*. Westminster Press: 1975.

Gillmor, Don. "Promised Land." In *Canadian Geographic*. July/August 1995.

Henson, Josiah. *The Life of Josiah Henson: Formerly a Slave, Now an Inhabitant of Canada*. Arthur D. Phelps: 1849.

Hill, Daniel G. *The Freedom-Seekers: Blacks in Early Canada*. Stoddart: 1992.

Riendeau, Roger, et al. *An Enduring Heritage: Black Contributions to Early Ontario*. Dundurn: 1984.

CHAPTER SEVEN: TADOUSSAC & THE SAGUENAY

Beattie, Benny. *Tadoussac: The Sands of Summer*. Price-Patterson: 1994.

Brooke, Rupert. *Letters from America*. Sidgwick & Jackson: 1916.

Cloverdale, William Hugh. *Tadoussac Then and Now: A History and Narrative of the Kingdom of Saguenay*. Canada Steamship Lines: 1942.

Cook, Ramsay. *The Voyages of Jacques Cartier*. Macmillan: 1993.

Davies, Blodwen. *Saguenay: The River of Deep Waters*. McClelland & Stewart: 1930.

Grescoe, Taras. "After the Deluge." Special Report on Saguenay Floods by *Canadian Geographic* and *L'actualité*. Spring 1997.
———. *Sacré Blues: An Unsentimental Journey Through Quebec*. Macfarlane, Walter & Ross: 2000.
Hémon, Louis. *Maria Chapdelaine*. Boréal: 1988 ed.
Jenkins, Phil. *River Song: Sailing the History of the St. Lawrence*. Penguin Viking: 2001.
LaPierre, Laurier. *Quebec: A Tale of Love*. Penguin Viking: 2001.
Laurence, Margaret. *Heart of a Stranger*. McClelland & Stewart: 1976.
Ouellet, Yves. *Tadoussac: The Magnificent Bay*. Guy Saint-Jean: 2000.

CHAPTER EIGHT: MADAWASKA

Carroll, Francis M. "Drawing the Line." In *The Beaver: Canada's History Magazine*. August/September 2003.
Collie, Michael. *New Brunswick*. Macmillan: 1974.
Doucet, Clive. *Notes from Exile: On Being Acadian*. McClelland & Stewart: 1999.
Griffiths, Naomi. *The Acadians: Creation of a People*. McGraw-Hill Ryerson: 1972.
Jones, Howard. *To the Webster-Ashburton Treaty: A Study in Anglo-American Relations, 1788–1843*. University of North Carolina Press: 1977.
Lenentine, Charlotte. *Madawaska: A Chapter in Maine–New Brunswick Relations*. St. John Valley Publishing Company, 1975, from a 1956 thesis.
MacNutt, W.S. *New Brunswick: A History: 1784–1867*. Macmillan: 1963.
McCue, Michael Westaway. "The Aroostook War." In *The Beaver: Canada's History Magazine*. August/September 2000.
Soucoup, Dan. *Historic New Brunswick*. Pottersfield Press: 1997.
Trueman, Stuart. *An Intimate History of New Brunswick*. McClelland & Stewart: 1970.
———. *Tall Tales and True Tales from Down East*. McClelland & Stewart: 1979.
Wright, Esther Clark. *The St. John River and Its Tributaries*. Esther Clark Wright: 1966.

CHAPTER NINE: ST. JOHN'S

Dobbs, Kildare. *Ribbon of Highway.* Little, Brown & Company:
    1992.
Fitzgerald, Jack. *Amazing Newfoundland Stories.* Creative: 1986.
———. *Strange But True Newfoundland Stories.* Creative: 1989.
Gordon, Charles. *The Canada Trip.* McClelland & Stewart: 1997.
Horwood, Harold. *Newfoundland.* Macmillan: 1969.
Horwood, Harold, and John de Visser. *Historic Newfoundland.*
    Oxford: 1986.
McCarthy, Mike. *The Irish in Newfoundland: 1600–1900.*
    Creative: 1999.
Mustard, Cam, Amy Zierler, et al. *Signal Hill: An Illustrated
    History.* Newfoundland Historic Trust: 1982.
O'Flaherty, Patrick. *Old Newfoundland: A History to 1843.* Long
    Beach: 1999.
Power, Rosalind. *A Narrow Passage: Shipwrecks and Tragedies in
    the St. John's Narrows.* Jeff Blackwood & Associates: 2000.
Stacey, Jean Edwards. *A History of Quidi Vidi.* DRC Publishing: 2002.

CHAPTER TEN: L'ANSE AUX MEADOWS

Ingstad, Anne Stine, and Helge Ingstad. *The Viking Discovery of
    America.* Breakwater: 2000.
Magnusson, Magnus, and Hermann Palsson, trans. *The Vinland
    Sagas.* Penguin: 1965.
Major, Kevin. *As Near to Heaven by Sea: A History of
    Newfoundland and Labrador.* Penguin: 2001.
McGhee, Robert. "Northern Approaches." In *The Beaver: Canada's
    History Magazine.* June/July 1992.
Munn, W.A. *Wineland Voyages,* 6th ed. Evening Telegram: 1946.
Nuffield, Edward W. *The Discovery of Canada.* Haro: 1996.
Seaver, Kirsten A. "Land of Wine and Forests: The Norse in North
    America." In *Mercator's World: The Magazine of Maps,
    Exploration, and Discovery,* January/February 2000.